Oliver Flügel-Martinsen, Franziska Martinsen, Stephen W. Sawyer,
Daniel Schulz (eds.)
Pierre Rosanvallon's Political Thought

Bielefeld University Press

OLIVER FLÜGEL-MARTINSEN, FRANZISKA MARTINSEN,
STEPHEN W. SAWYER, DANIEL SCHULZ (EDS.)

Pierre Rosanvallon's Political Thought
Interdisciplinary Approaches

BIELEFELD UNIVERSITY PRESS

Bibliographic information published by the Deutsche Nationalbibliothek
The Deutsche Nationalbibliothek lists this publication in the Deutsche Nationalbibliografie; detailed bibliographic data are available in the Internet at http://dnb.d-nb.de

This work is licensed under the Creative Commons Attribution-NonCommercial-NoDerivatives 4.0 (BY-NC-ND) which means that the text may be used for non-commercial purposes, provided credit is given to the author. For details go to http://creativecommons.org/licenses/by-nc-nd/4.0/
To create an adaptation, translation, or derivative of the original work and for commercial use, further permission is required and can be obtained by contacting rights@transcript-verlag.de
Creative Commons license terms for re-use do not apply to any content (such as graphs, figures, photos, excerpts, etc.) not original to the Open Access publication and further permission may be required from the rights holder. The obligation to research and clear permission lies solely with the party re-using the material.

© 2019 Bielefeld University Press
An Imprint of transcript Verlag
http://www.transcript-verlag.de/bielefeld-up

Cover layout: Maria Arndt, Bielefeld
Proofread and Typeset: Samia Mohammed, Bielefeld

Print-ISBN 978-3-8376-4652-8
PDF-ISBN 978-3-8394-4652-2
https://doi.org/10.14361/9783839446522

Contents

Preface | 7

1 Introduction
Stephen W. Sawyer, Oliver Flügel-Martinsen, Franziska Martinsen,
Daniel Schulz | 9

2 The Political Theory of Democracy
Pierre Rosanvallon | 23

3 Political Theory through History
Pierre Rosanvallon's Concepts of Representation and the People and
their Importance for Understanding Populism
Paula Diehl | 39

4 Rather Topics than Disciplines
Pierre Rosanvallon's Interdisciplinary Political Thought
Oliver Flügel-Martinsen, Franziska Martinsen | 61

**5 Writing the History of Democracy as a History of Tensions,
Antinomies and Indeterminacies**
Pierre Rosanvallon's Method of Conceptual History
Michel Dormal | 75

**6 On the Critical Potential of Rosanvallon's Wide Definition
of Democracy**
Wim Weymans | 99

7 Restocking the Storehouse of Democratic Ideas
Pierre Rosanvallon at the Collège de France (2002-2018)
Alain Chatriot | 119

8 Democracy and the Press in Rosanvallon's Historiography
Greg Conti | 133

9 Pierre Rosanvallon in Context
The Crisis of Republicanism and the Democratic Experience
Daniel Schulz | 159

10 Organizing the Political
Understanding the Crisis of Democracy with Rosanvallon
Felix Heidenreich | 175

11 Governing Democratically
A Reconceptualization of the Executive based on Pierre Rosanvallon
Anna Hollendung | 199

12 Coals to Newcastle
Samuel Moyn | 217

13 Pierre Rosanvallon's Pragmatic Turn
Stephen W. Sawyer | 229

The Authors | 247

Preface

The present volume has its origins in a colloquium that took place on the occasion of the awarding of the Bielefeld Scientific Award 2016 to Pierre Rosanvallon at the Center for Interdisciplinary Research, Bielefeld. As the papers from this conference and the intense debates with the author that followed during the colloquium proved once again, Rosanvallon situates his research beyond the usual distinctions between scientific disciplines. His reflections on urgent political challenges like the consequences of inequality on the conditions of democratic self-government or recent tendencies within western democracy to transfer decision-making authority from parliaments to governments draw upon and contribute to a wide variety of disciplines including political science, history, sociology, economics as well as philosophy and the humanities.

The colloquium assembled a group of experts in modern political thought, having already widely published in the field and being particularly interested in Rosanvallon, it gave birth to the idea of publishing such a volume. And because the *genius loci* of the Center for Interdisciplinary Research underpinned once more the interdisciplinary character of Rosanvallon's political thought, it quickly became clear that the volume had to highlight this important dimension present throughout Rosanvallon's writings. We would like to thank the participants of the colloquium who have contributed to this book and those who have contributed chapters to its final version. We would like to extend our thanks to Pierre Rosanvallon for publishing the lecture he gave in the context of the Bielefeld science award to this volume. Finally, we are very grateful to the rectorate of Bielefeld University for the financial and organizational support which made this publication possible. We also thank the Center for Interdisciplinary Research at Bielefeld for hosting the colloquium in honor of Pierre Rosanvallon in November 2016.

Oliver Flügel-Martinsen, Franziska Martinsen, Stephen W. Sawyer,
Daniel Schulz

1 Introduction

Stephen W. Sawyer, Oliver Flügel-Martinsen, Franziska Martinsen, Daniel Schulz

In 2015, Pierre Rosanvallon published *Le Bon gouvernement* (English edition 2018), bringing an end to his tetralogy on the contemporary transformations of modern democracy (2006b; 2008b; 2011b; 2015). With this volume, he not only concluded the series of books that had occupied the better part of almost two decades of research, lecturing and writing at the Collège de France, he also unavoidably, shed new light on his previous work. The key idea behind this final volume – that a contemporary democracy must surpass a simple electoral authorization through a reinvention of public confidence and reappropriation – provided an important contribution to his project to articulate the foundation of a democratic theory of government (2015). This last installment therefore captured an essential ambition that has animated Rosanvallon's work for more than three decades: the interconnection between historical analysis and a robust conceptual terminology to inform a theoretical approach to democracy.

Since the publication of the first book of the tetralogy, *La contre-démocratie. La politique à l'age de la defiance* (2006b) [English edition, *Counter Democracy. Politics in an Age of Distrust* (2008)], Rosanvallon's work has drawn increasingly widespread attention. Nonetheless, no major edited volume in English dedicated to his work has yet to appear. As a result, in spite of the growing interest in Rosanvallon's intellectual production, scholars and curious readers have had surprisingly few resources for making sense of his democratic conceptualization and his historico-theoretical method. Indeed, the shape of reception of Rosanvallon has unfortunately been subject to only partial and fragmentary commentaries on his previous works.

Among the most common modes of reception prior to the tetralogy, especially in the Anglophone world, was a reading of his books through the narrow lens of a history of French liberalism. This reception was largely the product of specific readings of his book on the French liberal thinker and statesman of the nineteenth century, François Guizot (*Le Moment Guizot* 1985), which, while playing a key role in stirring new interest in this figure, was also read by some as an apology of early nineteenth-century French liberal doctrinaires. The reception of Rosanvallon as a historian of French liberalism received a new impulse with the first translation of his work into English in Mark Lilla and Thomas Pavel's *New French Thought* in 2000. Lilla had opened this book series in 1994 with a tone of liberal triumphalism, summarizing the history of French political thought, and French political history more generally, since the Revolution under the sign of a deep-seated anti-liberalism. According to him, however, with the help of Raymond Aron, this trend began to finally crumble in the 1970s when a new interest for liberalism emerged in France. The French, he argued, finally contributed to a conversation that had been largely the preserve of Anglo-Americans. A number of Rosanvallon's colleagues from France, especially those at the Raymond Aron Studies Center, found their first audiences in the US through the *New French Thought* project, including, Marcel Gauchet and Pierre Manent. And though Rosanvallon was absent from the first collective volume of this project as was the other great influence on the work of Rosanvallon, Claude Lefort, Rosanvallon was translated later in the book series with an English version of *The New Social Question* (2000b). Thus even if Rosanvallon was not part of the seraglio of this project, many of his close colleagues were (Sawyer/Stewart 2016).

The reading of Rosanvallon as a historian of liberalism could be found in the reception of his works as late as the translation of his *Le Modèle politique français* (2004) into English [*The Demands of Liberty* (2007)]. While the beginning of the book explicitly states its intent to explore a new history of democracy, numerous book reviews continued to understand Rosanvallon's major ambition to be a history of liberalism. Cheryl Welch, for example, proposed that Rosanvallon's book offered a way to understand the French inclination to criticize liberalism. "French public opinion is strikingly negative towards the discourse of globalization, identifying it with liberalism run amuck…Pierre Rosanvallon helps us to understand this evasive impulse." As a result, while she recognized that democracy was an important theme within the book, she argued: "Compelling to those who want to use historical work to clarify the possibilities of a more inclusive liberalism, these claims [for a history of democracy] nevertheless remain elusive and difficult to unpack." She concluded by bringing the book back to the common tension in Franco-American historiographical exchanges on the issue of liberalism, reminding potential readers of "the gulf between Anglophone and Francophone sensibilities around the discourse of liberty." This break was characterized by what she referred to as "Rosanvallon's determined avoidance of the 'L' word." The fact that

Rosanvallon did not use the word liberalism – though extensively employed the word democracy – meant in her eyes then that the book was "yet more evidence of the French penchant for a reformism that dares not speak its name: liberalism by stealth." (Welch 2009) In the same vein, the review on the network of French historians H-France by James Smith Allen announced that the contribution of Rosanvallon's book resided mostly in what he has to say about "the struggle between liberalism and republicanism ... since the Revolution and [that] is not yet finished." So, according to him, Rosanvallon "contends that the republican-liberal dichotomy in the history of modern French politics is simplistic and misleading." (Allen 2007) And the conclusion of the review joins Welch: "The author is correct, I think, to call for comparative study on the model of a liberal Jacobinism despite itself." Andrew Jainchill's review was more attentive to the democratic questions in the book, explicitly recognizing Rosanvallon's main arguments about democracy. But, he also concludes that there is at the same time "an important sense in which the *Demands of Liberty* [...] also reaffirms the very narrative of French illiberalism that Rosanvallon expressly seeks to challenge." (Jainchill 2009) The review of Philip Nord avoided the question of democracy, focusing more on the question of civil society seen through a liberal prism of a certain Tocqueville that he emphasizes with a reference to Putnam when he concludes: "It may well be asked: who is today 'bowling alone'? And the answer to the question, but the citizens of the United States, that once-celebrated homeland of associational activism." (Nord 2008)

All this is not to say that Rosanvallon has not been interested in liberalism or that the issues raised in these reviews were unfair. Rosanvallon has explored many of the key authors in the liberal canon, and some elements of his work are certainly compatible with a broader interest in liberalism that began in the 1970s in France. It does however highlight the overly dominant role that liberalism has taken in many of the English reviews of his work, at the expense of the democratic, especially in the reception of the earlier phases of Rosanvallon's work. Rarely, one might suggest, has the displayed motivation of the work and the horizon of reception gone in such different directions. Samuel Moyn and Andrew Jainchill offered an ambitious and fruitful second interpretive framework for Rosanvallon's work when they published a landmark article in English on Rosanvallon in the *Journal of Modern History* in 2004. Here, they explicitly attempted to pull Rosanvallon out of the shadows of liberalism and toward the field of anti-totalitarian thought. At the heart of Rosanvallon's work, as Moyn would argue forcefully once again in the introduction to his edited volume of Rosanvallon's writings in 2006, was an engagement with a historical exploration of political history and theory from the perspective of the anti-totalitarianism that had played such an important role in the

French political theory of the mid-1970s and early 1980s. As wide-ranging and influential as this article was, however, it did privilege the relationship between Rosanvallon and one of his mentors François Furet. "No book has affected the study of modern French history in the last twenty-five years more than Francois Furet's *Interpreting the French Revolution*," Jainchill and Moyn argued. "This paper interprets the intellectual career of Pierre Rosanvallon as an attempt to test the flexibility of Furet's paradigm for the understanding of French history and its amenability to new ends."

Insisting on this connection to Furet had two consequences, however. First, it situated Rosanvallon largely as a scholar of French history. While this is certainly not incorrect, such a rendering tended to imply that the wide range of activities – from syndicalism to direct involvement with the Second Left under Rocard and his connections with the Finance Minister and later President of the European Commission, Jacques Delors (much of which they discussed in their well-researched essay) – seemed to lead ineluctably toward his ultimate interest in the history of nineteenth-century French democracy. Second, such a reading of Rosanvallon in the context of Furet's later writings – in particular his *Passing of an Illusion* –, his position within the Committee on Social Thought at the University of Chicago where Allan Bloom was leading a kind of conservative intellectual crusade, and Furet's own conscious liberal political positioning did little to assuage a sense that those who had worked closely with him, like Rosanvallon, were also liberal. Thus even as the ambition of Moyn and Jainchill's article, as well as Moyn's introductory essay to the Rosanvallon reader, attempted to send readers in the direction of anti-totalitarianism, the fact that one of the first major articles on Rosanvallon introduced him first and foremost as the disciple of Furet, did little to challenge Rosanvallon's association as a French historian of liberalism.

The completion of this most recent cycle of Rosanvallon's work however clearly places Rosanvallon far beyond the fields of liberalism and modern French history. The balance has plainly shifted toward a historically-informed political theory, offering a radical new conceptual vocabulary for thinking the democratic. It may therefore be helpful in this new moment to provide a brief look back at Rosanvallon's work to present, especially since only a small portion of Rosanvallon's considerable oeuvre (he has published more than 25 monographs to date) has been translated into English and, as a result, important aspects of his work as well as a collective volume in the English language on its different aspects and its interdisciplinary character have until now remained unavailable. Indeed, outside *The New Social Question*, which appeared in Mark Lilla and Thomas Pavel's New French Thought series at Princeton University Press in 2000, the serial translation into English of Rosanvallon's work only began with his entry into the Collège de

France with the publication of *The Demands of Liberty: Civil Society in France since the Revolution* in 2007. Since then, the four major works of his tetralogy: *Counter-Democracy: Politics in an Age of Distrust* (2008), *Democratic Legitimacy: Impartiality, Reflexivity, Proximity* (2011), *The Society of Equals* (2013) and *Good Government: Democracy Beyond Elections* (2018) have all appeared in English. While the English translation of these works has provided an important entry point into Rosanvallon's larger oeuvre for Anglophone readers, the focus on his later investigations has also raised the stakes of the present volume. As a number of the chapters in this collection explicitly demonstrate, Rosanvallon's work in his Collège de France years (2001-2018) drew directly from the topics and subjects he had been developing since the mid-1970s, which in many cases were only partially related to the French history of liberalism. Alongside the tetralogy, then, it is possible to establish five other thematic projects.

First, between 1976 and 1981, Rosanvallon published three books: *L'Âge de l'autogestion* (1976), *Le Capitalisme utopique. Histoire de l'idée de marché* (1979), and *La Crise de l'État-providence* (1981). Without imposing an artificial synthesis on these works, one may note that they shared three broad themes: an ambition to bridge the gap between scientific or academic works and civic engagement for a wider public audience; an attempt to shift the terrain, especially on the left, from an overwhelming focus on economic struggle toward the importance of the political (note that the initial subtitle of *L'Age de l'autogestion* was "la politique au poste de commandement"); and, at the same time, an interest in pushing beyond a tradition of statism – or a "state-centered" society [*social-étatisme*] – to favor instead a reevaluation of the potential development of civil society. These three books, along with his co-authored volume (with Patrick Viveret), *Pour une nouvelle culture politique*, which appeared in 1977, cemented Rosanvallon's position as a public intellectual. It must be mentioned that his *La Nouvelle Question Sociale. Repenser l'État-providence*, which he published in 1995, was to serve as a companion volume to *La Crise de l'État-providence* published almost 14 years earlier, highlighting a key trait of Rosanvallon's work: his theoretical and historical vision of a given project often spreads across entire decades.

With the publication of *Le Moment Guizot* in 1985, Rosanvallon opened a second set of reflections, which continued with the publication of *La Monarchie impossible. Histoire des Chartes de 1814 et 1830* almost ten years later in 1994. Rosanvallon maintained an interest in confronting contemporary political and social problems in these two volumes, his work also took a more academic historical turn. It was in between these two sets of works that he entered the École des Hautes Études en Sciences Sociales in 1983. With these two volumes, Rosanvallon's work did indeed focus more specifically on the singularity of French liberalism, exploring the broader set of political and social questions that emerged in the post-revolutionary period between Napoleon and the 1848 Revolution. While these works clearly concentrated on French history, and even the specificities of the French political tradition, they also explored a series of themes that have become central within the fields of political history, political theory and social theory. Among the most important themes covered in Rosanvallon's exploration of liberalism was an attempt to uncover novel ways of conceiving of the relationship between the state and civil society. Far from looking to find answers for the present in early nineteenth-century French liberalism, Rosanvallon's account attempted to open up new possibilities within the fraught state-civil society relationship by revealing the variety of post-revolutionary conceptions and thereby denaturalizing those in the present.

These two works also confirm Rosanvallon's particular tendency to pursue the continuity in his research over long periods of time. Like the twin works on French liberalism, Rosanvallon inaugurated a third major project when he published the first book in another, two-volume investigation that also spread across 15 years with his *L'État en France de 1789 à nos jours* (1990). The second volume, *Le Modèle politique français* (2006) showed its relationship to the first through its subtitle *Civil Society in France since the Revolution*. Continuing his larger set of investigations on the state-society relationship, these two books remain Rosanvallon's chronologically sequential broadest historical works as they cover the entire period of modern France from the late eighteenth century to the last decades of the twentieth. While the latter was translated soon after publication, the former remains unavailable in English, highlighting one of the challenges of situating Rosanvallon's recent works within his larger research program without a broader understanding of his oeuvre. While the structure and style of the two works remain distinct, rarely has a theoretically-minded political historian provided such an in-depth account of the civil society and state traditions within a specific national context across 200 years.

In spite of the ambition and scope of these previous works, Rosanvallon's most important research project in this earlier period is no doubt the fourth project: his trilogy on French democracy across the long nineteenth century (from the Revolutionary period to the decades leading up to and surrounding World War I) including *Le sacre du citoyen. Histoire du suffrage universel en France* (1992); *Le peuple introuvable. Histoire de la représentation démocratique en France* (1998); and *La démocratie inachevée. Histoire de la souveraineté du peuple en France* (2000a). These books highlight Rosanvallon's theoretical and historical ambition by illustrating the method he had been elaborating since the mid 1980s in his "Pour une histoire conceptuelle du politique (note de travail)" which appeared in the *Revue de synthèse* in 1986. Focusing respectively on three key "concepts" of the political – citizenship, representation, and sovereignty – these books are the strongest illustration of Rosanvallon's recurrent statement that it is insufficient to understand democracy from a historical perspective because democracy *is* a history. He offers at once a genealogy of these three concepts, which remain at the heart of so much work in political theory, while at the same time situating them within the development of revolutionary and post-revolutionary democracy in France (with occasional references to the US and the UK). One of the important contributions of the present volume is the way a number of authors return to this trilogy to find resources for thinking through Rosanvallon's historical and theoretical contributions.

Since the trilogy, and alongside the tetralogy, Rosanvallon's fifth project may be captured in his wide range of editorial activities. The importance of some of these endeavors is highlighted in the chapters that follow. This aspect of his intellectual engagement goes back to the early 1970s when he edited the journal of the CFDT union, CFDT-*Aujourd'hui* and later starting in 1975 co-edited the journal *Faire* with Patrick Viveret. His first book series came in 1971 when he edited the collection "Objectifs" for the Éditions du Cerf – it is worth noting that this series was already designed to provide easily accessible books for a large politically engaged audience. Rosanvallon was involved in many other editorial projects over the years, but it is worth mentioning his most ambitious recent projects including the *Books and Ideas* (*La vie des idées*) website, the *Republic of ideas* (*La République des idées*) book series, the *Life Stories* (*Raconter la vie*) book series which has become the *Raconter le travail* project and his book series at the Seuil, *Books of the New World* (*Les livres du nouveau monde*). All of these projects testify once again to the interdisciplinary nature of Rosanvallon's investigations. These series include authors from almost every field from creative fiction writing to geography to philosophy to economics (the French edition of economist Thomas Piketty's best-selling *Le Capital au XXe siècle* appeared in the *Books of the New World* series). They also stand as a testament to Rosanvallon's consistent efforts to break down barriers between the high towers of academia and varying modes of public action.

It is our sense that the set of questions that has emerged out of the tetralogy and these five projects have focused on four major themes: first, an analysis of the *structural aporias* of political modernity; second, the role of *indetermination* in modern democracy; third, the ways in which the political forms out of society working upon itself, especially in modern democracy; and fourth, a methodology focused on both *historical and conceptual definitions of the political*. The ways

Rosanvallon has integrated these themes and questions into his work pushes far beyond the limits of this introduction. But for the purposes of providing an introduction to this volume and its ambition to provide a first synthetic and interdisciplinary exploration of his work in English, it is possible to observe that Rosanvallon has structured his work on the history and theory of the democracy by elaborating the conceptual aporias that he argues underpin self-government. Second, these structural aporias, can never be resolved, revealing a fundamental uncertainty or indetermination at the heart of the modern political. It is because of this unremitting indetermination, or modern society's inability ever to be entirely consonant with itself, that society is constantly working on itself. Furthermore, it is out of this ceaseless operation that the symbolic imaginaries emerge which give meaning to social action understood in all of its diversity. Finally, it is precisely because of this constant generation of an interpretive social framework that a method is required that is both historically grounded – accounts for change over time – and conceptual to reveal the structural similarities across distinct historical experiences of democracy and its pathologies.

Given the completion of the tetralogy, this is an opportune time to attempt an initial retrospective study of Rosanvallon's work. With its emphasis on democracy, interdisciplinarity and political theory, the present volume consciously attempts to take stock of this new moment in the reception of Rosanvallon as his political thought increasingly stands among the most insightful in current debates in democratic and political theory. It includes two essays which were previously published in French and/or German. The other chapters, including Rosanvallon's essay were written for this book.

Rosanvallon's lecture, which inaugurates the volume, represents a condensed outline of his reflection on the fate of contemporary democracy. As the following contributions also show, this text reveals Rosanvallon's interest in thinking outside the borders of academic disciplines. Neither the label "history" nor the label "political science" nor "political theory" sufficiently situate the particular perspective pursued in this piece. It is rather a classical example of how Rosanvallon's situates political theoretical interrogations alongside a historical and sociological mode of investigation, thus reflecting at a conceptual level on the historical genealogy of our political order, and trying to grasp the problem of the political in a world where democracy has become the most important contested concept in our political vocabulary.

Here, Rosanvallon lays out two of democracy's structuring antinomies: the problematic representation of the people and the uncertainty of the forms of popular sovereignty. The first antinomy has produced a series of attempts to determine the fundamental subject of democracy between its two forms, the social and the symbolic. The second is the ongoing challenge to translate democratic legitimacy into an institutional setting that mirrors the expectations of self-legislation and autonomy under the sign of popular sovereignty. Both aspects have been discussed at length in Rosanvallon's historical studies and are resumed here to show in which sense the ultimate goal of an investigation of the political may grasp the "structure of this indetermination" (Rosanvallon 2019: 32). The existence of this inner void is the reason why democracy regularly produces a variety of pathologies that are not exterior to the democratic experience but a part of its own history. This is why according to Rosanvallon's political theory of democracy must be capable of including the deceptions linked to democratic expectations. In summing up his reflection, democracy is thus "the regime that must ceaselessly interrogate itself as to its definition" (ibid: 35), reaffirming his conclusion that democracy not only has a history, but more importantly is a history. The task of exploring the democratic political is thus to reconstruct the unfolding of that history and to reflect upon its antinomies and blind spots. At a time when it has become clearer than ever that the narrative of democracy is much more than just a linear story of successes, this openness to the ambivalences and the different paths of democracy are the reason why the interdisciplinary investigations of Rosanvallon provide important insights into our contemporary condition.

Paula Diehl focuses on the increasingly pressing topic of populism in contemporary democracies and goes back to the concept of political representation, which is at the core of Rosanvallon's work. Diehl shows why representation in a democracy can never be described as having come to a successful finish, but rather as something that is in a permanently flowing process. This process contains ruptures and flaws, which are highlighted by Rosanvallon and which contribute to a better understanding of the populist phenomenon.

Oliver Flügel-Martinsen and *Franziska Martinsen* expound the framework in which Rosanvallon's work is best to be considered as a genuine interdisciplinary attempt to reflect upon the political with regard to its complex methodological approach and especially with regard to its participation-oriented access to democratic practice. They hold that Rosanvallon's intrinsic research interest lies in the critical pervasion of crucial political and social topics rather than in elaborating academic methodologies to describe these political and social phenomena.

Michel Dormal highlights the way Rosanvallon conceives political thought in a historical perspective in showing the differences to the Cambridge School as well as to Reinhart Koselleck and his history of concepts. Both approaches have had a deep influence on Rosanvallon's work, nonetheless he has developed his own position in writing the history of the political. It is thus the relation to the present that makes his approach valuable for political theory because he is adding historical depth of field to the democratic aporias by reconstructing their genealogy.

Wim Weymans revisits the central concept of Rosanvallon's work in political theory, by exploring his original and capacious definition of "democracy." Revealing how democracy pushes far beyond the confines of a legal, institutional, or organizational framework, Weymans explores Rosanvallon's understanding of democracy as a social form and the wide variety of forms it has taken historically. He therefore disagrees with claims that Rosanvallon's conception of the democratic is insufficiently critical, while at the same time offering a diagnosis for such misinterpretations: Rosanvallon's conception of democracy may be, paradoxically, too broad and not broad enough.

Greg Conti explores the political and philosophical challenge of the role of the press in Rosanvallon's treatment of two nineteenth-century conceptions of governance: François Guizot and Napoleon III's caesarism. Conti highlights the pathological nature of both of these conceptions, showing how, in Rosanvallon's view, neither adequately conceptualize the relationship between a free press and a democracy. At the same time, according to Conti, there is an asymmetry in Rosanvallon's critique in that he ultimately finds the Bonapartist conception particularly dangerous. Conti concludes by drawing lessons from these two conceptions for providing a more precise account of the place of the free press in modern democratic systems.

Alain Chatriot focuses specifically on Rosanvallon's research and civic engagement during his almost two-decade tenure at the Collège de France. Chatriot explicitly attempts to draw out the connections between Rosanvallon's earlier work, in particular the trilogy on French democracy and his histories of the state and civil society, to highlight the broader thematic and methodological continuities across his oeuvre. Within this analysis he also emphasizes the interdisciplinary variety and historical range of Rosanvallon's seminars within the Collège de France and introduces the broad outlines of his editorial activities of the past two decades.

In his contribution *Daniel Schulz* contextualizes Rosanvallon within the crisis of French republicanism, interpretating his approach as a liberalization of the republican paradigm. At the same time, he argues, Rosanvallon maintains central aspects of republican thought, notably in showing why a democracy cannot be understood without constant reference to its own historical narrative. A theory of democracy according to Rosanvallon is thus irreducible neither to a pure functional analysis nor to a normative justification of principles. It is rather a medium where the positive and the negative experiences of democratic practices are kept present, are interpreted and transformed.

Felix Heidenreich focuses on the concept of counter-democracy. After a comparative reconstruction of counter-democracy, which is as distinguished from the alternative concept of monitory democracy proposed by Keane as it is different from the "romanticism of being against," Heidenreich comes to a critical conclusion. On the one hand, Rosanvallon's model is offering multiple inspirations to conceptualize contemporary democracy in a complex way. On the other hand however, he could have given more space to the role of parties in modern democracies, since political parties have always represented a counter-democratic aspect.

Anna Hollendung discusses the recent focus on the question of good government. Her chapter deals with Rosanvallon's attempt to theorize a specific form of democratic government. Starting from his analysis of the "presidentialization of democracies," she demonstrates how his theory of counter-democracy is best understood as supplying a supplement, and not a substitution of democratic institutions as some critics may fear. In her line of interpretation, Rosanvallon is therefore delivering empirical evidence of the transformation of democracy and at the same time proposing an agenda of reform that, while it may not fulfil all of its promises, makes new forms of democracy visible.

In his article, *Samuel Moyn* points toward an obstacle in the reception of Rosanvallon in the Anglophone world. The American discourse on French Theory has long been dominated by the demand of radical chic, whereas Rosanvallon's theory of democracy hardly fits into such narrow schemes. Running against the usual expectations towards theoretical productions from French origins, Moyn shows how Rosanvallon was only hesitantly received in the US. At the same time, Rosanvallon's combination of liberal and republican arguments might have numerous possibilities of connecting to American discussions of problems of democracy, thus enlarging the range of perspectives and examples commonly discussed in the Anglophone discourse of political theory.

The book concludes with *Stephen Sawyer's* essay. Sawyer takes Rosanvallon's principal methodological statements on a conceptual or philosophical history of the political as his point of departure to trace a subtle but important shift in his oeuvre. While Rosanvallon placed the political at the heart of his intellectual project since the mid 1980s, building on the work of Claude Lefort, he also underlined the proximity between the political and secularized religious concepts, and their emergence within exceptional moments of political life. Rosanvallon's diagnosis in the mid-2000s that the crisis of contemporary democracy was driven by a generalized disenchantment therefore obliged him to consider the conditions for a re-symbolization of contemporary political life. Sawyer shows that this resymbolization in Rosanvallon's later work – both within his editorial project *Raconter la vie* and his tetralogy – largely took place through a shift from a focus on the exceptional toward a renewed investment in the pragmatic and the everyday.

Together these chapters offer one of the first attempts in English to collect a plurality of voices and approaches on Pierre Rosanvallon's work. It is our ambition that they be precisely that: an opening statement in a long and engaged discussion with his oeuvre and the past, present and future of the democratic.

BIBLIOGRAPHY

Allen, James Smith (2007), "Review of Pierre Rosanvallon, The Demands of Liberty: Civil Society in France since the Revolution." In: H-France Review 7/106

Jainchill, Andrew (2009) "Review of Pierre Rosanvallon, The Demands of Liberty: Civil Society in France since the Revolution." In: The Journal of Modern History 81/2, pp. 429-430.

Jainchill, Andrew/Moyn, Samuel (2004): "French Democracy between Totalitarianism and Solidarity: Pierre Rosanvallon and Revisionist Historiography." In: The Journal of Modern History 76, pp. 107-154.

Nord, Philip (2008): "Review of Pierre Rosanvallon, Demands of Liberty: Civil Society in France since the Revolution." In: Social History 33/3, pp. 351-354.

Rosanvallon, Pierre (1986): "Pour une histoire conceptuelle du politique (note de travail)." In: Revue de synthèse, 107/1-2, pp. 93-105.

Rosanvallon, Pierre (1992): Le sacre du citoyen. Histoire du suffrage universel en France, Paris: Gallimard.

Rosanvallon, Pierre (1998): Le peuple introuvable. Histoire de la représentation démocratique en France, Paris: Gallimard.

Rosanvallon, Pierre (2000a): La démocratie inachevée. Histoire de la souveraineté du peuple en France, Paris: Gallimard.

Rosanvallon, Pierre (2000b): The New Social Question, Princeton: Princeton University Press.

Rosanvallon, Pierre (2006a): Democracy Past and Future, Samuel Moyn (ed.), New York: Columbia University Press.

Rosanvallon, Pierre (2006b): La contre-démocratie: La politique à l'âge de la défiance, Paris: Seuil.

Rosanvallon, Pierre (2007): The Demands of Liberty: Civil Society in France since the Revolution, Cambridge: Harvard University Press.

Rosanvallon, Pierre (2008a): Counter-Democracy: Politics in an Age of Distrust, Cambridge: Cambridge University Press.

Rosanvallon, Pierre (2008b): La légitimité démocratique: Impartialité, réflexivité, proximité, Paris: Seuil.

Rosanvallon, Pierre (2011a): Democratic Legitimacy: Impartiality, Reflexivity, Proximity, Cambridge: Harvard University Press.
Rosanvallon, Pierre (2011b): La société des égaux, Paris: Seuil.
Rosanvallon, Pierre (2013): The Society of Equals, Cambridge: Harvard University Press.
Rosanvallon, Pierre (2014a): Le Parlement des invisibles, Paris: Seuil, Raconter la vie.
Rosanvallon, Pierre (2015): Le bon gouvernement, Paris: Seuil.
Rosanvallon, Pierre (2018a): Good Government: Democracy beyond Elections, Cambridge: Harvard University Press.
Rosanvallon, Pierre (2018b): Notre histoire intellectuelle et politique – 1968-2018, Paris: Seuil.
Rosanvallon, Pierre (2019): "The Political Theory of Democracy." In: Oliver Flügel-Martinsen/Franziska Martinsen/Stephen W. Sawyer/Daniel Schulz, Pierre Rosanvallon's Interdisciplinary Political Thought, Bielefeld: transcript, pp. 23-38.
Sawyer, Stephen W./Stewart, Iain (eds.) (2016): In Search of the Liberal Moment: Democracy, Anti-totalitarianism, and Intellectual Politics in France since 1950, Basingstoke/New York: Palgrave Macmillan.
Welch, Cheryl (2009) "Review of Pierre Rosanvallon, The Demands of Liberty: Civil Society in France since the Revolution." In: French Politics, Culture and Society, 27/1, pp. 120-124.

2 The Political Theory of Democracy*

Pierre Rosanvallon

INTRODUCTION

I propose to define political theory as a specific field within the social sciences dedicated to the analysis of the *political*. It must be differentiated from political science, the object of which is *politics*. As I understand the term, the "political" is at once a field and a project. As a field, it refers to a site where the multiple threads of human life come together, so that their activities and discourses can be understood in a comprehensive framework. It exists by virtue of the fact that there is such a thing as a "society," whose members, by acknowledging it as a totality, afford meaning to its constituent parts. As a project, the political is the process whereby a human collectivity, which can never be reduced to a mere "population," gradually becomes a full-fledged community. It is constituted through an always contentious process whereby the explicit or implicit rules of what can be shared and accomplished in common – the rules which give form to the life of the polity – are elaborated. Whatever the catalogue of cultural and social facts, economic variables, and institutional rationales, it is impossible to decipher society at its most essential level without bringing to light the nerve center from which the very fact of its institution originates.

Political science analyzes the functioning of institutions, unravels the mechanisms of public decision-making, illuminates the reasoning of actors and the ways they interact, disentangles voters' rationales, and describes the rites and symbols that structure political life. It develops models, calculates correlations, and defines typologies for a better understanding of politics as a specific field of human action.

---

* This chapter was translated from the original French by Michael Behrent.

In referring to the "political" rather than to "politics", one is speaking of democracy and law, state and nation, equality and justice, identity and sovereignty, and citizenship and civility – in short, of everything that constitutes in its essence political life beyond the immediate field of partisan competition for political power, everyday governmental action, and the ordinary function of institutions.

Political science seeks the formal conceptualization of empirical data (it is thus "theoretical" in a technical sense, as it attempts to define internally consistent propositions). Political theory, however, has a *normative* dimension. But there are two different conceptions of normativity. Normativity is most often understood as a coherent set of concepts or values defined *a priori*, in a way that defines a question in universalistic terms. This is *ex-ante* normativity. Rawls and Habermas are two prominent and remarkable examples of this approach in our own time. But another conception of the political is also possible – one that tries to make sense of the conflicts and perplexities that structure the definitive concepts of the political (sovereignty, equality, identity, legitimacy, democracy, and so on). What are the implications of considering these terms in the historical and sociological conditions in which they were formulated, in order to attain a different kind of normativity, an *ex-post* normativity, corresponding to a different definition of universalizing concepts? A theory of democracy understood in this way can be approached in concrete terms. But it must begin with the indeterminacy of the word "democracy" itself.

AN ELUSIVE WORD

In an eighteenth-century dictionary, one finds the following definition: "democracy: archaic term used to describe ancient Greek constitutions and the remnants of medieval practices in several small Swiss counties." These archaic – and almost technical – connotations of the word "democracy" in the eighteenth century explain its absence from French revolutionary discourse in 1789. In fact, the idea of a regime in which the people was both legislator and magistrate inspired no one, as it seemed to hark back to a bygone age, an antiquated and unstable stage of political development. To the generation of 1789, the word recalled a past that combined utopian theory with a practice marked by failure and outbreaks of unrest. Thus democracy's pejorative connotations were almost as strong as its utopian and archaic dimension.

Of the many revolutionary newspapers, not one used the word "democracy" or "democratic" in its headlines between 1789 and 1800. The adjectives "national," "patriotic," and "republican" (the letter first appearing in 1792) were most common on the front pages of papers from this period. Moreover, the word "democracy" was not used a single time during the debates over the right to vote occurring between 1789 and 1791. The relative absence of the word "democracy" from revolutionary discourse is confirmed by an examination of dictionaries dating from this era. Of the ten sociopolitical lexicons published between 1789 and 1801, only one contained an entry for "democracy." On both the right and the left, the concept seems to have been largely ignored.

"Under democracy," wrote Sieyès, one of France's founding fathers, "the citizens themselves make the laws, and name their public officials directly. Under our plan, the citizens decide – more or less directly – on their deputies to the legislative assembly." With the size of the country making any direct exercise of the general will technically impossible, Sieyès concluded that "France is not, and cannot be, a democracy." The representative form of government that Sieyès desired should thus not be confused with democracy, which he continued to perceive as it was commonly understood in the eighteenth century. Like Thomas Paine, he defined a "republic" as a government by representation, and on this ground rejected the democratic model: "The republicans of France," he said, "do not desire the pure democracy of old Athens." At the time of the American Revolution, the word "democracy" was also used in a purely negative sense. In the language of the founding fathers, it was related to three images: images of disorder (the "mob," the populace), images of irrationality (in connection to instances of rage, madness, passion, and imprudence), and immorality. When it was said in these times that the people was the "the font of all powers," no one considered using the term democracy to describe the regime founded on this principle. It was, rather, the term "republic" that was used to refer to the political good they sought to establish. How and when did the term democracy enter both countries' vocabularies?

In France it began to be used in the early nineteenth century, around 1820, but it came then to connote modern egalitarian *society*, not the political regime associated with the classical Greek and Roman republics. The semantic shift was completed in 1835, when Alexis de Tocqueville published the first volume of his *Democracy in America*. By making equality of conditions modern society's great revolutionary engine, he posited (in the first volume of *Democracy in America*) the sociological definition of democracy. Our interest in his work, however, lies in the way in which it exemplifies the impossibility of limiting oneself to this definition. In his work, the meaning of democracy is never settled; modern civilization remains forever subject to the irresistible pressure that popular sovereignty exerts on governing institutions. Tocqueville's private papers show this very clearly: "Democracy," he writes in once place, "constitutes political right. These two things are not analogous. Democracy is a way a society can be, whereas popular sovereignty is a form of government." But some pages later he retreats from this clear-cut distinction, writing that "popular sovereignty and democracy are terms that are perfectly correlated: one presents the theoretical idea, while the other presents its practical realization." His vacillation testifies at once to the semantic shift and its limit, as if it were impossible to dissociate completely the social from the political and to build the new independently of the old. After the Revolution of 1848, a new layer of meaning was added to the word, but in a way that was very vague. Democracy began to be celebrated, but at the time it remained feared; it was considered inevitable, but also obscure and problematic.

In the US, in the early nineteenth century, to be called a democrat was considered an insult (democracy being seen as the equivalent of *mobocracy*). The term was at that time an equivalent to the denomination of "populists" in contemporary Europe. The federalists thus called Jefferson's supporters "democrats" in order to demean them. This insult would then be inverted and positively embraced, as a valorizing attribute, resulting in the founding of the "Democratic Party" in 1828. The Democrat was the "common man" who accused the federalist elites of being "Brahmins" or aristocrats. The opposing side valued what was known as the "nose-count democracy" or "coonskin democracy" (i.e., democracy of those who wore a trapper's hat, with a raccoon's tail), celebrating the authentic America of these nose-counts and coonskins. The Federalists, however, who founded the "Whig" party, which later become the "Republican" party, soon came, by the same token, to emphasize their "popular touch" in electoral competitions. And they ultimately said that they were as "democratic" as Jackson's supporters, whose candidate was elected president in 1830. Thus it was also a sociological variable that explains the shift to the positive use of the term "democracy" in the United States – yet in the blurriest of ways, even more than in France. The American cult of democracy would ultimately be associated with a form of messianism, referring to a divine project. It was this will to appropriate "democracy" as a synonym for American exceptionalism that completed its acclimatization and placed the term at the heart of the American political vocabulary. Its consecration would come when it transformed America into a country that conceived itself as promoting a new universalism (an idea whose naïve arrogance produced, over the course of the twentieth century, effects with which we are all familiar). A famous writer from this period stated: "For us, democracy is now merely Christianity put into practice." This meant that democracy had become a religion and that it was no longer simply a political regime.

The semantic triumph of the word "democracy" has consequently been a triumph of ambiguity. Behind a facade of clarity, the word "democracy" conveys modern society's perplexities concerning its ultimate political foundations.

If democracy is now readily supported by nearly all voters, embodying as it does the most desirable type of political regime in the eyes of the great majority of our contemporaries, its definition is far from meeting with similar consensus, at least if one refuses to content oneself with the usual paraphrases and conventional formulas (democracy as the "power of the people," for example). There is scarcely another word in political usage whose practical definition is more variable. Hence the recurrent tendency to prop it up with some adjective or other. Like an insipid dish that has taste only when spiced up, democracy has no real character except when it is specified that it is "liberal," "popular," "real," "radical," or "socialist." Hence also the constantly demonstrated difficulty of drawing a clear dividing line between democracy and its pathologies (such as demagoguery or populism), as well as the perplexities manifested in questions surrounding the proper use of the referendum. The word "democracy" is at once a solution and a problem. In it coexist the good and the vague. This coexistence does not principally stem from democracy's status as a distant and utopian ideal upon which everyone agrees, with disputes over its definition pertaining only to questions of the means for realizing it. Far from corresponding banally to a sort of methodological indeterminacy, the fluctuating meaning of democracy reflects its history and its essence, inextricably mixing the question of popular sovereignty with that of equality.

This ambiguity is hardly new. In the ancient Greek world the terms *eleutheria* (liberty as a capacity to resist tyranny), *isonomia* (norms applying to all, implying the absence of aristocratic privileges), *isegoria* (equal right to speak in an assembly) were in use much before the appearance of the word *demokratia* to express ideals of equality and participation. But the fact is that this new word had never been defined. There was not a single *Treatise* dealing with democracy. The reason is that it appeared as controversial, saddled with *aporias*. Its very etymology testifies to this fact. Thus the verb *kratein* is equivocal. While at a functional level it meant to exercise power, in common usage its connotations were more aggressive. It referred to the idea of victory in combat, specifically winning a trial of strength: it means to seize the advantage, assert one's ascendency, and establish a relationship of domination. It indicated a superiority of an almost physical nature of a man or a group over a third party. Applied to the *dèmos*, it suggested a show of strength in which the people triumphed, one side gaining the upper hand over the other. It has, in this way, a brutal and unilateral quality. To explain what some saw as the threatening connotations of the *dèmos* wielding *kratos*, one contemporary historian has rather provocatively suggested that its meaning was roughly equivalent to that, in the twentieth century, of the concept of "dictatorship of the proletariat" (Cartledge 2009). Perhaps this explains why the word *dèmokratia* has been primarily used pejoratively (i.e., as government of the poor and ignorant mob) – that is, as having the threatening character of power wielded as a form of class revenge. It has of course been invoked positively and politically, in response to more critical views. (cf. Hansen 1999) But most evidence leaves little doubt that it gave rise primarily to questions, suspicion, and controversy. By the same token, it is most frequently mentioned by its detractors rather than by its proponents. Thus Nicole Loraux (1979) speaks of *kratos* as a "cumbersome word" that is "surrounded by silence," since it was missing from great flights of oratory as well most historical accounts, which preferred to emphasize *arkhe*. It was as if it could never be a glorious standard or be held up as an eminently definable good. Hence, she explains, the "unrelenting avoidance by democrats of the word *dèmokratia*," insofar as it referred to a division of the polis into two parts, with one dominating the other. In this instance, democracy referred simply to the *tyranny of the majority*.

Consequently, defining democracy means making sense of these semantic ambiguities. Formulating a theory of democracy requires starting from the premise that it is an "elastic word," to borrow the well-known phrase of Auguste Blanqui, the revolutionary. It is thus on the basis of its indeterminacy, its tensions, and its contradictions that one must build a theory of democracy. Far from simply referring to a practical uncertainty concerning the conditions under which it is organized institutionally, democracy's floating meaning is fundamental to its essence. It evokes a type of regime that has never ceased resisting undeniable categorization. This is, moreover, the source of the distinctive malaise which underpins its history. The parade of deceptions and the sense of betrayal that have always accompanied it have been all the more intense insofar as its definition continues to be incomplete. This vagueness is the inner spring of a quest and dissatisfaction that struggle, by the same token, to become explicit. To understand democracy, one must begin with this fact, in which the history of a disenchantment blends into the history of an indeterminacy.

DEMOCRACY'S TWO STRUCTURING ANTINOMIES

1. The Problematic Representation of the People

If by definition "the" people lays claim to being the political subject of a democratic order, the idea that this power should be anonymous and commanding is not self-evident. The people is a master that is inseparably imperious and problematic. It is a "we" or a "one" whose representation always remains contentious. Between the people as a body, conceived as a sovereign, and its multiple concrete manifestations, a considerable gap exists. The former is presumed to constitute a unified and homogeneous block, whereas the latter appears pluralistic and divided; it exists only in the form of differentiated social classes and contradictory opinions. This gap does not result solely from the difficulty of superimposing an abstract category on tangible entities. It is also, more structurally, the consequence of the contradiction between democracy as a political principle, on the one hand, and as a sociological principle, on the other. Indeed, modern politics conferred power upon the people at the very moment when its emancipatory project rendered society abstract by sanctifying the individual through the affirmation of human rights. Its political principle consecrated the power of a collective subject whose sociological principle was dissolving its tangible consistency and minimizing its visibility. Initially, the idea of popular sovereignty had no trouble accommodating this tension, when it was limited to defining a principle of opposition to and differentiation from the past (in the form of a critique of tyranny and absolutism) or the outside. It only seemed uncertain when sovereignty had to conceive of itself as an acting and instituting force.

This reduced visibility of the social was not the consequence of the sudden entrance of the "individual" onto the social stage, taking the place of old regime corporate bodies. Its source at first lies in the fact that the imperative of equality, which is required to make each person a full-fledged citizen and legal subject, means considering people in relatively abstract terms. All their differences and distinctions must be kept at arm's length, so that they are considered solely from the standpoint of the essential quality they share: that of being autonomous subjects. Put differently, it is the *juridical* consecration of the individual which leads to the rejection of substantive conceptions of the social as archaic and unbearable. For this reason, democratic society leads to the radical rejection of the organic, a permanent critique of institutions that might chain human beings to nature and thus make them dependent on an external power. The requisites of equality and the conditions of autonomy impose, in this way, their imperatives, seeing as legitimate no form of social bond other than those emanating from voluntary contracts, established between individual relations whose artificiality ensures that one is freed from natural determinations and historical legacies. The enterprise of modernity thus makes it necessary de-substantialize the social, reducing it to a pure quotity; that of conditions of equivalence and commensurability between independent individuals. The social loses, in this way, all particular consistency, yielding its place to a formal principle of juridical construction.

In democracy, the people, by the same token, has no form: it loses all bodily density and becomes, positively, a *number*, that is, a force composed of equals, of individuals who are purely equivalent only under the reign of law. This is what, in its radical way, universal suffrage expresses: it represents the advent of a sequential order. Society consists of nothing but identical, completely substitutable voices, reduced, in the foundational moment of elections, to numerical units that pile up in the ballot box: it becomes a pure fact of arithmetic. Substance is completely hidden, in such instances, behind number, reinforcing the effects of abstraction tied to a purely procedural constitution of the social. By disincorporating the social, the modern world must automatically resort with increasing frequency to fiction. Indeed, it is all the more compelled to bestow legal personhood on the people when the latter has no obvious consistency. It no longer exists except as an assemblage of bodies. The first theorists of the social contract resolved this difficulty by giving the institution of the monarchy the role of representing society. Thus, for Hobbes, it is the sovereign who gives the people, who at first glance are simply a multitude, a recognizable albeit fictitious form: the process of representation becomes indistinguishable, in this case, from that of embodiment. Representation, here, mediates identity. As the author of the *Leviathan* emphasized, to represent is to personify.

To resolve the "ambiguity of the word 'people'," the task of political representation has consisted, from this perspective, in creating a people that is a fiction, in the legal sense of the term – that is, in forging a symbolic body to stand in for the actual people, which has become un-localizable and un-representable. This is the task of symbolic representation, which changed character with the advent of the democratic imperative. The function of mediation and embodiment that once belonged to the monarchy had to take a different path. This is the source of the structural incompletion that underpins the democratic project. From the beginning, there has been an opposition between the instituting and the instituted, the people in the street and the people embodied in their representatives, the diversity of social conditions and the unity of the democratic principle. It is a tension between the one and the multiple, endlessly reconstituting itself in a way that engenders doubt and dissatisfaction. The contradiction between the nature of democratic society (a society without constituted bodies) and the presuppositions of democratic politics (the creation of a represented legal person) has thus entailed a permanent identity quest that may never be entirely achieved.

Seen in these terms, the constitutive disease of democratic experience is not tied solely to the aporias of representing the people (which could also correspond to the opposition between formal democracy and what real democracy should be). What must be emphasized is that the *people as a concrete entity* also remains indeterminate. The latter refers not to a self-evident sociological fact upon which the imperative of popular sovereignty could establish itself. The difficulty arises from the fact that the people itself has no clear form. There is no real difference whether it takes the form of an electorate, public opinion, social classes, a history, or a principle. These figures are constantly encapsulating different and perhaps competing peoples. A theory of democracy thus consists, in the first place, in constructing a typology of these figures of the people, or their modalities of appearance and expression, as well as the ways in which they become institutional.

2. The uncertainties of representative democracy (the forms of popular sovereignty)

The uncertainties inherent in giving popular sovereignty a form derive from the fact that the latter cannot be exercised directly: it can take form only when mediated and instrumentalized by representative procedures. This conclusion lies at the heart of the constitutional endeavors of America's and France's founding fathers. Yet this seemingly self-evident fact has historically concealed a major ambiguity. On the one hand, the representative system has been perceived as a mere *technical artifice* resulting from purely material constraints (how can power be organized in a large society?). Such an approach would implicitly suggest that this system was no more than a stopgap, a necessary substitute for the impossibility of direct rule by the citizenry, the latter being, in absolute terms, the ideal political system. But establishing representative procedures has, on the other hand, been explicitly tied to a *genuinely positive assessment* of their inherent value. Representative government was, in this context, seen as an original and specific political form, defining an unprecedented kind of regime, adding a fourth type to the traditional typology. These two approaches were contradictory insofar as representative government was perceived, in the first instance, as the equivalent of democracy, whereas it represented, in the second, an *overcoming* or even a *limitation* of the latter. The boundary between these approaches has become, in practice, blurred, as the term *representative democracy*, which oscillates between two extreme ideal types – *elective democracy* (a term from Rousseau) and *immediate direct democracy* – has asserted itself.

The conception of representative government as an elective democracy is based on four dimensions. 1) *The concept of election*. The latter is perceived as a means of *selection* – a term that is constantly found in the writings of the American and French founding fathers. It is a kind of process of classification, of triage, and for collecting various qualities. In this way, it resembles a test or a competitive examination. This similarity was, incidentally, frequently pointed out during the nineteenth century, with some speaking of "scientific or intellectual elections" when discussing the latter. 2) *The relationship between representatives and the represented*. This is established on the basis of a difference, which constitutes a kind of intellectual and moral hierarchy (witness the reference on both continents to the terms "capacity," "virtue," and "wisdom"). Representatives are, in this way, seen as forming an elite. The term *natural aristocracy* is often used in this context by the American founding fathers (unutterable in France during the first years of the Revolution, it resurfaced under Napoleon with the idea of meritocracy). 3) *The epistemology of the general interest*. It is in terms of knowledge that the latter was brought up to date. It is not deduced from disparate social demands but is constructed on the basis of a comprehensive understanding of society's condition and needs at a particular moment. In the language of the federalists, one finds terms such as "knowledge of the general interests of society" (Hamilton), "chains of communication" (Wilson), and "information" for describing the representative bond. At the same time, the "variables of connection" are also emphasized: faithfulness, trust, and dependence. 4) *The nature of representative government*. It is different from democratic government.

Immediate democracy differs from this conception point by point. 1) *The concept of election*. In this instance, it is conceived as reproduction. It is the idea of a mirror-representation, as Mirabeau defined it, when he observed that the proper composition of an assembly should be "for the nation what a reduced map should be for physical expanse; whether partially or as a close-up, the copy should have the same proportions as the original." In this case, it is compared not to a test or a competitive examination, but to a randomly selected sample. In contrast to an election, which is a "selection of distinction," we have, rather, the model of drawing straws, functionally adapted for reproducing randomness. 2) *The relationship between representatives and represented*. This is constituted through similarity and proximity. "Your elected representatives are still you," wrote Necker (stigmatizing the defenders of this approach) in his *Philosophical Reflections on Equality*, "and you with perfect exactitude. Their interests, their will are yours, and no abuse of authority, on the part of these new twins, seems possible to you." Noting that the term representative suggested "the idea of another self", the very same Necker emphasized the importance of the conception of a relationship based on similarity.

In America, this theme was also a leitmotif of the anti-Federalists' opposition to Hamilton and Madison. They, too, spoke of "substantive" representation, which should be "the true image of the people"; and the terms "likeness" and "resemblance" recur constantly in their written and spoken words. 3) *The epistemology of the general interest*. One can see it arising from experiences shared with ordinary people, in direct confrontations with social expectations, or in sympathy for social suffering. 4) *The nature of representative government*. It is conceived in this instance as the functional equivalent of the ideal of a democracy grafted onto society's needs and feelings.

These two ideal types do not delineate two concurrent positions or ideologies structured along these lines, even if each has its most expressive interpreters. They constitute, rather, two poles of a tension the effects of which are constantly felt, albeit in ways that are specific to each case. Voters aspire to be governed by people whom they think are capable of performing the necessary tasks, but they simultaneously wish to choose people who articulate their expectations and speak their language. This tension also manifests itself in the difference between the language of election campaigns (which value possibilities and stress candidates' proximity to their voters) and that of governmental action (which reminds us of constraints).

The goal of political theory on this terrain is to build an analytical framework that describes the structure of this indetermination and thus makes it possible to understand its successive historical manifestations.

THE WEIGHT OF VARIABLES OF PRACTICE

These different categories of indetermination must be analyzed while taking account of two "variables of practice": that of democratic temporality and space.

Democratic institutions and procedures cannot be first considered independently of the regime of temporality to which they belong. This dimension has not, in my view, been adequately taken into account. The study of the political has, in general, focused on the analysis of actors, procedures, and institutions, in which temporality is treated as a basically neutral element – that is, as duration. But if democracy refers to the regime through which society institutes itself, it is necessary to grasp time as an active and constructive factor. Thus it is not sufficient, for example, to say that a president is elected on the basis of universal suffrage. Indeed, the institution of the presidency does not have the same meaning if the term in question is for three years or seven, if it is limited to one term, two terms, or is unlimited – or if it can be conferred for life! To grasp the phenomena of democracy, with all the expectations and disenchantment it produces, one must include this first "variable of practice": *temporality*. It is necessary to think of *political rhythms*, and not merely political mechanics. The importance of this "temporality of concepts" becomes all the greater as ecological anxieties ask us to integrate long-term concerns into democratic procedures. This leads to unprecedented questions: how are future generations to be represented? What status should be given to pre-commitments limiting future choices? Classical democratic theory is, in fact, based entirely on a valorization of the present. "Every age and generation," Thomas Paine once said, "must be as free to act for itself, *in all cases*, as the ages and generations that precede it." For American or French revolutionaries of the late eighteenth century, the affirmation of the general will presupposed a permanent – or at least generational – capacity to invent the future, meaning that what one generation freely chose could not become the inevitable fate of those that followed. Whence the crucial debate, on either side of the Atlantic, over the correct way of conceiving of constitutional documents, to ensure that their legal force did not approximate a binding constraint. All democracies have thus evinced the same concerns as Karl Marx when he railed against "the tradition of all dead generations [that] weighs like a nightmare on the brains of the living."

Today, democratic time faces two kinds of temporal difficulties: an excessive concern with the immediate in relation to long-term concerns, and an excessive emphasis on duration in relation to the urgencies of the moment. In both cases, the appropriateness of the concept of generality is called into question. These issues are also connected to the very definition of the *subject* of democracy. This subject must be understood as inseparably juridical – the people as citizens and electors – and historical, with the nation linking memory to the promise of a shared future. And *humanity* as a new democratic subject must also be taken into account. The redefinition of sovereignty has vast consequences.

Next, one must take into account a second variable of practice, that of democracy's relevant space. The question of democracy's size – that is, of the nation state – was for a long time derived from the conditions and forms of emancipatory movements, which were themselves constituted through the communal ordeal of shared experiences of domination. The problem at present is that perspectives on democratic space have been completed altered by the development of separatism and secessionism of various kinds, which sever the bond between (internal) democracy and (external) self-determination. The idea of democratic "homogeneity" is thus deeply modified. At the same time, the prospect of an expansion of the democratic sphere in a directly cosmopolitan direction or in more limited contexts, such as that of the European Union, lead to different conceptions of democracy's form and content. The "spatiality of concepts" becomes, in this way, essential.

DEMOCRATIC PATHOLOGIES

A theory of democracy must propose an analytical framework for understanding the deception associated with regimes that describe themselves as democratic. If the history of democracy is woven from numerous deceptions, it is also inseparable from democratic pathologies. Contrary to the "reactionary" denial of democracy (that of radical anti-modernists, such as Burke, de Maistre or Donoso Cortès), these pathologies also participated in this history. They constitute the deformed, contracted, exacerbated, or completely inverted image of democracy itself – interpretations that are minimalistic or radically expansive. But they have always derived from a claim to realize democracy's truth. These pathologies – this is my hypothesis – can always be grasped as a reduction, polarization, or simplification of the structuring tensions and forms of indeterminacy that underpin the question of democracy.

A number of words, if not concepts, have been forged over the past two centuries to characterize the historical forms that many authors see as participating in this category of pathologies. One can cite, in no particular order, Jacobinism, formal democracy, elective oligarchy, Caesarism, populism, and totalitarianism. I use them here without trying to rank their effects. The goal is to propose a general theory of these pathologies, one that could place them in a unified conceptual framework while accounting for the specificity of each of them, in order to resist the temptation, to which many analysts succumb, of drawing hasty equivalencies that are rarely illuminating (such as Rousseauism = Jacobinism = totalitarianism). The perspective to be adopted must tie the unification of categories to the diversification of interpretations of historical examples. One can, in this way, distinguish between these pathologies' *forms* and *figures*: similar forms can correspond to figures that are very divergent and even opposed from the standpoint of practical criteria. Indeed, each figure corresponds to an institutional form and to specific practical modalities. From the standpoint of a pathology of representation such as the "one man-one people," some Caesarist regimes exhibit forms that are very close to those of fascism and Nazism, even if the figures to which they correspond are far removed from them (if only in terms of their relationship to freedom and repression), making it impossible to equate them.

In undertaking a study of forms, one can begin by distinguishing two *families*: pathologies of realization and pathologies of channeling. Let us begin with pathologies of realization. They seek to provide answers to what is perceived as a kind of betrayal, an incompleteness, a reduction, a caricature of existing democracies and dominant models. These pathologies are born from deception and disenchantment. One can distinguish:

- pathologies of representation-figuration;
- pathologies of legitimacy;
- pathologies of sovereignty;
- pathologies of equality.

It is within this family that one finds the figures evoked by the terms such as Jacobinism, Caesarism, populism, and totalitarianism. If one takes the case of pathologies of representation, they consist for the most part in the pretense of resolving the antinomies that structure it through a principle of embodiment and the identification of representatives with the represented (resulting in the idea that it is the represented who in fact exercise power). In the case of pathologies of sovereignty, what is at play is the idea of "power-as-society." These pathologies result from exacerbation and radicalization, which delivers a kind of *semantic blow*, resulting in a belief in an enchanted reality.

The *pathologies of channeling* seek, for their part, to provide answers to perceived threats or dangers, imbalances or wayward drifts in existing democracies. They result from a reduction which leads to a *nominative blow*. In this category, one can place the so-called "realist" theories of democracy (Pareto, Mosca, and so on), for whom power always remains a form of domination, or as Pareto wrote, "history is a cemetery of aristocracies." Faith in the possibility of the power of people is merely a superstition to which lucid people would never subscribe. Arising out of this normative blow are the so-called "minimalist" theories of democracy (such as Schumpeter and Popper), for whom deception is the result of excessively ambitious definitions of democracy. There would be no deception, according to these authors, if one "understood" that democracy's sole object is the avoidance of tyranny by allowing, through elections, the rotation of leadership. Their call for "democratic modesty" was a response, it must be acknowledged, to totalitarian hubris. Yet by the same token, they did not take seriously democracy's antinomies.

It is important to emphasize that the boundaries between the denial of democracy and democratic pathologies have often been porous. Consider a few brief examples:

- If Italian fascism and Nazism exalted the sovereign people, these two examples of totalitarianism were also tied to the articulation of deeply anti-egalitarian sentiments, which took the form of a racial hierarchy as well as, more generally, the celebration of strongmen and elites who would guide the people.
- The critique of democratic egalitarianism has also frequently expressed itself in a more derivative fashion, notably in the Romantic form of a disgusted rejection

of bourgeois society and the equalizing power of money. Burke set the tone for this critique when he observed nostalgically: "The age of chivalry is gone [...]. That of sophists, economists and calculators has succeeded."

- While the properly theological terms of Joseph de Maistre's critique of democratic abstraction and human rights are still confined to traditionalist circles, this critique has been far more widespread in the "secularized" version that Burke proposed in his *Reflections on the Revolution in France*. It was often picked up during the nineteenth century by conservatives and Marxists.
- At present, a virulent critique of "human rightsism" often runs alongside the discourse of the populist far right; the critique of democratic individualism and "democratic civilization" can be found, for their part, in the discourse of some "republicans."

REDEFINING DEMOCRATIC UNIVERSALISM

Having theorized democracy on the basis of its indeterminations and the antinomies that shape it, and having included its pathologies in the latter, I define democracy as *the regime that must ceaselessly interrogate its definition of itself*. In this sense, democratic theory is inseparable from its history and the explorations to which it is tied. It has, therefore, been my goal to rethink democracy by following the thread of the history it has spun. But the point is not simply that democracy *has* a history. What matters, more radically, is that democracy *is* a history. Its task has consisted irreducibly of exploration and experimentation, as it has set out to understand and elaborate itself.

There can, according to this conception, exist no model of democracy that some have been appointed to impose on the rest of the world. There are only experiences and the results of trial and error, which we must all carefully and lucidly assess. Understood as an experience, democracy opens the door to a genuine universalism – an experimental universalism. By acknowledging that in the workshop of democracy, we are all apprentices, this approach allows us to establish a political dialogue between nations that is more open because it is more egalitarian. There have been many experiences of deliberation, collective decision-making, and equality; there have been experiences of failures as well. They can all be included in a single comparative framework. The only positive universalism is, consequently, a universalism of problems and questions that remain to be solved. This universalism is not imposing and arrogant, but open. Only on this basis does what it might mean to identify shared values become apparent. A universalism of this kind also makes it possible to lower the boundary separating democratic theory –

which is assumed to be academic – and civic conversation. Both can interact in a positive way that makes citizens more active and more lucid.

BIBLIOGRAPHY

Cartledge, Paul (2009): Ancient Greek Political Thought in Practice, Cambridge: Cambridge University Press.
Hansen, Mogens Herman (1999): The Athenian Democracy in the Age of Demosthenes: Structure, Principles, and Ideology, J.A. Crook (trans.), Norman: University of Oklahoma Press.
Loraux, Nicole (1979): La Cité divisée, Paris: Payot.

3 Political Theory through History

Pierre Rosanvallon's Concepts of Representation
and the People and their Importance
for Understanding Populism*

Paula Diehl

INTRODUCTION

Pierre Rosanvallon is one of the leading contemporary thinkers of modern democracy in France today. His analysis of the development of democracy is saturated historically at the same time that it opens new perspectives in political theory. With this in mind, he attempts to understand democracy by considering its contradictions and failures instead of focusing on its successes and requirements. Rosanvallon's numerous publications are the impressive culmination of an ambitious research program. Within this project, two key concepts structure his work: the concept of "representation" and the notion of "the people." While representation is a key element for understanding the political, the notion of "the people" enables us to better comprehend modern democracies and their contradictions. Rosanvallon has argued that the concept of the people is two-dimensional. It is at once a sociological condition and, at the same time, a political abstraction. Thus he circles around the tension between those two dimensions in order to develop a theory of democracy that focuses on the representation of the people and its crisis.

For this reason, Rosanvallon's "history of the political" offers a promising approach, especially regarding phenomena such as populism. It enables us to understand populism as a response to a failure of democratic representation. Yet, surprisingly, to date, Rosanvallon has only marginally addressed the question of populism in his publications. In books like *La contre-démocratie* (2006a) and *Le bon government* (2015a), a few short passages on populism can be found. And at the time this paper was written (the end of 2016), Rosanvallon had published just one short essay on the topic (Rosanvallon 2011c). His own conceptual definition and a systematic examination of populism as a political phenomenon was still missing.* And yet, the relevance of Rosanvallon's reflections is evident, as is apparent in the fact that in the past years, several scholars explicitly refer to his work (cf. i.a. Rovira Kaltwasser 2012; Müller 2014; Urbinati 2014). Rosanvallon's core argument draws attention to populism's roots and causes. According to the author, the emergence of the phenomenon is based on the intrinsic malaise of democracy. Following Rosanvallon, populism offers a response to this malaise by lifting the people as a homogeneous unit and through the embodiment of this homogeneous people by a leader (Rosanvallon 2011c: 5). This line of argumentation is one of the fundamental contributions of Claude Lefort's theory of totalitarianism. Lefort himself characterized totalitarianism as an attempt to fill the empty space of power and determine the people as an unchangeable unit. In this sense, totalitarianism modifies the dynamic of democratic representation in a fundamental way: it builds a homogeneous unity of the people, while the leader or the leading party embodies the power generated by this homogeneity (Lefort 1981).

As previously indicated, I follow Rosanvallon up to this point, but suggest another path when it comes to the application of Lefort's theory of totalitarianism in diagnosing populism. Nevertheless, Rosavallon provides a valuable approach, which makes it possible to identify the operative areas of populism. Therefore, I first focus on Rosanvallon's conceptualization of democracy, representation, and the people. Second, the chapter turns to their significance for understanding populism. Finally, based on this analysis, I present an alternative interpretation of populism which diverges from Rosanvallon's, mainly with regard to the aforementioned dynamic of totalitarianism. My argument is that populism relocates democratic representation and walks a thin line between democratic and anti-democratic dynamics. But these dynamics are not identical to those of totalitarianism. Moreover, as of yet, I argue, it may not be determined whether populism leads to totalitarianism or not. Populism remains an ambivalent phenomenon.

---

* Editor's note: Rosanvallon announced in his last lecture at the Collège de France on February 7, 2018 that he was preparing a book on the history and theory of populism. In this lecture he provided a broad outline of his approach to this question.

THINKING ABOUT DEMOCRACY
AMIDST ITS IMPERFECTIONS

When Pierre Rosanvallon was elected to the Collège de France, he stated his research focus to be the "history of the political." In this context, his first aim was to grasp the transformation of the modern political system by taking its problematical dimension into account (Rosanvallon 2006b). Accordingly, the history of the political does not appear as an affirmative historiography of political emancipation, but rather becomes visible in the fractures and imperfections of democracy (Rosanvallon 2006b: 36), accompanied by several crises, namely the crisis of political representation (Rosanvallon 1998), trust (Rosanvallon 2006a), equality and political institutions (Rosanvallon 2011a). For Rosanvallon, all of these crises are an inherent part of democracy which reveal the blind spots and imperfections of democracy and thus form the center of his research program.

Within this specific perspective on democracy, it is fundamental to assume that democracy itself is not stable. Instead, its sense is rather "floating." It is here that the influence of his mentor Claude Lefort is obvious.[1] For Rosanvallon, "Democracy, in fact, constitutes the political in a field largely open to the very fact of the tensions and uncertainties that underlay it" (Rosanvallon 2006b: 36). He incorporates two interconnected arguments from Lefort. First, like Lefort, Rosanvallon chooses the political and not politics as the starting point for his analysis of democracy (Rosanvallon 2006b; Lefort 1988a) – even though Rosanvallon takes the developments of political institutions and decision-making bodies into account. Rosanvallon regards the political as "a modality of existence of life in common as a form of collective action that is implicitly distinct from the functioning of politics" (Rosanvallon 2006b: 36). Lefort, already defined the political in a similar manner in his famous essay "The Question of Democracy" (1988). Thus, the political is at once a space and an organizational principle. It becomes visible "in the double movement whereby the institution of society appears and is obscured" (Lefort 1988a: 11). Rosanvallon's choice of placing the political at the center of his research can therefore be interpreted as an attempt to apply Lefort's concept within an approach of historically guided research.

The second argument which Rosanvallon incorporates from Lefort's work, appears in his understanding of democracy as a social form "without positive determination" (Lefort 1988b). Lefort derives his concept of democracy from historical processes, which have been initiated by democratic revolutions. Similar to Lefort,

---

1   In this context, it is important to note that Claude Lefort was Rosanvallon's doctoral supervisor, which explains the conceptual proximity.

Rosanvallon recognizes the birth of modern democracy in the rupture caused by the French Revolution. With the revolution, a new configuration of the political took place. This involved "a new mode of legitimation, not only of power but also of social relations as such [*un mode nouveau de légitimation, non seulement du pouvoir, mais des rapports sociaux comme telles*]" (Lefort 1981: 92), which changed access to the social and the political spheres in a fundamental way. This also applies to the American Revolution. However, following Lefort, the conditions for the rupture and the symbolic turning point which were necessary for the "democratic invention" were far more radical in France than in America (Rosanvallon 2011a: 67). Accordingly, the political history of France is on the one hand a particular one, while at the same time its essence says something general about democracy. Therefore, the political history of France produces symbolic events that reveal the configuration of the political in democracy.

One of those significant events is the beheading of Louis XVI (Rosanvallon 2000: 59). It was at once an institutional and symbolic act, which marked the end of monarchy and released a new social imaginary. In the period prior to the revolution, the king embodied the institutional and symbolic center of society, so that the king visibly embodied the nation as whole. The term nation subsumed both in this case: the state and society. So, the physical elimination of the king's body was above all the execution of a symbolic act, which banished the embodiment of political representation by the king. On that basis, a new form of representation arose, which put autonomy and the sovereignty of the people in the foreground and, at the same time, banished any possibility of embodiment of power. Henceforth, power was to be symbolized as an empty place. The intrinsic connection between the elimination of the king's body and the founding of the French Republic, in line with the emergence of the principle of people's sovereignty, becomes clear at this point. This connection is present in both Lefort's theory of democracy and Rosanvallon's historical approach. From that moment on, power has been shifted toward the people and belongs correspondingly to all. As a result, it cannot be embodied by any one single individual (Lefort 1981: 92; Rosanvallon 2000: 104). The place of power must remain symbolically empty (Lefort: 1988a 17), even if power is executed by political representatives. In this context, Lefort speaks of a democratic invention, which changes political representation in a radical way and eliminates any possibility of embodiment.

The society, which emerges from this rupture, is fundamentally shaped by self-reflexion (Rosanvallon 2006a: 170). And the fact that society becomes aware of the possibility of transforming itself constitutes the central source of democratic renewal. In light of this process, the option to understand oneself as a monolithic and unchangeable unity, which Rosanvallon expresses as "*l'un*" (the One), loses its validity. Individualization and pluralization become the sociological characteristics of modern society. In this context, Rosanvallon barely distinguishes between sociological processes and political changes and the terminology which specifies society as "modern" and "democratic" merges. The important point here is that the political and the social order are understood as changeable and are both open for modification by the people's will. For that reason, democratic society and its understanding of the people no longer form an embodied unity. At the same time, the principle of sovereignty and the related idea that power belongs to everyone prevent rulers from taking on an embodied form of representation, which was a typical characteristic of absolutism. This is precisely why Lefort refers to a "society without a body," or "a society which undermines the representation of an organic totality" (Lefort 1988a: 18). Rosanvallon builds on this approach (Rosanvallon 2015a: 51 et seq.) and describes power in democracies as a "pouvoir sans tête" (power without a head) and following Lefort, as a "disembodied society" (Rosanvallon 2015a: 52 et seq.;1998: 23).

These are factors that renew democracy and as such legitimize democratic power and determine the new relationships within democratic society. But at the same time, these factors are the main reason why democracy incorporates uncertainty (Lefort 1988a). Therefore, democracy must constantly negotiate its form, in contrast to its counterparts in the shape of pre-democratic or, later on, totalitarian systems, which try to fix a symbolic and social form forever. Democracy requires a continuous debate on the understanding of political legitimacy, political practices, norms and values. If this continuous process of negotiation is strenuous, it has the advantage to allow the political order and its representation to adapt to society and to social changes (Diehl 2015: 128). A glance at Lefort's theoretical work illustrates that such an uncertainty is not problematic. It rather involves a "productive, a generative device that helps to foster ever new claims for legitimacy" (Näsström 2007: 626). Uncertainty therefore appears as a precondition for democracy as a continuous process. From a more pessimistic perspective, however, democracy is always under pressure in order to cope with uncertainty. Rosanvallon himself seems to take this pessimistic point of view (Rosanvallon 2006a: 170). His focus is not placed on the renewal of resources for democracy coming from openness and uncertainty, instead he is interested in the failure of the democratic promise, frustration, and disappointment caused by uncertainty. In his inaugural lecture at the Collège de France in 2002, Rosanvallon summarizes this perspective as follows: Democracy, he writes, "implies a type of regime that resists any attempt of unequivocal classification. The specificity of the malaise that has dogged its history stems from this fact too. The train of disappointments and the perpetual feelings of its betrayal that have always accompanied it have stung just as much as the debate over its definition has resisted closure. From democracy's unmoored wandering has followed both a question and a nagging absence of destination. One must begin with this fact in order to understand what democracy is: the history of a disenchantment and the history of an indeterminacy are bound up with one another." (Rosanvallon 2006b: 37)

THE MALAISE OF DEMOCRACY AND THE POPULIST MOMENT

Against this background, it is understandable that the "malaise" of democracy has become an ongoing topic in Rosanvallon's work (cf. i.a. *Le people intouvable* 1998; *La contre-démocratie* 2006a; *La démocratie inanchévée* 2000). In one of his earlier essays, Rosanvallon identified this malaise, manifested in a specific moment of French history which he elaborates as an example within this framework. The electoral success of the *Front National* in the first round of elections in 1988 gave Rosanvallon the reason for this diagnosis. At that time, the party in question was clearly allocated to right-wing extremism and not to right-wing populism and the presidential candidate was Jean-Marie Le Pen and not his daughter. In 1988, Le Pen polled 14 percent of the vote and shocked the French public. In 2002, the shock was even greater, as the second round of election pitted Jean-Marie Le Pen against the conservative candidate Jacques Chirac. Similarly, in the regional elections of 2015, the socialist party recommended at the time that their voters should choose the conservative party in order to save France from right-wing extremism. In this context, some of the socialist members of parliament demonstratively cast their vote by wearing gloves as they put their ballot in the voting box. Chirac, as is commonly known, received 82 percent of the vote.

Rosanvallon argued that the success of the Front National in 1998, as well as in 2002 and 2015, was an expression of the intrinsic malaise of democracy. Characteristic of this context was a general retreat of politics behind pragmatism, the dominance of the market, and the "somnolence of political imagination" (Rosanvallon 1988: 137). This situation was accompanied, he argued, by a lack of political vision which blurred the differences between left and right. At the same time, Rosanvallon observed how political discourse became dominated by a "*langue de caoutchouc*", an elastic and rubberlike political language. According to Rosanvallon, this language became too soft and elastic to establish clear political differences. Yet this also explains why the political imagination "fell asleep" (Rosanvallon 1988: 137). In such a situation, the confrontation between different political programs was forced back and instead an opposition between the masses and elites emerged. With civil society on the one side and the political system or rather political institutions on the other, alienation was rising to the point, that their bond, which is crucial for democracy, might dissolve. These are the key elements of the "populist moment" (Goodwyn 1978; Dubiel 1986).

With a view to the events of the year 1988, Rosanvallon locates the populist moment in a specific social framework since, at that time, the situation was supported by a fundamental transformation of society: In the 1980s, the flexibilization of the working conditions made political representation of workers more difficult, while trade unions lost their political weight (Rosanvallon 2011b: 64). Since then, no social group could claim to speak for the majority of society (Rosanvallon 1988: 152). Against this background, neither the representation of the people as a whole, nor the representation of their diversity seemed possible. The latent crisis of democratic representation became acute and the scope for populist and anti-democratic reactions increased.

While the crisis of representation may grow, depending on potential social as well as political conditions, the crisis remains inherent to modern democracy. It arises out of a structural distance between the political system and society and is therefore a crucial characteristic of political modernity (Rosanvallon 1988: 156, 172 et seq.).[2] This is one of the main reasons for the disenchantment of democracy. Frustration and delusion have spread to the extent that one could even speak of a "narcissistic wound" (Schulz 2008: 105), which originates from the impossibility of a complete and comprehensive representation of the people. On this point, Rosanvallon identifies the potential of populism from which Jean-Marie Le Pen benefited in 1988 (Rosanvallon 1988: 138-142) and which also paved the way for today's right-wing populist parties like the German AfD (Alternative for Germany) or the Front National, under the leadership of Marine Le Pen. The consistency between a characterization that emphasizes how populism is "always anti-institutional, anti-elitist, or anti-systemic" (Priester 2005: 305) and the relationship between the latent malaise of democracy and the populist moment quickly becomes recognizable: populism gives an expression to the malaise of democracy in the form of criticism of political elites and institutions, allegations of corruption, and reacts to it by calling for more direct democracy. This is similar to the general

---

2   In his essay from 1988, Rosanvallon describes the distance between society and the political system also as a distance between the political and the social.

criticism of the political system at the end of the nineteenth century, as previously described by Rosanvallon (Rosanvallon 2000: 305 et seq.). Already at that time, the first populist moment emerged, in the shape of most of the agriculture-populist movements like Narodniki in Russia or the People's Party in the USA (Rosanvallon 2011c: 5). These movements could be understood as a reaction to the transformation of modern society and moreover, as a reaction to the crisis of representation in democracy.

REPRESENTATION AS A KEY TO UNDERSTANDING DEMOCRACY

The idea of representation serves as the key concept for understanding modern democracy and is closely connected to the concept of the people. Therefore, it is not surprising that the representation of the people is the central topos of Rosanvallon's work and its failures participate in the history of the democratic delusion. However, Rosanvallon's concept of representation is not limited to the idea of "acting for others." In addition, the author incorporates symbolic and imaginary components of representation. In this context, the influence of his mentor, Claude Lefort, is more than evident. Rosanvallon adopts Lefort's thesis of the democratic invention in order to substantiate the fundamental role of political representation in modern democracy. Representation has the task to connect the representatives with their constituents and the government with the citizens.

The necessity of mediation between the political and the social grows as the society becomes aware of itself. In this regard, one witnesses literally the birth of a "political society" (Rosanvallon 1988: 158), since, from this moment on, the society starts to recognize itself as a political actor. In this context, representation is crucial. It offers the necessary articulation between the social and the political, civil society and the state. Representation occurs, when the representatives act in the name of the constituency ("acting for") and when symbolic processes take place ("stand for").[3] Here, the symbolization and social imagination of society on the one hand, and the articulation of social diversity and different understandings of the political on the other, become fundamental. Rosanvallon reconstructs these

---

3   The conceptual distinction between representation as "acting for" or rather "standing for" has been introduced by Hanna F. Pitkin, who disqualified symbolic representation as a form of democratic representation (cp. Pitkin 1972). Rosanvallon by contrast revised this thesis, but nevertheless incorporates Pitkin's terminology.

processes exemplarily through his examination of French social and political history – for example by describing the development of political representation and the political disputes and debates from the French Revolution to present.

Representation, however, is not only a solution, but also a problem that reveals itself on a number of levels. There are primarily three reasons why representation emerges as a problem. First, it is always inscribed in a fundamental tension between the symbolic and the real (Rosanvallon 1998: 41). Second, the exercise of a mandate – and of power – by political representatives is always in a competition with the symbolic representation of the political community, even, if both are – as required – general partners (Rosanvallon 2011b: 88). Third, representation is a challenging endeavor because the people cannot be represented adequately as a political subject. As a sociological reality, the people are undetectable and have no coherent and total form since they change in a twofold manner: biographically and from one generation to the next (Rosanvallon 2000: 419). The impact of these factors must be taken seriously, particularly if it is put into the context of Lefort's characterization of democracy's indeterminacy. It is a difficult task for society to develop appropriate structures, which are suitable to give expression to democratic representation. With this in mind, the representation of the people and the role of representation become a problem. Populism and totalitarianism can be considered as a misguided answer to the previously indicated difficulties. Both address the frustration, which arises out of the impossibility to shape the people as a single unit and to determine a perpetual form of representation and symbolization of society.

By connecting the political and social transformations to the changes of the symbolization of society and the people, Rosanvallon's history makes the problems of democratic representation visible. The link between social and political development on the one hand, and the simultaneous shift of imagination on the other, is thus Rosanvallon's methodological trademark. His book *Le peuple introuvable* (1998) gives a good example of his methodology. In this book, Rosanvallon traces the emergence of a split between the symbolic and the real, which manifests itself in the dissatisfaction caused by the chasm between the imagination of the people as a unity and a conflicting, fragmented social reality. In the aftermath of the French Revolution it was primarily the republican or rather the Jacobin discourse that promised national unity. This promise found expression in revolutionary symbols, celebrations and rituals. Yet these visualizations could not cover the fact, that this unity would never be achieved (Rosanvallon 1998: 74 et seq.). In this sense, one may speak of a basic tension between the representation of unity and the heterogeneity of modern society.

The social developments in the course of the nineteenth century – a century which embodied for Rosanvallon the diversification of modern society – the underlying tension in the political and in the scientific discourse took shape progressively. There was first and foremost, the progressive urbanization and industrialization that give rise to a society that understood itself as diverse and therefore sought suitable forms of representation. The representation of the people as one unit and the representation of social diversity were, as a result, in competition with one another. Rosanvallon elaborated this argument by linking the emergence of social science with the political debate. Early social science attempted to express social diversity by categorizing social groups and functions within society, which led to the development of sociology and social psychology. At the same time, a growing interest in the representation of social groups arose within politics. Rosanvallon shows how social science and politics participate in a common search to represent the diversity of a society (Rosanvallon 1998: 139 et seq.). This does not mean that the idea of a representation of unity disappears. Politicians, social scientist and intellectuals at that time were rather seeking for complementary principles which could do both: presenting a society as whole while at the same time recognizing its diversity.

Although the discussion provides a specific inventory of the nineteenth century, for Rosanvallon its significance spreads far beyond. The discussion on the representation of diversity bears an element that reaches beyond its own context. In his view, the nineteenth-century debate illustrates key points that bring the "*déception démocratique*" to the fore (Rosanvallon 1998: 136). Such a disappointment arises from the transition from a society best captured by the metaphor of the body ("*une société de corps*") to a society of individuals ("*une société d'individus*"), in which diversity becomes visible. Facing these conditions, the representation of society becomes increasingly difficult (Rosanvallon 1998: 44).[4] Thus, Rosanvallon concludes, the people do not become visible as a coherent bloc. They must rather be grasped as fundamentally multidimensional.

THE DIFFERENT DIMENSIONS OF THE PEOPLE

Rosanvallon begins by conceptualizing two dimensions of the people: as a political abstraction and as a social reality in the form of a concrete assemblage of individuals. In democracy both dimensions are in a fundamental state of tension,

---

4   Quotation from the original: "le passage d'une société de corps à une société d'individus rend la société moins représentable."

produced by the rise of the sovereignty of the people. Popular sovereignty creates a new political subject and establishes a new political and a sociological imperative: it presupposes the people as the principle of authority (*"un régime d'autorité"*) and – at the same time – recognizes them as the concrete author (*"un sujet exerçant"*) (Rosanvallon 2000: 15). Correspondingly, the people are divided into a political principle and a social fact. Political representation intervenes in a tension between the political and the philosophical moment of democracy and its sociological realization (Rosanvallon 2000: 13). Representation promises to connect the abstract idea of the people with its concrete social form. Political institutions, elections and representatives as well as symbols, pictures and discourses express this promise. However, it is important to point out that Rosanvallon is not entirely optimistic when it comes to the performance of representation.

For instance, in *La démocratie inachevée* (2000), he tries to grasp the two dimensions of the people – as political abstraction and as a given social fact – referring to the idea of the "two bodies." In doing so, the influence of Ernst Kantorowicz, especially with regard to *The King's Two Bodies* (1997) becomes evident. In accordance with this idea, the first body is branded a *"peuple-nation"* (nation-people), which subsist on the unity principle. It is an abstract understanding of the people, which has to be symbolized in order to exist. The second body – namely the *"peuple-société"* (social-people) – is the ensemble of specific individuals, which do not constitute a unit, because they are characterized by plurality and variability in a historical sense (Rosanvallon 2000: 40 et seq.). In the political history of France, the abstract people are symbolized in the constitution from 1793 – due to the fact that they are referred to in the text. The people are cited as a "principle and promise of democracy." They symbolize the configuration of society as a "block" and serve to promote the universalization of national identity (Rosanvallon 1998: 40).

The nature of the concrete, or social-people, is entirely different. As a social reality, the people are amorphous, elusive and improbable (*"sans forms, corps fuyant et improbable"*) (Rosanvallon 2000: 40). Here, categories like the ones developed by social scientists in the nineteenth century are needed in order to conceptually approximate the concrete people. Therefore, Rosanvallon's understanding of the people as a political category is embedded in the framework of the complexity of modern society. The *"peuple-société"* is plural by nature and in this sense, it participates in a process of permanent change, which makes it "untraceable" (Rosanvallon 2000: 419).[5] This is fundamental for the understanding of the

---

5 Rosanvallon's perspective is comprehensible, if the idea of autonomy and self-reflexion are understood as principles of modern societies. In this sense, the innovation appears

incongruence between the abstract and the concrete social people. The problem is that the abstract concept of the people refers to a political possibility long before this possibility has become a sociological fact. Furthermore, it is improbable that this abstract conception of the people can ever become a sociological fact (Rosanvallon 1998: 40). It invokes a promise with a high risk of failure. Hence, the gap between the abstract and the concrete remains a source of frustration and constant insult.

Rosanvallon varies the people's terminology depending on the particular research focus and in so doing elaborates other dimensions of the people as well. In *Democratic Legitimacy* (2011) he speaks of three bodies: (1) "people as principle"; (2) "social people"; (3) "electoral people." He thus adds the term "electoral," and a slight terminological alteration: instead of using the term "*peuple-sociologique*" – sociologically conceived – Rosanvallon refers to "*peuple-social*" (social-people) (Rosanvallon 2011b: 130). The "electoral people" describes the expression of the "social people" in the election results, an expression of the people's will as a majority will at the moment of the vote. Since "it takes on a numerical reality at the ballot box" (ibid.). In elections, the constitution of minority and majority comes to the fore, because the "electoral people" fix the will of the majority and provide it with a political-legal function. What is problematic is, first, that the will and identity of minorities are neglected. Second, the "electoral people" only provides an image, or a snapshot of a dynamic society, but nevertheless makes a definitive political statement for the society as a whole. The existence of the electoral people is fleeting. It appears whenever there is an election, briefly and sporadically (ibid.). Yet, at the same time, it has a claim on "expressing social generalities" (ibid.) since the majority vote is a compelling argument.

The abstract concept of the people is not modified by Rosanvallon. He moreover relates it to the concepts of the "social-people" and to the "electoral people." While the "social people" depicts the concrete and varying conditions of the people and the "electoral-people" materializes its current expression in the form of voting results, the "ideal-people" do not have any "substantial reality" (Rosanvallon 2011b: 139). However, the abstract people provide an orientation for the common good, but this is exactly the reason why it reveals the imperfections of democracy.

In his article *A Reflection on Populism* (2011c), Rosanvallon develops a fourth dimension of the concept of the people, which he names "random people"

---

in the fact that the modern society is aware of its own self-constitution, transformation and that self-reflection is an option for its individuals – in contrast to the societies in previous periods such as the medieval world.

– in the French version of the article *"people aléatoire"* (Rosanvallon 2011c: 8) – but he does not elaborate more on the concept. However, the concept of the "random people" is not an entirely distinct category. For Rosanvallon, it is rather an opportunity to give the people a voice, which arises out of a lottery – comparable to jury elections for trials or the filling of positions within decision-making bodies or advisory boards. In the course of his analysis of populism, Rosanvallon continues to use the terms "social-people" and "ideal-people" or rather "people as a principle" ("people-principle"), but he modulates the term "electoral people" once again: it appears now as an "arithmetic people" (Rosanvallon 2011c: 7-8). For Rosanvallon, this differentiated view and the dimensions involved perform an important function for the success of political representation, given the fact that the people never speak with one voice. With this in mind, Rosanvallon emphasizes the need for a multiplication of voices and expressions to let the people speak and, in consequence, "multiplying the terms of a continuous democracy" (Rosanvallon 2011c: 8). According to his conception, there "has to be a polyphony" (ibid.). Populism rests on exactly the opposite.

In order to better understand populism, two distinctions have to be made regarding the concept of the people in Rosanvallon's work: the first concerns the difference between the "ideal people" and the "social people." For Rosanvallon, the coexistence of these two dimensions is one of the crucial conditions of democracy, at the same time that they build a *"double indétermination"* and, in this sense, a source of disappointment, which begins with an essential *"regime de la fiction"* (Rosanvallon 2000: 16). At this point, the limits of the democratic promise become visible. Democracy promises to connect both dimensions of the people by elections and by representation. This applies because the distance between the people as a political principle and as sociological reality is insurmountable. For Rosanvallon totalitarianism as well as populism operate at this point and promise to merge both dimensions. The second distinction made by Rosanvallon which can make a fruitful contribution to a better understanding of populism, is the distinction between the will of the majority, expressed by the "electoral people" and the actual plurality of the "social people," that is the collection of different opinions, identities and interests. Populism equates the "electoral people" and the "social people" by blocking out the existing differences between the majority will and the general will.

These two differences in representing the people are permanent sources of malaise, because they demonstrate that democracy can never fully keep its promise. The "electoral people" and the "social- people" will never be identical, and similarly, the majority can never express the general will of the people. Only the idea of the people as a homogeneous unity and therefore, the imagination of the society as a body, can mask and hide these differences. However, this would be a relapse in non-democratic conditions. For Rosanvallon, this is a phantasm of democracy – the manufacturing of "*l'un*" (the One) (Rosanvallon 2006a: 270, 276), which on the one hand accompanies and on the other threatens the democratic imaginary. Populism, in his view, represents a promise to re-establish this homogeneous unity.

THE PHANTASM OF DEMOCRACY: MANUFACTURING THE "THE ONE"

In several of his books, Rosanvallon returns to the configuration of "*l'un*" (the One) as an idea of a monolithic unity (cf. Rosanvallon 1998: 445; 2000: 78; 2006a: 270; 2015a: 315). Rosanvallon follows Claude Lefort's argument on the idea of a configuration of the people and society as a unit. Lefort himself uses the term "*l'un*" (the One) with reference to people and power. He speaks in the context of the "*peuple-un*" (People-as-One) and as "*pouvoir-un*" (Power-as-One) (Lefort 1981). The idea of a total unity builds the center of his theory of democracy and – moreover – marks his analytical discussion of totalitarianism. For Lefort, democratic society is characterized by the impossibility of being identical with itself (Lefort 1981: 151). This is based on the differentiation of the social: Democratic society is too plural and transformable to form a coherent unity. This impossibility also refers to the internal conflicts and divisions of a society, which in turn need a forum to be carried out. The voice of the people, which find its expression in elections, is only the voice of the majority and can never be the expression of the general will. In addition, democracy is – as already described – based on the principle of the popular sovereignty that marks power as an "empty place." Therefore, it comes to a split between the people and the power, between civil society and the state, which is fundamental for Rosanvallon's argument. These two factors indeed prevent society and its representation from becoming identical. At this point, the previously discussed democratic indeterminacy takes effect (Lefort 1981: 146-151).

Totalitarianism inverses this logic and promises a society which is free of conflict and difference, where power and civil society merge. That is the reason why Lefort speaks of an "*affirmation de la totalité*," or an affirmation of totality (Lefort 1981: 99). Lefort applies the idea of "*l'un*" specifically to these two inversions: first, he identifies the image of the "*peuple-un*" (people-as-one) as an attempt to construct the people as a homogeneous unity (Lefort 1981: 101), so that the differences and conflicts within the society disappear. Following Rosanvallon's terminology, the "ideal people" and the "social people" are assumed to be identical. The second inversion is linked to this assumption because the image of the "*peuple-un*" (people-as-one) merges with the image of the "*pouvoir-un*" (power-as-one). In this setting power is concentrated in the government and is embodied by an individual that furthermore embodies the unity of the people and the people's will (ibid.).[6] Thus, representation as a modus of embodiment – which had been abrogated during the French Revolution – returns. But at this point, it is not the King that embodies the power, it is the "Egocrat" (Lefort 1981: 101; Lefort 1986: 299-300). Thereby, the two preconditions of democracy are being destroyed: plurality and the persistence of social conflicts and divisions on the one hand, and the symbolization of power as an empty place on the other. For Lefort, the "*peuple-un*" and the "*pouvoir-un*" are two versions of the same phantasm, since the people as a unit cannot be configured other than as the embodiment of a "larger other" (Lefort 1981: 101), in other words by a powerful individuum (the leader).

The idea of "the One" is a primary phantasm within democracy and at the same time the most powerful instrument of totalitarianism. The special characteristic of a totalitarian society is correspondingly the configuration of the people as a unit, which eliminates social, cultural and identity differences and conflicts in the name of a homogeneous society. Power is imagined accordingly as a "*pouvoir-un*." In this situation, power is not only concentrated in the state apparatus and in bureaucracy. In addition, the "Egocrat" and the party appear as the embodiment of power and the people. Rosanvallon adopts the concept of "the One" and, following Lefort, identifies this concept as characteristic of totalitarianism.[7] The distinguished traits of totalitarianism are based on the "effective fantasy of a power that could fully absorb society" (Rosanvallon 2006b: 51). This "involved the desire to bring about, artificially and at the same time, a society perfectly legible in its unity

---

6 Original text: "Or, cette image se combine avec celle d'un pouvoir concentré dans les limites de l'organe dirigent et, finalement dans un individu qui incarne l'unité et la volonté populaires." Lefort makes no terminological distinction between "incorporer" (to incorporate – in the text translated as embodiment) and "incarner" (to incarnate).

7 In the epilogue to the volume of Sarah Al-Matary and Florent Guénard, Rosanvallon tries to distinguish himself from Lefort by extending the concept (cp. Rosanvallon 2015b: 240 et seq.). However, as shown above, in his earlier works the conformity with Claude Lefort and his concept of "the One" (l'un) is visible (cp. Rosanvallon 2015b).

and a power supposed to be completely identified with it, with the goal of reabsorbing it in its very origin the gap between the social and the political" (ibid.). So the question that arises is then: Is this true in the case of populism as well?

POPULISM AS THE MAKING OF "THE ONE"

Following Rosanvallon, the answer is clearly yes. Rosanvallon links the constitution of "the One" to the main theme of his research program, the malaise of democracy. From this perspective, populism appears to be a "pathology" (Rosanvallon 2006a) which serves as a simplified and perverted response to the different variations of the crisis of representation. Thus, populism transforms the ideals and the procedures of democracy (Rosanvallon 2006a: 269).

This perversion finds its procedural expression in the anti-parliamentary attitudes and distrust towards the representative system, which within populism is accused of corruption (Rosanvallon 2011c: 6). However, according to Rosanvallon, the distrust that is linked to the concept of counter-democracy does not necessarily have a negative effect on democracy. Nevertheless, he also refers to a destructive effect of populism, which radicalizes distrust and erodes the trust in political representation and institutions. In this light, populism can be understood as a "political form of expression [...] within [which] the democratic project is completely absorbed and vampirized by counter-democracy." (Rosanvallon 2006a: 276) Indeed, populists propagate the immediacy of the people's voice as an expression of popular sovereignty and combat institutional mediation. Rosanvallon interprets this position as anti-parliamentary and identifies a first populist moment already in the nineteenth century (Rosanvallon 2006a: 270). In the end, the growth of counter-democratic distrust within populism leads to an extreme form of anti-politics.

On the ideal dimension, populism manifests itself in its conception of the people. According to Rosanvallon, this conception implies the construction of "the One" and, relating thereto, a vision of a homogeneous society (Rosanvallon 2011c: 5). In this context, populism conceals the distinction between the "ideal people" and the "social people" as well as the differences within the "social people," effacing the plurality of society. For Rosanvallon this represents the analogy to totalitarianism (ibid.). Societal cohesion is therefore based on the identity of the group and not on social relations (Rosanvallon 2011c: 7). For this purpose, populism promises a homogenous identity by drawing an outline of the people – e.g. the elite, oligarchy, foreigners or the enemy (Rosanvallon 2006a: 270; Rosanvallon 1998: 446). Surprisingly, Rosanvallon does not distinguish between these two forms of demarcation. A demarcation between the people and foreigners or other ethnic groups follows the same pattern as the one between the people and the elite or rather oligarchy. This is possible because Rosanvallon considers both distinctions to be ways of creating "the One."[8] For him, populism is based on a "vital identity."

According to Rosanvallon, populism uses the mental figure of the "the One" to activate the embodiment of power and the people. This aspect is discussed in *Le bon gouvernement* (2015a) under the term "*l'homme-peuple*" (the people's man). This figure describes the attempt to embody the modern and complex society in one person. Rosanvallon always uses the masculine gender, so that it is a "*he*" who personalizes the power that is provided by the image of the people. Rosanvallon recognizes this figure in political leaders like Napoleon, Lenin, Perón and Chávez. This kind of leader is the "egocrat" and is associated with the totalitarian dynamic of the "*pouvoir-un*" (Rosanvallon 2015a: 314 et seq.). Rosanvallon finds in Chávez and Lenin prototypical "egocrats" that present themselves as the image of "the One". The "egocrat" operates within its own set of contradictions. He tries to create a form of a personalization of power that makes him appear as the radicalization of democratic representation (Rosanvallon 2015a: 320), but he plays a double game by showing himself as the "people's man" and as the "master" (Rosanvallon 2015a: 317). This dynamic fills a gap, because in democracy the people no longer have a form. They are "a number," a "force," whose components are "the same," as "the equivalent individuals under the law" (Rosanvallon 2011c: 2). The embodiment by the "people's man" makes it possible to deliver a unified image to the scattered parts of the people. This is not a democratic dynamic.

In sum, Rosanvallon is accusing populism of a triple simplification. First, he refers to a "political and sociological" one, as populism considers the people to be an evident subject, which is definable as a distinction from its exteriority (Rosanvallon 2011c: 6). The problem of this simplification lies in the fact that a "negative principle simply cannot define that society" (ibid.). The second simplification is a procedural and institutional one. Because populism starts from the assumption that the representative system and democracy are structurally corrupted by politicians, the only democratic procedure – according to populism – is an appeal to the people by holding a referendum (ibid.). Finally, populism simplifies the concept of social

---

8   In *A Reflection on Populism* Rosanvallon drops the above-mentioned distinction with regard to foreigners and enemies, but he does not correct his original definition (cp. Rosanvallon 2011c).

cohesion, because it reduces the asserted identity of the people (Rosanvallon 2011c: 7).

CONCLUSION

By enrolling populism within the dynamics of the constitution of "the One" as well as its embodiment, Rosanvallon leaves little space to distinguish between populism and totalitarianism. However, within his publications *La contre-démocratie* and *Le bon gouvernement* a possible distinction between the two is implied (Rosanvallon 2006a: 271; Rosanvallon 2015a: 319), although this distinction concerns neither the constitution of "the One" nor the mechanism of embodiment. Rosanvallon rather discusses the specific mechanism of counter-democracy, which is radicalized by populism (Rosanvallon 2006a: 271). Another important distinction that Rosanvallon mentioned in *A Reflection on Populism*, relates to the aspect of the institutionalization of power: while totalitarianism defines a form of power and shapes in this sense state institutions, the structure of populism seems to be rather vague with a less direct impact on political culture, compared to totalitarianism (Rosanvallon 2011c: 5). Yet, Rosanvallon does not pursue this analytical path further.

At this point, a critical review is appropriate. Populism indeed shifts the democratic representation of the people, which Rosanvallon rightly emphasizes. But populism is always balancing on a thin line between democracy and totalitarianism, without however, ever becoming identical with the latter. It remains an open question whether populism leads to totalitarianism or not. In this sense, populism's relationship to democracy remains ambivalent. Subsequently, I want to substantiate this thesis by focusing on the two main points of Rosanvallon's argumentation: the populist construction of the people as "the One" and the mechanism of embodiment.

Rosanvallon describes the construction of the people and the establishment of exteriority, which moreover serves as a point of departure for defining the people. Here, he does not distinguish between different forms of exteriority. Martin Reisigl has analyzed the discourse of right-wing populists and discovered a significant difference between populism and right-wing populism. Populists idealize the people and oppose the people to the elite in a vertical line: "we, on the bottom, against those at the top" (Reisigl 2002). So in this sense, the elite is being identified as the "powerblock" and the people can be recognized as the real sovereign (Mouffe 2005; Laclau 2005). Therefore, Carlos de la Torre refers to this dynamic by using the expression "inclusion of the excluded" when he elaborates on Latin

American populism, even if he recognizes the related ambivalences (De la Torre 2013: 9).

The discourse of right-wing populism is more complex because the top-bottom perspective and the internal-external perspective are crossed. The rhetoric of "we against those at the top" is linked with "we, from the inside, against those outside" (Reisigl 2002). Accordingly, the anti-elite-attitude is complemented by an idea of the people as a body, which can be contaminated and destroyed by external intruders. For Chantal Mouffe, who understands populism as an articulated democratic discourse, the problem of right-wing populism is located in its specific construction of the people. Its xenophobic character, in conjunction with the generalization of migrants as a threat of the people, has an undemocratic effect on the construction of the political subject. On the contrary, "We are here dealing with a very perverse mechanism, since it allows people to assert their virtuous nature through an act of rejection" (Mouffe 2005: 66). The demarcation from the outside is a typical ideological element of right-wing extremism and can be found in fascism and national socialism as well. In contrast, the demarcation from the elite is a characteristic element of populism. The combination of both demarcations in right-wing populism can be explained by the fact that populism is not consistent. It is rather a form of "thin ideology" (Canovan 2002; Mudde 2004) that may be combined with other ideological elements. The right-wing extremist definition of the people as a body, which is vulnerable to high levels of contamination, has something totalitarian in itself and creates an inside-outside-opposition that serves as an act of rejection. In general, populism potentially includes all individuals – under the condition that it identifies with the people against the elite. A comparable inclusion is not possible in right-wing populism because of the inside/outside demarcation. In fact, inclusion is no longer possible, because right-wing populism does not operate with a position within the society regarding power structure only. Moreover, it is based on an ontological concept of the other, who can only be the enemy. As already indicated, in Rosanvallon's work the two types of constructing the people – in populism and in right-wing populism – are blurred due to a lack of conceptual distinction.

The second point of my critique addresses Rosanvallon's thesis of embodiment of the people and of power by the populist leader. It is true that the claim of populism to be the only representative of the people is dangerous (Müller 2013: 68). But, populism also plays with these ambiguities. In contrast to totalitarianism it does not put the totalitarian claim to embody the people and power in concrete terms. For this reason, Carlos de la Torre refers to populist representation as a "semi-embodied-power" (De la Torre 2013). This means that the populist leader is offering himself as the embodiment of the people, but this embodiment is not and cannot be carried out completely because populist leaders submit themselves to elections. "Differently to totalitarianism, under populism power is not embodied permanently in the proletariat, the nation, the party, or the Egocrat." (De la Torre 2013: 14) It is a "semi-embodied power," because populists obtain their legitimacy from free and open elections. Hence, populism admits democratic accountability in contrast to totalitarianism. Populist leaders even explicitly refer to democratic election procedures as an expression of the people's will in order to legitimize themselves (Diehl 2019: 140).

Rosanvallon's approach offers important elements for a conceptual critique and analysis of populism. However, it is necessary to relocate the construction of "the One" and the mechanism of embodiment in the context of totalitarianism. Rosanvallon is right, when he alleges that populism is providing false answers to the intrinsic tensions within democratic representation. This means that populism is not just a contextual phenomenon, but inherent to democracy. Rosanvallon clearly recognizes the dangers which come from the "simplistic and perverse" populist solution to this tension. They reside (1) in the equation of the "ideal people" and the "social people"; (2) in the non-consideration of minorities generated by the equation of the "electoral people" and the "social people"; and (3) in the radicalization of the counter-democratic distrust. Finally, Rosanvallon's negative perspective on populism also draws attention to its inherent risk potential of turning into totalitarianism.

BIBLIOGRAPHY

Canovan, Margaret (2002): "Taking Politics to the People. Populism as the Ideology of Democracy." In: Yves Mény/Yves Surel (eds.), Democracy and Populist Challenge, New York: Palgrave Macmillan, pp. 25-43.

De la Torre, Carlos (2013): "The People, Populism, and The Leader's Semi-Embodied Power." In: Rubrica Contemporanea 2, pp. 5-20.

Diehl, Paula (2015): Das Symbolische, das Imaginäre und die Demokratie. Eine Theorie politischer Repräsentation, Baden-Baden: Nomos.

Diehl, Paula (2019): "Twisting representation." In: Carlos de la Torre (ed.): Routledge Handbook of Global Populism, London/New York: Routledge, pp. 129-143.

Guénard, Florent (2015): "Introduction. Le système conceptuel de Pierre Rosanvallon." In: Sarah Al-Matary/Florent Guénard (eds.): La démocratie à l'œuvre. Autour de Pierre Rosanvallon, Paris: Seuil.

Goodwyn, Lawrence (1978): The Populist Moment. A Short History of Agrarian Revolt in America, New York: Oxford University Press.
Kantorowicz, Ernst H. (1997): The King's two Bodies. A Study in Mediaeval Political Theology, Princeton/New Jersey: Princeton University Press.
Laclau, Ernesto (2005): On Populist Reason, New York: Verso.
Lefort, Claude (1981): L'invention démocratique. Les limites de la domination totalitaire, Paris.
Lefort, Claude (1986): "The Image of the Body and Totalitarianism." In: Claude Lefort: The Political Forms of Modern Society. Bureaucracy, Democracy, Totalitarianism, John B. Thompson (ed.), Cambridge: Polity Press, pp. 307-319.
Lefort, Claude (1988a): "The Question of Democracy." In: Claude Lefort (ed.): Democracy and Political Theory, Cambridge: Polity Press, pp. 9-20.
Lefort, Claude (1988b): "The Permanence of the Theologico-Political?" In: Claude Lefort (ed.): Democracy and Political Theory, Cambridge: Polity Press, pp. 213-255.
Mouffe, Chantal (2005): "The 'End of Politics' and the Challenge of Right-wing Populism." In: Francisco Panizza (ed.), Populism and the Mirror of Democracy, New York: Verso, pp. 50-71.
Mudde, Cas (2004): "The Populist Zeitgeist." In: Government & Opposition 39, pp. 541-563.
Müller, Jan-Werner (2013): "Anläufe zu einer politischen Theorie des Populismus." In: Transit 44, pp. 62-71.
Müller, Jan-Werner (2014): "The People Must Be Extracted from Within the People: Reflections on Populism." In: Constellations 21, pp. 483-493.
Näsström, Sophia (2007): "The Legitimacy of the People." In: Political Theory 35, pp. 624-658.
Pitkin, Hanna F. (1972): The Concept of Representation, Berkeley/London/Los Angeles: Berkeley University Press.
Reisigl, Martin (2002): "Dem Volk aufs Maul schauen, nach dem Mund reden und Angst und Bange machen. Von populistischen Anrufungen, Anbiederungen und Agitationsweisen in der Sprache österreichischer PolitikerInnen." In: Wolfgang Eismann (ed.), Rechtspopulismus. Österreichische Krankheit oder europäische Normalität, Wien: Czernin, pp. 149-198.
Rosanvallon, Pierre (1988): "Malaise dans la représentation." In: François Furet/Jacques Juillard/Pierre Rosanvallon (eds.), La République du centre. La fin de l'exception française, Paris: Calmann-Lévy, pp. 132-182.
Rosanvallon, Pierre (1998): Le peuple introuvable. Histoire de la représentation démocratique en France, Paris: Gallimard.

Rosanvallon, Pierre (2000): La démocratie inachevée. Histoire de la souveraineté du peuple en France, Paris: Gallimard.

Rosanvallon, Pierre (2006a): La contre-démocratie. La politique à l'âge de la défiance, Paris: Seuil.

Rosanvallon, Pierre (2006b): "Inaugural Lecture, Collège de France." In: Pierre Rosanvallon: Democracy past and future, Samuel Moyn (ed.), New York: Columbia University Press, pp. 31-58.

Rosanvallon, Pierre (2011a): La société des égaux, Paris: Seuil.

Rosanvallon, Pierre (2011b): Democratic Legitimacy. Impartiality, Reflexivity, Proximity, Princeton: Princeton University Press.

Rosanvallon, Pierre (2011c): "A Reflection on Populism", September 27, 2011, (laviedesidees.fr), pp. 1-10.

Rosanvallon, Pierre (2015a): Le bon gouvernement, Paris: Seuil.

Rosanvallon, Pierre (2015b): "Postface de P. Rosanvallon." In: Sarah Al-Matary/Florent Guénard (eds.), La démocratie à l'œuvre. Autour de P. Rosanvallon, Paris: Seuil, pp. 229-250.

Rovira Kaltwasser, Cristóbal (2012): "The Ambivalence of Populism: Threat and Corrective for Democracy." In: Democratization 19, pp. 184-208.

Schulz, Daniel (2008): "Minderheit, Mehrheit, Allgemeinheit: Die Krise der Repräsentation im Spannungsfeld des Französischen Republikanismus bei Pierre Rosanvallon." In: Soraya Naour (ed.), The Minority Issue: Law and the Crisis of Representation, Berlin: Duncker & Humblot, pp. 103-116.

Urbinati, Nadia (2014): Democracy Disfigured. Opinion, Truth, and the People, Cambridge: Harvard University Press.

4 Rather Topics than Disciplines
Pierre Rosanvallon's
Interdisciplinary Political Thought

Oliver Flügel-Martinsen, Franziska Martinsen

1. INTRODUCTION

Pierre Rosanvallon's political thought is to be characterized as an inventive approach to exigent socio-theoretical problems of representative democracies. One of Rosanvallon's concerns is the rending of democracy as a regime resulting from the withering of democracy as a social form (Rosanvallon 2013: 1). Another challenge is identified by him in the so-called paradox of representative democracies, e.g. the fact that although representative democracy as a constitution guarantees democratic structures in terms of free and equal elections, the people do not self-govern themselves in a literal sense because of a structural asymmetry between government and the governed (Rosanvallon 2018: 134). However, Rosanvallon deals with these two issues (among many others) not only from a political theorist's perspective, but he refers also to their socio-historical lineages, respectively as a historian and as a theorist of the history of ideas. Moreover, here and there he takes a sociological perspective on the discussed phenomena and involves in addition to that moral or anthropological points of view.

In the following, we aim to depict how Rosanvallon's work is best to be grasped as a genuine interdisciplinary attempt to reflect upon the political with regard to its complex methodological approach and especially with regard to its participation-oriented access to the democratic practice. We hold that Rosanvallon's intrinsic research interest lies in the critical pervasion of crucial political and social topics rather than in elaborating academic methodologies to describe these political and social phenomena.

Our article is structured as follows: In the second section we give an overview on the process of disciplinary differentiation within the field of modern science (part 2) and then situate Pierre Rosanvallon's unusual methodology consisting in a historical reconstruction which is enriched with empirical experience (Heidenreich 2016: 55) within the context of current democratic theory (part 3). Two examples discussed and developed in Rosanvallon's recent books might very well illustrate his interdisciplinary approach to certain political topics. We will reconstruct his diagnosis of a crisis of equality (Rosanvallon 2013) (part 4) and after that turn to the problem of a predominance of the executive (Rosanvallon 2018: 5-6) (part 5). Both diagnoses deliver, as we will see, a background explanation for the current crisis of representative democratic systems and the strengthening of nationalist and right-wing populist movements. In examining Rosanvallon's considerations we will be particularly interested in how he develops these diagnoses by combining the epistemic means of different disciplines such as history, history of ideas, political philosophy, political theory, political science and political sociology.

In our article we will mainly concentrate on the diagnostic parts of Rosanvallon's political thought. Even when the constructive parts, where he seeks solutions, seem to him very important, his diagnoses appear to us much more interesting and convincing, whereas the solutions he proposes are sometimes a bit too idealistic and appear to be even a bit too optimistic. We will come back to this problem in our conclusion (part 6).

2. IN BETWEEN SCIENTIFIC DISCIPLINES AND BEYOND

To a certain extent interdisciplinarity could be interpreted as a reaction to the diagnosis of an intrinsic deficit in modern scientific research. Modern science has undergone an intense process of differentiation during the last centuries. What is true for science in general also took place within its different branches such as natural sciences, social sciences, humanities and so forth – all of them are nowadays subdivided into various and often highly specialized disciplines, sub-disciplines and fields.

What thus appears to be a necessary development – taking into account the need to reduce the enormous complexity – does in fact nonetheless come at a price. Today even single disciplines such as political science are confronted with the fact that their different sub-disciplines no longer speak the same language – sometimes even when they are investigating very similar phenomena. What is true for the situation within single disciplines becomes even reinforced with regard to different disciplines sharing the same subjects of interest. Considering the investigation of the political, which is the task of Pierre Rosanvallon's work, one has to state that many different disciplines with sometimes completely different epistemic and methodological self-understandings are involved – often without even communicating with each other. Political science, sociology, history, law and philosophy, to name only a few among them, are looking from different angles at what could in a very broad sense be called the sphere of the political.

Even if the process of differentiation might epistemologically have been inevitable (if something could be called inevitable in a contingent social world), it leads to a situation characterized by the loss of a comprehensive or at least connected perspective. This is in a way the price of modernization in the reflection of phenomena like (in the case that interests us here) the political. The process of differentiation thus calls at least sometimes for an exchange between these different perspectives on similar phenomena. And this demand leads to interdisciplinary research. But interdisciplinarity can be understood in at least two different ways, often not sharply enough distinguished from each other. On the one hand interdisciplinary research could simply refer to the exchange between scholars looking at phenomena from different disciplinary perspectives. This exchange might be fruitful, but it does not necessarily improve the deficit we have identified above: the lack of a more or less comprehensive perspective or at least a perspective not being limited by the mutual disconnectedness of different epistemic and methodological points of view. Here, on the other hand, another sense of interdisciplinarity comes into play: a reflection being in itself interdisciplinary in its character. This second understanding is even more demanding than the first one, since it not only calls for an exchange of different insights, but also for a genuine interdisciplinary kind of reflection. It aims at connecting and embracing different disciplinary perspectives without having the illusion of being able to reconstitute something like a lost comprehensive point of view. If one succeeds in opening this second notion of interdisciplinary research it might become possible to overcome the limitations of the often rather narrow perspectives on phenomena implied by a strictly scientific perspective.

Claude Lefort, one of Pierre Rosanvallon's academic teachers with a very significant influence on the development and the character of his work, accused political science and political sociology of narrowing the reflection of the political by conceiving of it as a mere object of social science (Lefort 1986). From his point of view the social science perspective leads to an objectification of the political that eventually misses its most important characteristic: being a mode of instituting society.[1] What Lefort aims at, instead of this limited point of view, is reopening political philosophy as a practice theory – one that is able to understand the political institution of society more deeply. What is important within this approach for our discussion of Pierre Rosanvallon's political thought, is that it not simply implies a turning away from the perspective of social science but rather a re-conceptualization of the relationship between theoretical reflection and empirical research. Lefort does not try to reanimate an ancient notion of a comprehensive understanding of political philosophy abstracted from the social and political world, as it might be implied in certain lines of thought in Plato's political writings. Instead, he is conceptually aiming at a new notion of political philosophy being in touch with empirical phenomena without limiting itself to an objectivist understanding of social science and being able to reflect normative questions without trying to give time-transcending foundations to them. Such a project requires an intimate connection of the different perspectives of political philosophy, history and a reworked notion of political science and political sociology.

Pierre Rosanvallon's political thought can be best understood as such a deep and intrinsically interdisciplinary attempt to reflect upon the political – or at least this is what we are trying to argue for in what will follow.

3. INTERDISCIPLINARITY IN PERSONAL UNION

A very important feature in Rosanvallon's considerations lies within the fact that they are first of all interested in reflecting topics; to which kind of discipline such a topic might belong then is a marginal question. Moreover, according to Rosanvallon's self-conception as both "a historian and political philosopher" (Rosanvallon 2013: 11), his work takes a broad intellectual perspective rather than a certain methodology into account. Thus, instead of situating himself within the narrow borders of scientific disciplines, Rosanvallon refers to several methodologies and epistemic perspectives that seem to him most suitable for his investigations. Historical reconstructions are being confronted with conceptual questions derived from a normative political philosophy and institutional reflections derived from political theory; all of this is enriched with current empirical insights in order to understand the present by taking history into account. By doing this, Pierre Rosanvallon's political thought is able to provide two things at once: a deep insight into the genesis of the political and social context we are living in today and an

---

1   Ernesto Laclau defends a very similar perspective; cp. Laclau 2014.

ability to develop critical diagnoses of these contexts, that shed a very sharp analytical light on the challenges and problematic developments we are witnessing today. His hypothesis of a crisis of political representation and of a predominance of executive powers in contemporary politics (Rosanvallon 2018) do deliver for example a background explanation for the threat of populist successes[2] we are facing today – be it Brexit or the result of the presidential elections in the USA that brought Donald Trump into office.

From our point of view a strong reason for the pertinence of these diagnoses can be found in the specific character of Pierre Rosanvallon's work: In a situation where on the one hand the humanities are under pressure and called into question in many western university systems (Brown 2017) while on the other hand empirical branches of the social sciences have proven to be lacking in understanding and analyzing – not to mention predicting as they normally claim to do – the populist challenges our democracies are facing, it is in a way relieving to read books like those written by Pierre Rosanvallon. Since the very systematic point of his work targets putting the crisis of equality across in order to dampen potentially high expectations for representative democracy, Rosanvallon is not so naïve as to provide fixed solutions (Heidenreich 2016: 55). He is entirely aware of the difficult undertaking of actively arranging a vivid, popular and reciprocal democracy by institutionalizing socio-political actions of 'the people'. In this respect the challenge of a democracy which comprises both the political and the social citizenship (Rosanvallon 2013: 1) is based mainly on the possibility to fight social and economic inequalities efficiently in order to prevent discriminatory structures which tend to weaken the necessary mechanisms of solidarity of political citizens (Rosanvallon 2013: 276 ff.). In giving historical examples of this fight for both political and social equality, Rosanvallon does not only illustrate the lack of democratic rights within former political communities. In drawing parallels to the current situation, he rather stresses the necessity to gaze critically at the problematic decrease of social equality, which results from the democratic institutions themselves (Rosanvallon 2018).

Rosanvallon's work is one of the best examples to prove that a combination of interpretative methods in history, philosophy, political science and sociology are perfectly able to help us understand the problem of social inequality and its undermining of equal and reciprocal democratic institutions, and to reflect upon counter-strategies (Rosanvallon 2011). In his work, Rosanvallon reminds us that it is time to bring this insight back into public debates, and that it is important to

---

2   For a brief and informative analysis of the temptation of populism cp. Rosanvallon (2011: 265-273).

reflect on the challenges of our time with the help of theoretical attempts, thereby having history and history of ideas in mind and taking insights from political theory and political sociology into account.

4. THE SOCIETY OF EQUALS – SOCIAL INEQUALITY AS A THREAT TO DEMOCRATIC EQUALITY

"Democracy is manifesting its vitality as a regime even as it withers as a social form" (Rosanvallon 2013: 1) is Rosanvallon's central diagnosis in his book *The Society of Equals*. He is convinced, that it is "a whole era that is coming to an end: an era based on a certain conception of social justice involving redistribution of wealth" (Rosanvallon 2013: 9). Historically, modern representative democracies might be a relatively new phenomenon, first and foremost founded towards the end of the 18th century in France and in North America. So Western democracies may be considered as being still in an ongoing process of development, with a tendency to politically include an increasing number of individuals – slaves, proletarians, and women. Against this assumption Rosanvallon points out that the deployment of Western democracies is characterized by a certain change. Whereas both the American and the French Revolution did not separate the idea of democracy as a regime of popular sovereignty from the idea of democracy as a society of equals (Rosanvallon 2013: 4), current democracies, however, do not any longer entail an accordance of the political and the social. Moreover, the situation of representative democracies seems rather inverted, because there can be witnessed a growing social and economic inequality within democratic societies – even though citizens do have equal political rights. Without the specific historian's perspective it would not be possible to recognize the characteristics of this development in the long run and it would therefore be difficult to capture the complex dimension of the current situation. The first historical break of the secular trend to minimize inequalities both in the political and in the social realm occurred in the first third of the 19th century, "when capitalism began to undo the achievements of the revolution" (Rosanvallon 2013: 9). Since then, the idea of the welfare state came into being as a solution to the social question. Yet, the same pathologies like nationalism, protectionism or xenophobia that have been engendered by the first crisis of equality seem to be having a comeback these days. Instead of a remake of the 'old idea' like redistributive welfare mechanisms within a corporatist framework, Rosanvallon insists on the urgent need to rethink and to re-conceptualize the very idea of equality (Rosanvallon 2013: 9-10). From his point of view the crisis of equality, which threatens to undermine the fundament of society, is to be grasped as a "total social fact" that cannot be reduced to a question of unequal income (Rosanvallon 2013: 7). Therefore, he warns emphatically against taking a populist or a nostalgic path to reconsider the terms of a society of equals, because the first option would turn out to be a purely negative vision of equality by discriminating against foreigners and non-citizens, whereas the second option fails to take the irreversible character of individualism and societal heterogeneity seriously by exaggerating the idea of civic republicanism. A third option that can be labeled as the social-liberal one is also to be rejected, because it simply proposes a radicalization of the notion of equality merely in terms of liberal opportunities, e.g. in the sense of a so-called 'luck egalitarianism' (Rosanvallon 2014: 252-253). In contrast, Rosanvallon points to the intellectual dimension of the crisis of equality, for that it reflects the collapse of the whole set of old ideas of justice and injustice. So, we must make an advance to a comprehensive understanding of the nature of inequality in order to regain the political potential to restore democratic action in an emphatic sense (Rosanvallon 2013: 7-8; Weymans 2015): "Therein lies the difference between the idea of a community of equals and that of a society of equals. The latter defines a horizon; it is an objective, a goal whose precise contest is continually subject to public debate and criticism" (Rosanvallon 2013: 121). Here, the harmless-sounding term 'society of equals' contains a genuinely political programmatic which can be associated with the post-fundamentalist approach to the concept of radical democracy that is brought into discussion by his former academic teacher Claude Lefort, to whose memory he dedicated the book *The Society of Equals*. Like Lefort, he holds that a democracy is *the* political mode of institutionalizing the social realm (Lefort 1986). In other words, the act of abstracting from individual differences the radical idea of political equality (Lefort 1994: 148) enables us to generate a realm where all people, the rich as well as the poor, the learned scholar as well as the simplest spirit, are regarded as "equally capable of thinking about the common good and drawing the dividing line between the just and the unjust" (Rosanvallon 2013: 35). Other than Lefort, Rosanvallon refers firmly back to the ideas of the 18th century by emphasizing that "equality then was understood primarily as a relation, as making a society, of producing and living in common" (Rosanvallon 2014: 255). It is this specific heritage of history that he tries to tie on again and to re-conceptualize for the present, yet he is convinced that the idea of relational equality provides the genuinely democratic quality modern societies are in need of in order to establish a solidary community (Rosanvallon 2014: 255). The last chapter of *The Society of Equals* consists of a draft for such a societal approach, which mainly refers to historic ideas of Aristotle, Marx, and Mill (Rosanvallon 2013: 255-301). At this point it may become obvious that the historical reconstruction of political and social ideas is challenged by the need to be thoroughly reflected by the discipline of comparative government or sociology (Heidenreich 2016: 69).

5. *GOOD GOVERNMENT* – THE PARADOX OF REPRESENTATIVE DEMOCRACY

In his most recent book, *Good Government* (Rosanvallon 2018), Rosanvallon starts with the diagnosis of a "failing of democracy" (Rosanvallon 2018: 2) very common today among critical political theorists.[3] At first sight we are dealing with a kind of paradox, because two things seem to be true at once: "Our regimes are democratic, but we are not governed democratically." (Rosanvallon 2018: 1) That our regimes are democratic refers to the fact that political systems in Western democracies have successfully institutionalized free and equal periodic elections. But at the same time the successful institutionalization of free and equal periodic elections does not necessarily lead to a democratic government in the emphatic sense of the concept. Rosanvallon refers to different epistemic means from several disciplines in order to analyze and explain this diagnosis. As Rosanvallon points out, the whole notion of democratic self-government is sociologically and conceptually problematic: Rousseau's famous introduction of the principle of the sovereignty of the people (Rousseau 1964) has been dedicated to solving the problem of the legitimation of laws. Rousseau's simple and beautiful formula is, as is well known, that laws can only be legitimate if those being their subjects are at the same time their authors (Rousseau 1964: 380).[4] But this is only true for legislation and cannot be transferred to the executive power, because, as Rosanvallon puts it, there is always a "*structural asymmetry* between the governed and their governors" (Rosanvallon 2018: 134, original emphasis), which cannot be resolved by any means. According to Rosanvallon, Rousseau was perfectly aware of this point. It is the reason why he argued for a democratic legislation while completely refusing the possibility of a democratic government – which he reserved to gods (Rosanvallon 2018: 135). From the conceptual perspective of political philosophy, Rousseau "solved the problem by demoting executive power to a secondary position and placing it outside the sphere of popular sovereignty" (Rosanvallon 2018:

---

3   Cp. for example the debate on post-democracy: Crouch 2004; Rancière 1997.
4   This solution is still quite popular in contemporary political theory and philosophy. Habermas's very influential approach of a deliberative democracy basically consists in an attempt to re-actualize this revolutionary notion. Though Habermas rather refers to the Kantian adoption of Rousseau's original insight. Cp. Habermas 1994.

135). As Rosanvallon demonstrates by reconstructing the history of modern democracies historically, this has also been the institutional solution of the first democratic systems as they have been established during the revolutions in France and the United States of America at the end of the 18th century: The founders of these democratic systems understood legislation as the central power, "whereas the executive was considered secondary" (Rosanvallon 2018: 7). But as a further historical reconstruction – informed by the perception of this tension from the perspective of political theory – shows, things went differently in the course of history up to the current era. Following Rosanvallon's argumentation today we are confronted with a global trend towards a predominance of the executive (Rosanvallon 2018: Introduction and ch. II). Even those nation states that aren't witnessing a formal presidentialization of their democratic systems have nonetheless a strong tendency towards a predominance of the executive power. As research in political sciences has worked out since the late 1990s, this development is strongly enforced by a global trend towards governance beyond the nation state, shifting decision-making processes from parliaments to governments (Wolf 2000). Whereas governments are mainly involved in international negotiations, parliaments are often restricted to confirming decisions *de jure*, which are *de facto* already made in long-term negotiation processes between governments.

Against this historical background a conceptual problem immanent to common institutionalizations of the majority rule in democratic systems becomes reinforced: According to Rosanvallon "the problem of the majority rule [...] is that it conflates a *principle of justification* with a *technique of decision*, two quite different things that do not entail the same consequences" (Rosanvallon 2018: 111, original emphasis). Its qualities as a means of decision are obvious, since it is a mere technical operation to determine that, as Rosanvallon illustrates, "51 is greater than 49" (Rosanvallon 2018: 111). Decisions are thus very easy to make with the help of the majority rule. But as Rosanvallon underpins at the same time from the perspective of political sociology "the majority cannot be said to speak for the people as a whole, for it designates only a fraction of the people, even if it is a dominant fraction" (Rosanvallon 2018: 111). Liberal thinkers like John Stuart Mill were very well aware of that effect of the majority rule, wherefore Mill wrote: "The 'people' who exercise the power are not always the same people with those over whom it is exercised; and the 'self-government' spoken of is not the government of each by himself, but of each by all the rest." (Mill 1998: 9) If one distinguishes, as Rosanvallon proposes, between the majority rule as a principle of justification and as a means of decision it becomes very quickly clear that the current tendency of a loss of significance of legislation and a shift of power towards the executive increases this tension: Whereas the legislation is to a certain degree able to represent the pluralist character of the democratic people, the government primarily represents the majority. Thus the minorities and with them the pluralistic will of the democratic people are being silenced through the shift of decision-making processes from legislation to the executive. From Rosanvallon's perspective this is also an important reason for the demise of political parties we are witnessing today in many democratic political systems: Since they are becoming more and more "auxiliary forces" (Rosanvallon 2018: 14) of the executives, they are simply no longer able to fulfill their function as "intermediaries between society and political institutions" (Rosanvallon 2018: 13).

With these considerations in mind one can critically call into question the so-called new form of democratic legitimacy claimed by populist movements and populist leaders already in office. While populist movements and parties claim to represent the true will of the people against elites, being considered as corrupt, and against immigrants and divergent opinions, both being accused of putting the unity of the people into danger (Rosanvallon 2011: 266), it becomes obvious that something like *the* will of *the* people simply does not exist, because there is no such thing as *the people*.[5] Lefort has already brought forward this argument against totalitarian attempts to refer to something as obscure as a unified people – "le fantasme du people-Un" (Lefort 2007 [1986]: 468). According to Lefort such a totalitarian temptation is inherent to modern democratic societies, because they are characterized by uncertainty and thus lack any form of substantial, unified notion of the people and any kind of foundations at all (Lefort 2007 [1986]: 465), which gives room for what Lefort calls the totalitarian temptation of a re-constitution of a substantial unified people. Even if this totalitarian temptation has to be considered as a phenomenon occurring within democratic societies it is absolutely clear to him that it is deeply anti-democratic in its character, since it tries to end the unending openness and indeterminacy of democratic societies. Rosanvallon makes a similar point against populism; he even speaks in a Lefortian manner of a populist temptation (Rosanvallon 2011: 265).[6] So in the end it turns out that the strengthening of the executives on the one hand and the populist movements – making false promises of re-constituting popular sovereignty against the predominance of the executives – on the other hand do in fact both, although in quite

---

5   This is also the main thesis of Judith Butler's attempt to re-think the democratic people as a pluralist entity: Cp. Butler 2015. For the critical debate on the democratic people in contemporary political theory cp. Badiou et al. 2016.

6   Even if there are certain parallels, it is important to mention that Rosanvallon does not conflate totalitarianism and populism (cp. Rosanvallon 2011: 267).

different ways, prevent the pluralist will and character of the people from expressing itself properly. Thus it is not by chance that Rosanvallon illustrates his diagnosis of presidentialism's tendency towards illiberalism (Rosanvallon 2018: 110-112) with the examples of Putin and Erdogan, two obviously populist presidents.

What is maybe most interesting here for an understanding of our time and the challenges we are facing today, is that these examples of populist presidents, often legitimately being accused of putting democratic institutions in danger, are in fact only particularly clear examples of an anti-pluralist trend implied by the shift of power towards the executive, which is taking place in most democratic countries all over the world. As we have seen, Rosanvallon is offering us a very in-depth diagnosis of these disturbing developments of our time by examining them against an intensely sketched out historical background, while referring to analytical means of political theory as well as normative categories of political philosophy, concepts established in the history of ideas and explanations derived from political sociology.

6. CONCLUSION

As already mentioned in section 4 of this article, Rosanvallon's writings can be considered as contributions to the ongoing debate on the political and the perspectives of (radical) democracy, since Rosanvallon shares two important assumptions with many positions in these debates. Firstly, like his teacher Claude Lefort (1986) and also like Cornelius Castoriadis (1999) or Jacques Rancière (1997) and recently Chantal Mouffe (2013) he is deeply convinced that we have to understand the political in general and democracy in particular as a mode of "self-institution of society" (Rosanvallon 2018: 137). Secondly, he is, like the authors mentioned above and many others participating in the debates on radical democracy, convinced that "[t]he time has come to fight for *integral democracy*, which will come about the mutual interaction of two ideas that have been kept apart for too long: namely, socialism and democracy" (Rosanvallon 2013: 11, original emphasis). Thus, the ability of Rosanvallon's political thought to open up a critical understanding of the social and political world we live in today is of the highest importance. Whereas Rosanvallon enriches these debates by bringing in historical considerations which give material substance to a very often overly abstract discussion, his propositions for what to do regarding the problems and challenges he identifies are all in all too conventional and do lack a radical criticism required today, when the emancipatory project of democratic self government tends to be endangered by two threats: a neoliberal politics within and beyond Western democratic nation states (Brown 2017) and unfortunately very successful right-wing populist movements. These movements give the false promise of a reconstitution of popular sovereignty, while they are in fact trying to reintroduce into the political arena the fatal tradition of xenophobic nationalism that almost destroyed European countries (and with them half of the world) in the first half of the 20th century.

BIBLIOGRAPHY

Badiou, Alain et al. (2016): What Is a People?, New York: Columbia University Press.
Brown, Wendy (2017): Undoing the demos. Neoliberalism's Stealth Revolution, Cambridge, MA/London: The MIT Press.
Butler, Judith (2015): Notes Towards a Performative Theory of Assembly, Cambridge, MA/London: Harvard University Press.
Castoriadis, Cornelius (1999): L'institution imaginaire de la société, Paris: Seuil.
Crouch, Colin (2004): Post-Democracy, Cambridge/Malden, MA: Polity Press.
Habermas, Jürgen (1994): Faktizität und Geltung. Beiträge zur Diskurstheorie des Rechts und des demokratischen Rechtsstaats, Frankfurt am Main: Suhrkamp.
Heidenreich, Felix (2016): "Die Organisation des Politischen. Pierre Rosanvallons Begriff der 'Gegen-Demokratie' und die Krise der Demokratie." In: Zeitschrift für Politische Theorie 7:1, pp. 53-72.
Laclau, Ernesto (2014): The Rhetorical Foundations of Society, London: Verso.
Lefort, Claude (1986): "La question de la démocratie." In: Claude Lefort, Essais sur le politique, Paris: Seuil, pp. 17-32.
Lefort, Claude (1994): L'invention démocratique, Paris: Fayard.
Lefort, Claude (2007) [1986]: "Démocratie et avènement d'un 'lieu vide'." In: Claude Lefort, Le temps present. Écrits 1945-2005, Paris: Belin, pp. 461-469.
Mill, John Stuart (1998): "On Liberty." In: John Stuart Mill, On Liberty and Other Essays, Oxford/New York: Oxford University Press, pp. 5-128.
Mouffe, Chantal (2013): Agonistics. Thinking the World Politically, London: Verso.
Rancière, Jacques (1997): La mésentente. Philosophie et politique, Paris: Galilée.
Rosanvallon, Pierre (2011): Counter-Democracy. Politics in an Age of Distrust, Cambridge/New York: Cambridge University Press.
Rosanvallon, Pierre (2013): The Society of Equals, Cambridge, MA/London: Harvard University Press.

Rosanvallon, Pierre (2014): "The Society of Equals. Restoring Democratic Equality in Relations." In: Juncture 20:4, pp. 249-257.

Rosanvallon, Pierre (2018): Good Government. Democracy beyond Elections, Cambridge, MA/London: Harvard University Press.

Rousseau, Jean-Jacques (1964): "Du contrat social ou principes du droit politique." In: Jean-Jacques Rousseau, Oeuvres completes III, Paris: Gallimard, pp. 349-470.

Weymans, Wim (2015): "Demokratie als Gesellschaftsform. Pierre Rosanvallon und die vielfältigen Stimmen des Volkes." In: Franziska Martinsen/Oliver Flügel-Martinsen (eds.), Demokratietheorie und Staatskritik aus Frankreich, Stuttgart: Franz Steiner, pp. 167-185.

Wolf, Klaus-Dieter (2000): Die neue Staatsräson. Zwischenstaatliche Kooperation als Demokratieproblem in der Weltgesellschaft, Baden-Baden: Nomos.

5 Writing the History of Democracy as a History of Tensions, Antinomies and Indeterminacies
Pierre Rosanvallon's Method of Conceptual History

Michel Dormal

Discussions of Pierre Rosanvallon's oeuvre most often focus on his thoughts on contemporary challenges of democracy – like the emergence of a 'counter-democracy' or the strengthening of an executive orientation of politics (Rosanvallon 2006a; 2015a). His innovative contribution to conceptual history and the history of ideas has, however, so far received only marginal attention. In the eye of the hasty reader, who does not bother to comprehend the specifics of this approach, the numerous passages pertaining to the 'long 19th century', which can be found in most of Rosanvallon's books, might even seem somewhat tedious and superfluous, only of interest to a small circle of historians. But this would be a serious misunderstanding. Rather, Rosanvallon's investigations into the problems of contemporary politics are inseparable from the very form in which they are developed – the form of a historically saturated self-enlightenment of democracy. Since his early writings, the refoundation of a 'history of the political' has thus constituted a Leitmotiv of Rosanvallon's work.

Rosanvallon himself describes his method as an "histoire conceptuelle du politique" (Rosanvallon 1986; 2003) – a term which has sometimes been translated literally as "conceptual history of the political" (Rosanvallon 2006b: 46) and sometimes more freely as "philosophical history of the political" (Rosanvallon

2001).[1] But in contrast to other prominent authors like Quentin Skinner or Reinhart Koselleck, who shaped the recent historiography of ideas and concepts, Rosanvallon has not elaborated much on his own method. In an afterword to an anthology dedicated to his work, edited by Al-Matary and Guénard (2015), Rosanvallon tells his readers that, over the years, he has been invited many times to formalize his method, in order to found a recognizable 'school of thought' and secure his influence in academia, but that he deliberately abstained from this (Rosanvallon 2015b: 236). Instead, he preferred the practical demonstration of his approach (and its potential) by means of his own proper analyses of different historical subjects (Rosanvallon 2011b: 193).

With all this in mind, the present article[2] nevertheless tries to pin down some constituent elements of what can be seen as Rosanvallon's contribution to the methodological debate. Because even if it was never his intent to found his own school of thought, a better comprehension of his method can help us to re-think the boundaries both between past and present, and between theoretical concepts and practical experience. This kind of critical self-reflection is highly called for in the contemporary context, as traditional history of ideas has come under external and institutional pressure to explain what makes it a legitimate part of Political Science and Political Philosophy, beyond being a mere 'archive' of thoughts that would otherwise long be forgotten. But such a process of self-reflection requires turning the messy factual pluralism of methods into a more 'structured paradigmatic competition' from which scientific progress can arise (Straßenberger/Münkler 2007: 52; my transl.). Rosanvallon adds a coherent and inspiring paradigm to this competition – and, what is more, one that is closer to Political Theory than the established methodological triad of *Cambridge School, Begriffsgeschichte and Foucauldian analysis of discourse* (cf. Eberl and Marciniak 2011).

---

1   Rosanvallon (1995: 26f.) himself has conceded that the term could have been coined more precisely; thereby suggesting that he does not concern himself primarily with a catchy denomination.
2   This is a revised and updated version of an article first published in German in the 2016 special issue of the *Zeitschrift für Politische Theorie* on Rosanvallon. I thank Heike Mauer for helping me with the translation.

1. A CRITIQUE OF CONVENTIONAL INTELLECTUAL HISTORY

Rosanvallon sharply distinguishes his 'conceptual history of the political' from conventional 'history of ideas' and even situates his own approach at a "great distance from intellectual history" (Rosanvallon 2006b: 55). Of course, this does not mean that he sees no point in engaging himself with the thoughts of authors from the past. Rather, he opposes a certain kind of intellectual history, which – much to his regret – can still be found in many introductory textbooks.[3] His critique – but, as we will see, not the consequences he draws from it – is very similar to the attack mounted by Quentin Skinner on conventional historians of ideas in *Meaning and Understanding in the History of Ideas* in 1969.

First and foremost, Rosanvallon opposes the widespread inclination to produce yet another historical 'compendium'. That is to say, that all too often the history of ideas amounts to a mere juxtaposition of single facts and summaries, mostly in chronological form, but without any overarching research problem (Rosanvallon 1986: 97). However, in Rosanvallon's view, a certain style of writing the history of single doctrines, for example socialism or liberalism, that confines itself to the genealogy of a doctrine whose supposedly fully developed, 'final' shape one believes to know, is equally misconceived. This kind of historiography (which is common with Marxists, but not limited to them), does not take seriously the process of history itself (Rosanvallon 1986: 98). This stance of Rosanvallon is similar to Skinner's critique of a "mythology of doctrines", denouncing a "form of non-history which is almost entirely given over to pointing out earlier 'anticipation' of later doctrines" (Skinner 1969: 11). The same accusation of anachronism is put forward with regard to 'text-centered comparativism' – by which is meant an approach where texts and thoughts from very different contexts are compiled and compared with reference to seemingly timeless concepts like freedom, equality or justice, ignoring that the same words and phrases can take on very different and specific meanings. Again, the similarities with Skinner's warnings not to confound the "persistence of [...] expressions" with a "persistence of the questions which the expressions may have been used to answer" are quite obvious (Skinner 1969: 39). Furthermore, Rosanvallon opposes any attempt to generate a unified 'grand theory' in retrospect out of dispersed fragments or statements by an

---

3   Busen and Weiß (2013: 33) have analyzed a selection of introductory German textbooks used for teaching the history of political ideas and concepts. It is their conclusion that pretty much all of these books neglect the 'methodological reflexivity' which is common in other domains of political science.

author (i.e. trying to bridge the gap between Rousseau's second *Discours* and his *Contrat Social* even though Rousseau himself never claimed this kind of coherence). To both Rosanvallon and Skinner, who on his part criticizes a "mythology of coherence", this is nothing but an act of cheating in order to falsely attribute one's own ideas to more authoritative authors, instead of taking their texts seriously and treating them in the same way one does other historical sources (Rosanvallon 1986: 99; Skinner 1969: 18f.). In Rosanvallon's view, the desire to quickly classify all oeuvres and authors in ready-made categories and subcategories constitutes a final aberration: the ability to differentiate and label ten different substrands of liberalism without hesitation, a posture by which some writers superficially show off their scholarship, simulates false intellectual sovereignty and basically substitutes technical classification for real understanding (Rosanvallon 1986: 99).

In short: Rosanvallon opposes a kind of writing history which treats historical works as the mere "imposing wreckage of failed voyages since left on the shores of the past" (Rosanvallon 2006b: 45), subsequently disposing of these stranded goods as one thinks fit. In Rosanvallon's view, in contrast, 'ideas' and 'theories' do not exist independently of historical experience and therefore cannot be labeled, canonized or exploited without taking into account the larger context. They have to be understood along the lines of historical conflicts and challenges resulting from practical, political life (Rosanvallon 1998: 362). In order to make sense of it, the fragmented intellectual 'wreckage' of bygone days needs to be resituated "in a general framework of interpretation and exploration" (Rosanvallon 2006b: 45). This requires that we not only focus on canonized works, but equally take into account newspaper pieces, political speeches, anonymous brochures, 'grey literature' and other sources (Rosanvallon 1986: 101; Rosanvallon 2006b: 46). Up to this point, Rosanvallon seems to concur with Skinner's approach of analyzing a multitude of contemporaneous sources in order to retrace the meaning that the author might have wanted to give to a text within that very specific context (Skinner 1969: 49). Yet, when Rosanvallon refers to 'context', he does not quite mean the same thing as Skinner.

2. CONTEXT AND MEANING IN THE HISTORY OF CONCEPTS AND IDEAS

The relationship between historical context and political concepts can be analyzed from two different angles. One can try to *add* as much historical context as possible to the interpretation of a single work, in order to better understand what the individual author actually wanted to do. This, in a nutshell, is Quentin Skinner's method, who focuses not so much on the meaning of words but rather analyzes their use in concrete historical situations: "There is no history of the idea to be written, but only a history necessarily focused on the various agents who used the idea, and on their varying situations and intentions in using it." (Skinner 1969: 38; cf. Skinner 2002) Hence, writing Political Theory itself must be understood as a kind of political action with critical or legitimizing intent. For instance, according to Skinner, Thomas Hobbes' concept of political representation needs to be understood as a 'reply' to the specific political situation in mid-17th century England: Hobbes developed his theory of the fictional sovereign in opposition to existing proto-democratic forces, presumably trying to undermine their claims to legitimacy (Skinner 2005). It is only indirectly and in retrospect that these divergent intentions and contexts add up to recognizable patterns of theorizing the state (Skinner 2012).[4]

But there is a second angle. Ideas and concepts themselves can be understood as historical sources, as a kind of context, providing information about bigger, underlying social and political developments. This is – simply put – the method of Reinhart Koselleck and his *Begriffsgeschichte*, which tries to retrace the "dissolution of the old society of orders or estates, and the development of the modern world" by looking at how these twin processes have been "registered through language" (Koselleck 2011: 8).[5] What is of interest here is not merely the intention of a single author, but rather the trail of inertia and change, that can be traced throughout the centuries. Or, in Koselleck's words, the "long-term, profound, and at times convulsive transformation of everyday experience" that reveals itself in the evolution of concepts (Koselleck 2011: 9). Thus, if we look at the article on "representation" in the famous lexicon *Geschichtliche Grundbegriffe*, co-edited by Koselleck, the main focus is not on the (de-)legitimizing intentions that underlie a specific understanding of representation. Rather, the article tracks long-term

---

4   There is a vast literature on the Cambridge School. For an overview cp. Tully (1988) and Palonen (2002). I will not here address the question of whether, and to what extent, Skinner might have diverged from his own method in his more recent works (cp. Lane 2012).

5   To Koselleck, a concept is not the same thing as a word. Rather, it "bundles together the richness of historical experience and the sum of theoretical and practical lessons drawn from it in such a way that their relationship can be established and properly understood only through a concept" (Koselleck 2011: 20). For a discussion of the meta-theoretical premises and implications of this understanding of concepts, cp. Egner (2013: 88), Palonen (2002), Huhnholz (2015) and Koselleck (1989).

changes of the concept of representation since the middle-ages, the age of absolutism and the constitution of estates until modern parliamentarianism (Podlech 1984).

Rosanvallon's approach in turn can be interpreted as an attempt to systematically combine both angles. In his first text on methods, written in 1986, Rosanvallon himself speaks highly of Skinner, whom he praises for bringing new impulses and perspectives to the history of ideas. But at the same time, Rosanvallon takes great care to clarify that his own project is quite different from the one pursued by the protagonists of the *Cambridge School* (Rosanvallon 1986: 104f.). On the other hand, a proximity of Rosanvallon and Koselleck has occasionally been noted (Bernardi 2015: 40). And again, Rosanvallon does not deny mutual inspiration, but clearly distinguishes his work from Koselleck's *Begriffsgeschichte*. In an interview, he recounts: "I knew Koselleck well personally. [...] His *Begriffsgeschichte* was likewise a very important asset to me. But I wanted to go further, beyond a contextual and philological history of ideas [...] I've never wanted to separate a renewed history of ideas from a strictly political history." (Rosanvallon 2007: 711) His critiques of Koselleck and Skinner seem like two sides of a mirror: On the one hand, the project of *Begriffsgeschichte* is deemed too abstract and too philological, primarily analyzing dictionaries and, according to Rosanvallon, not sufficiently taking into account real political struggles and the expectations and disappointments that come with them. On the other hand, Skinner is accused of giving too much attention to single intents and contingent contexts of actions, failing to envision even the possibility that texts from different decades might still be understood with reference to the same political problems (Rosanvallon 1986: 105; cf. Bernardi 2015: 36).

Fittingly, Rosanvallon (1986: 96) characterizes his own approach as the writing of history *on a razor's edge* ("sur le fil du rasoir"). On one side, a rich and profound reconstruction of past political conflicts intends – in full accordance with Skinner – to give back to history its openness and its 'presence': "What interests me is understanding the political experience of the past all over again, making it come alive once more [...]. Therefore, the point is to re-invest the past with its dimension of indeterminacy." (Rosanvallon 2007: 710) Here, history is understood as an open "succession of presents", each of which is new and unprecedented (Rosanvallon 2006b: 38). But on the other side, Rosanvallon also wants – like Koselleck – to retrace the continuities and changes within the bigger patterns of interpretation and categorization, transcending single experiences and situations. This clearly presupposes that we can in some way discover a kind of 'structure' in political history that cannot be reduced to the actions and experiences of individual authors and agents. Rosanvallon himself even speaks of a "global social imaginary" (Rosanvallon 2006b: 45).

But can you have it all? One might question whether Rosanvallon's 'method' is really more than an improvised combination of existing approaches. And isn't he, in the end, sketching a 'methodological utopia'[6], which, due to its totalizing claims, cannot actually be put to use in practical research? Part of the answer is given in Rosanvallon's own books. There, he has proven "persistently and convincingly" (Raphael 2013: 19; my transl.) that not only can his research program indeed be put to practice, but also that it is possible to combine the respective approaches of Skinner and Koselleck in a way that is both novel, and that gives us original insights. For instance, Rosanvallon's own study of the history of representation is based on a rich and detailed account of the competing answers – that were given in different historical contexts by specific actors – to the question of where, how and by whom the people could be made present. This account is combined impressively with an analysis of different overarching 'imaginaries' of representation – from the ideal of an abstract representation of unity, passing through the attempts to give direct presence to different social groups, to the 'democracy of equilibrium' that is shaped by parties and labor unions (Rosanvallon 1998; cf. Weymans 2007). But the autonomy and originality of Rosanvallon's 'histoire conceptuelle du politique' can also be asserted with regard to methodology and metatheoretical premises. At the risk of schematizing matters a little too much, I will nevertheless outline three main points that – in my view – characterize this originality of Rosanvallon.

3. THREE BASIC ELEMENTS OF A CONCEPTUAL HISTORY OF THE POLITICAL

3.1 The political as a distinct object of history

A first fundamental theoretical decision that distinguishes Rosanvallon's approach from that of Skinner or Koselleck is already illustrated by the term he uses to name his project: a history of *the political*, thereby taking up a prominent distinction in French political philosophy.[7] At first glance, the term remains somewhat vague:

---

6   The expression stems from Rosanvallon (1995: 32) himself, who uses it to describe his ideal of finding those points of intersection where the history of empirical politics and the history of political ideas overlap.
7   Regarding the difference between politics and the political cp. Bedorf/Röttgers (2010).

"to refer to 'the political' rather than to 'politics' is to speak of power and law, state and nation, equality and justice, identity and difference, citizenship and civility – in sum, of everything that constitutes political life beyond the immediate field of partisan competition for political power, everyday governmental action, and the ordinary function of institutions" (Rosanvallon 2006b: 36).

Here, Rosanvallon is following his teacher Claude Lefort. Thinking about the political, according to Lefort (2001: 20 and 282), is to think about the specific forms and ways a political community is instituted – a question that has never been asked by a mainstream of Political Science oriented towards scientism. Rosanvallon develops this more philosophical attitude into a historical research program, thereby also distancing himself from the 'new political history' that Réné Remond tried to revive in France during the 1980s (Rosanvallon 1995: 27; cf. Jennings 2001 for the intellectual context in France). But unlike Carl Schmitt or Chantal Mouffe, Rosanvallon does not claim to have unveiled a timeless, ontological structure of the political that supposedly precedes historical experience and merely 'ontic' manifestations.[8] According to Rosanvallon, the concept of the political rather is a kind of "présupposé méthodologique" (Rosanvallon 1986: 96) – a conceptual prerequisite necessary in order to systematize and make sense of disparate sources and bodies of texts. The political, as Rosanvallon understands it, is both a social field and a process. Firstly, as a field, it is "the site where the multiple threads of the lives of men and women come together, what allows all of their activities and discourses to be understood in an overall framework"; secondly, the political can also be understood as an "always contentious process whereby the explicit or implicit rules" of what citizens "can share and accomplish in common – rules which give a form to the life of the polity – are elaborated" (Rosanvallon 2006b: 34). Writing the history of the political means, to start with, to understand this process in its indeterminacy and its richness in experiences. In a second step of analysis, the resulting historical patterns organizing the field of the political are to be retraced.

It is this twofold definition of the political which, in itself, connects both research angles that I have attributed before to Skinner and Koselleck – a context-based understanding of past actions on the one hand, and on the other the study of long-term structure and its transformations. Both aspects converge in what Rosanvallon

---

[8] Mouffe (2005: 9), following Carl Schmitt, thinks of the political in terms of an ontological "dimension of antagonism". This is alien to Rosanvallon, who has no great sympathies for 'radical thinkers' like Mouffe, Žižek or Badiou (cp. Rosanvallon 2011b: 195f.).

(1986: 99) calls political 'rationalities' – they link the processual aspect to a certain order of discourse. Examples of such rationalities, underlying the problematization of voting rights in 19th century France, are 'reason' or 'number' – the rationality of enlightened discussion vs. the rationality of majority decision (Rosanvallon 1992). These 'rationalities' describe somewhat stable patterns of interpretation, which for their proper understanding nonetheless require a reconstruction of those contexts of action, in which they were articulated in the first place to legitimate or weaken certain democratic claims. These patterns crystallize along certain concepts like election, representation or law, and sometimes they may be articulated in form of a coherent 'theory'. Nonetheless, they cannot be thought of as proper 'ideas' of one single author. An understanding of voting rights alluding to ideals of 'reason' cannot only be discovered in the writings of Guizot, but – among others – also in administrative voting regulations, parliamentary speeches or in the symbolism used by (official or unofficial) agents. In some respects, this concept of 'political rationality' comes close to what Foucault once designated as *épistème*. Indeed, Rosanvallon (1995: 34) characterizes his own approach to history as a "renewal of Foucault's original intentions" (my translation). But according to Rosanvallon, Foucault himself subsequently failed to really grasp the Political, conceiving of politics only in mechanical terms of power and opposition.

3.2 A phenomenology of structuring antinomies

Rosanvallon specifies his broad conception of the political by adding another assumption. He supposes that the political rationalities mentioned above develop along the lines of constitutive "contradictions and ambiguities" and sets of "equivocations and tensions that have structured political modernity since its inception" (Rosanvallon 2006b: 37f.). 'Reason and number' as possible rationalities of voting are an example of such an ambiguity, the effects of which can still be noticed today (as the ongoing debate on voting rights for minors illustrates).

It is crucial to point out that this kind of ambiguity does not result from an imperfect definition or an improper understanding on the part of scientists or citizens. Rather, the ambiguity lies in the object itself. In the example of voting rights, the tension is a result of two contradictory imperatives: individual rights on the one hand, requiring that every voice is counted equally, and collective self-government, which demands some kind of reasonable orientation towards the 'public good', on the other. In modern democracies, both principles seem equally and quite inextricably linked to voting rights and political participation in general. Hence, this ambiguity shaped the evolution of modern democracy since its early beginnings. But it is 'constitutive' for democracy in an even stronger sense: It was, according to Rosanvallon, ultimately impossible for contemporaries to conceptualize and to make sense of democratic rule outside or apart from this very tension. In *Le peuple introuvable*, Rosanvallon (1998: 31) analogously identifies a second constitutive tension: the antagonism between the abstract notion of 'the people' in constitutional law on the one hand and the empirical diversity and sociological representations of society on the other. These kinds of internal contradictions, occupying practitioners and theorists alike, organize and structure Rosanvallon's whole oeuvre. In *La contre-démocratie*, the argument is built around the tension between procedural legitimacy and societal distrust (Rosanvallon 2006a: 11). And his latest book, *Le bon gouvernement*, starts from the difference between democracy as an abstract institutional form and democracy as a tangible mode of action, namely of ruling and being ruled (Rosanvallon 2015a).

In a recent clarification regarding methods, Rosanvallon (2015b: 244ff.) distinguishes six specific kinds of ambiguity or antinomy. Firstly, he identifies a structural tension resulting from parallel, but contradictory aims (e.g. contradictory norms of what makes a 'good' representative). Secondly there are constitutive ambiguities resulting from necessarily different definitions of one single concept (e.g. 'the people' as a notion of constitutional law and as a sociological concept). A third antinomy results from effects of complexity and a fourth one from built-in functional asymmetries (take for example mechanisms to create public trust; they are required for democracy to work in the long run, but they are by nature opposed to the equally democratic, but more short-term function of distrust). Finally, and somewhat less elaborated, Rosanvallon cites variations of time and space as well as the plurality of forms: Democracy is not only a form of government, but also a form of praxis and a societal form in a more general sense. Whether this brief list is convincing may remain undecided here, and Rosanvallon himself would probably be the last person to dogmatize about it. The more important point here is the following: unlike Quentin Skinner, Rosanvallon claims that all of these tensions and aporias possess or develop to some degree a certain kind of obstinacy and permanence, thereby allowing to connect texts and theories independently of their authors' narrower intentions (cf. Bernardi 2015: 36).[9] Furthermore, Rosanvallon assumes that only a limited number of such ambiguities and antinomies are effective at a given time. It is along this limited number of

---

9   From this follows – despite remaining fundamental differences – a certain resemblance to the approach of Niklas Luhmann, who has analyzed the rise and fall of historical semantics such as 'representation' or 'sovereignty' as attempts to come to grips with certain irresolvable internal paradoxes of the political system (cp. Luhmann 2000: 323f.). To my knowledge, Rosanvallon has never elaborated on this affinity.

tensions and aporias, that a thick, synchronic reconstruction of elapsed presents à la Skinner can purposefully be combined with a diachronic analysis of the long-term changes in the meaning of concepts – without getting lost in the "odds and ends of historical sources" or even the bottomless project of an 'histoire totale' (Raphael 2013: 17; my transl.).[10]

In a next step, Rosanvallon develops from this premise a corresponding set of specific research methods and narrative techniques. Thus, his approach towards historical source materials is shaped by the methodological imperative to prioritize the oppositions, disappointments, tensions and doubts that might resonate in these documents – "to recover problems more than to describe models" (Rosanvallon 2006b: 39). While this recovering of structuring antinomies is – at first – inevitably influenced by intuition and our prior knowledge of the object at hand (cf. 3.3), the researcher nonetheless cannot simply and arbitrarily himself define what is to be treated as the relevant context of interpretation. Rather, the structuring antinomies must be retrieved and carefully scrutinized on the basis of a wide and diverse range of historical material. At this point, Rosanvallon is once again in complete agreement with Skinner. Both oppose an anachronistic interpretation of history.

Analyzing the nowadays widely discussed crisis of political representation using a Rosanvallonian approach, one could – instead of presupposing a deductively generated, timeless ideal against which messy empirical realities of political representation can then be juxtaposed – rather take as a starting point the heated debate about different modes of representation which sprung up in mid-19th century Europe. By then, the old majoritarian 'the-winner-takes-it-all-model' of representation was widely criticized as a fraud, and proportional representation was presented as a remedy to the pitfalls of majoritarian voting systems. This controversy took place simultaneously in different countries and its echo can be discovered in political pamphlets, parliamentary debates on franchise reform and in academic and theoretical writings alike (cf. Rosanvallon 1998: 154ff,). All these sources reveal traces of an internal tension within the very concept of political representation – a tension between personal representation, built on accountability, and the visible representation of dissenting opinions, between the ideal of integration, giving a shared sense of identity to citizens, and the counter-ideal of a depiction of fragmented social reality. The trail of this opposition could then be followed in

---

10 Raphael remarks that Rosanvallon has never been tempted by the idea of 'total history'. This is not completely true. At one point he actually claimed to pursue exactly this goal: "c'est vers 'une histoire totale' qu'il faut se diriger" (Rosanvallon 1995: 29). But this impulse is tamed by Rosanvallon's restricted focus on a limited number of structural tensions.

different historical directions – backwards to the French Revolution and its constitutional debates on popular sovereignty, and forward towards contemporary debates on populism. By this detour, ideally, one gains a deeper theoretical understanding of the complex developments that contributed to the recent feeling of crisis – a crisis which actually may have its deeper roots in the fact that ingenious political forms like parties which once managed to reconcile and balance *both* sides of the underlying antinomy are no longer functional (cf. the contribution of Felix Heidenreich in the present volume: Heidenreich 2019; for an analysis of the crisis of representation according to Rosanvallon see also Weymans 2007).

Following this pattern, Rosanvallon himself usually begins by introducing certain concepts that have come to be seen as problematic, tracing them back through history in order to subsequently unfold their internal non-identities, antagonisms and the centrifugal forces at work. This reconstruction of specific controversies, based on rich historical source materials, alternates with passages that take one step back, connecting the different parallel trajectories and identifying 'nodal points', thereby revealing the bigger historical motions and dialectics of the political (Rosanvallon 1986: 100). The image of the political resulting from this is that of an incessant, precarious work of exploration, continuously deciphering and balancing the ambiguities that set it in motion: "the object of such a history […] is to follow the thread of trial and error, of conflict and controversy, through which the polity sought to achieve legitimate form" (Rosanvallon 2006b: 38). According to Geneviève Verdo, this methodological approach itself has a 'centrifugal' spin. Seemingly stable and theoretically secured concepts burst into contradictory rationalities, and while at first these ambiguities might still appear to be reconcilable, in the ongoing process of research and also from book to book, Rosanvallon allegedly portrays them increasingly deeper and sharper (Verdo 2002: 698). The latter is only partially true, however, as Rosanvallon also takes into account learning processes and tentative solutions found by contemporaries. One example of such a solution would be the rationalized pluralism of party democracy, which bridged the gap between the abstract concept of 'the people' in constitutional law and the empirical diversity of opinions and identities. In other words: Rosanvallon's intentions are not merely deconstructive, but primarily 'reconstructive' (Schulz 2015: 155).

However, according to Rosanvallon, these temporary solutions, for which he crafts terms like 'democracy of equilibrium' (Rosanvallon 1998) or 'democracy of average' (Rosanvallon 2000), always remain precarious and experimental and, in the end, they need to be historicized themselves. His analysis does not lead to a generalizable conceptual synthesis, but rather provides a narrative reconstruction of explorative movements (cf. Rosanvallon 2008). Herein lies – to stick with the example of representation – a big difference from more traditional accounts like the one offered by Urbinati (2006). In her widely read book on the subject, she reviews canonized ideas on representation and democracy from Rousseau, Kant and Sieyès to Condorcet in order to distill one coherent model of how representative democracy ought to be properly understood – a model that Rousseau would have already arrived at, had he not built his reasoning on conceptual mistakes.

3.3 The continuum of democratic experience

From Rosanvallon's perspective, writing history along such internal antinomies as have been explained above is an exercise in "empirical phenomenology", which leads to the "very heart of the political" itself (Rosanvallon 2006b: 44f.). This raises epistemological questions. Thorough scrutiny of the historical material and the famous 'veto-power of the sources', postulated by Koselleck, might very well prevent the most fallacious anachronisms. But, putting this aside, how are past presents really accessible to us? How can it be guaranteed that our interpretations actually reflect the political experience of contemporaries? Many historians would not dare even to make such claims. Rosanvallon defends them – with a bold reasoning, specifically grounded in Political Theory. Here, we can no longer omit that Rosanvallon is actually not concerned with a history of 'the political' in general. Rather, all of his works up to now exclusively focus on modern democracy. He has not published an account of ancient democracy nor a history of the *Ancien Régime*, even if he mentions both sometimes for illustrative purposes. Even Rosanvallon's book on the French state restricts itself to the period since 1789 (Rosanvallon 1990) – a deliberate neglect of absolutism, arguably a quite important period in the history of the centralized modern state. This omission is not due to insufficient knowledge of the material. Rather it is closely connected to methodological considerations; for it is the very fact that we today live in a democracy too, which, according to Rosanvallon, gives us access to past presents. He assumes that there exist "resonances between our experience of the political and that of the men and women who were our predecessors", vouching for the possibility of an emphatic understanding of history (Rosanvallon 2006b: 39; Rosanvallon 1986: 102). While the actual form of democracy changes over time, all of these changes can be understood as answers to closely related original problems. Therefore, it might be misleading to characterize Rosanvallon as an "archeologist of democracy" (Verdo 2002). For the archeologist merely discovers fragments and ruins of sunken worlds, which all scholarly knowledge of facts notwithstanding, ultimately remain strange and foreign. In contrast, Rosanvallon's method presupposes that the researcher is situated in the same field of problems as his object of research:

He conceives of history as a "quest in which we stay involved", a search that also is ours (Rosanvallon 1998: 362; cf. Rosanvallon 1986: 102, my transl.). In this sense, Rosanvallon's latest books, which focus more on contemporary transformations of democracy – the erosion of parliamentarianism, the rise of 'counter-democracy' (Rosanvallon 2006a) or a 'democracy of exercise' (Rosanvallon 2015a) – can be read as seamless continuations of one and the same research program. This assumption of a certain continuity of problems, inherent to democracy, sharply distinguishes Rosanvallon from Skinner, who has always insisted on the incommensurability of problems and situations. Here, Rosanvallon seems closer to Koselleck, who deliberately chose to restrict his research to the history of such concepts which, "facing forward to our time", are familiar to us in the present (Koselleck 2010: 9).

However, Rosanvallon links this argument more specifically to his particular view of democracy. To him, democracy is not only one form of government among many. Much to the contrary, democracy establishes a historically new way of how society as such can relate to itself. Following Claude Lefort, Rosanvallon conceptualizes democracy as the rise of a society that is no longer fully comprehensible as a whole, that cannot be governed anymore from one single point, and in which the identity of the people is continuously called into question (Rosanvallon 1998: 18). To Lefort, democracy is defined by the fact that the space of power must remain empty (Lefort 2001: 28). This 'emptiness' at the heart of democracy not only renders any embodiment of unity impossible, it also entails a new relation to history. People experience a radical uncertainty regarding the foundations of power, order and knowledge. Therefore, they increasingly have to understand society as a product of their own making (Lefort 2001: 30). Following this lead, Rosanvallon explicitly identifies the dissolution of a unified body politic and the rise of democracy as the two crucial moments informing his approach to history (Rosanvallon 1995: 29). The aporetic, tension-ridden character of 'the political' thus reveals itself to be not a timeless constant, but, rather, a consequence of the structure of modern democracy – where indeed the political always needs to be understood as an "experiment in freedom" (Rosanvallon 2006b: 36), therefore manifesting itself more often in the form of a question than an answer.[11]

On several occasions, Rosanvallon has also insisted on what he sees as an important difference between his and Lefort's interpretation of democratic openness

---

11 The focus on democracy might also explain why Rosanvallon is largely ignoring important political events like the French colonial wars (cp. Raphael 2013: 17f.) – topics he probably considers external to democracy.

(or 'emptiness'). According to Rosanvallon, Lefort, strongly marked by the totalitarian perversions of communism, allegedly over-emphasized the necessity of liberal institutions that guarantee that the space of power remains empty. In contrast, Rosanvallon himself wants to focus more on the conceptual indeterminacy of democracy itself (Rosanvallon 2015b: 243f.; Rosanvallon/Schulz 2016: 117). This might not be as big a difference as Rosanvallon suggests, for the conceptual indeterminacy of democracy can only be fully experienced and processed if the basic openness of democratic politics is safeguarded by institutions, such as constitutions or a legally secured right to freedom of speech. Conversely, existing democratic institutions, even if initially the result of a rather flat opposition to totalitarianism, always have the potential to produce a 'surplus' of meaning and experiences that challenges and modifies the conception of democracy itself (one might think here of the German constitutional court, which was clearly founded in a strictly anti-totalitarian spirit, but since has become an important and distinct source of re-interpretations of democratic norms).

4. HISTORY AND THE QUESTION OF POLITICAL NORMATIVITY

The assumption that there exists an element of historical continuity, rooted in a shared experience of democratic freedom and openness, inevitably raises the question of how history relates to the present. To what end, and for whom, do we write the history of the political? What can and what should this history tell us? And what relevance does political normativity have for this whole endeavor? The answer is threefold.

To begin with, Rosanvallon distances himself strongly from traditional political philosophy, which aspires to generate an exhaustive and fully consistent normative framework for thinking about politics. The latter kind of political philosophy, as exponents of which Rosanvallon names authors like John Rawls and Jürgen Habermas, is accused of merely 'parasitizing' the idea of democracy (Rosanvallon 2011b: 177). By defining a priori criteria of justice or reasonable discourse, the aforementioned thinkers allegedly formalize reality in an inappropriate way. According to Rosanvallon (2006b: 44), they reduce all political problems to an obstinate non-compliance of reality with predefined principles discovered by the philosopher, leaving no room for the practical experience of ambiguities. Whether this critique really does justice to Rawls and Habermas may remain undecided here. In any case, Rosanvallon himself certainly does not want his project to be mistaken for what, for the sake of simplification, might be called Post-Kantian

Political Philosophy. Rather, much like Foucault and Bourdieu, he associates himself with a certain re-orientation of French scholars since the 1970s, increasingly opposing the very idea that incontestable foundations of reasoning, upon which norms could be built, are attainable or even desirable (cf. Raphael 2013: 16).

This certainly does not mean that Rosanvallon retreats to a kind of scientistic neutrality that refrains from all normative or moral judgement. For him, the real choice is not between neutrality and normativity as such, but between a 'foundational' kind of normativity a priori ("normativité de départ") and a process-oriented, a posteriori kind of normativity ("normativité d'arrivée") (Rosanvallon 2011a: 346). Rosanvallon clearly associates his own research with the latter kind of normativity, defining it as an attempt to clarify and reflect on empirical experiences and practices, based on which tentative offers of orientation can then be made – and false generalizations be refused. At first sight, this appears to be a weak form of normativity, hardly going beyond Quentin Skinner's modest hope that writing history would open our eyes to the fact that the present too is "the product merely of our own contingent arrangements", thereby inviting us to discover the "essential variety of viable moral assumptions and political commitments" (Skinner 1969: 52f.). Following a similar line of argument, Rosanvallon criticizes a 'closed' universalism centered on one privileged model. He advocates a more 'open' universalism that is able to preserve the totality of experiences of democratic freedom (Rosanvallon 2008).

Thus, what Kari Palonen says about Skinner and Koselleck equally applies to Rosanvallon: The normative value inherent to their work has little to do with conventional moral recommendations. Rather, it lies in a new way of theorizing as such: "Conceptual history offers a chance to turn the contestability, contingency and historicity of the use of concepts into special instruments for conceptualizing politics." (Palonen 2002: 92) For instance, the insight into the inevitable democratic tension between a sociological understanding of the people and an understanding in terms of constitutional law (a point that Rosanvallon reiterates on several occasions) allows for a critique of all models which unilaterally privilege one dimension of the concept without considering the other. At the same time, this insight stimulates our "institutional imagination", raising the question of how this tension can be mediated and dealt with in the present (Raphael 2013: 12). Here, one can very well remain skeptical about some actual answers Rosanvallon himself gives to such a question – I would, by way of example, not share his optimism regarding new, post-electoral forms of democracy and legitimacy (Dormal 2016). But these are questions of political judgement, something every one of us ultimately has to do for themselves – to rephrase Quentin Skinner (1969: 52). Rosanvallon sees it as his most important task to provide historical and conceptual insights in order to inform the autonomous political judgement of citizens – while refusing, most of the time, the posture of the omniscient expert giving lessons to a passive audience (Rosanvallon 2015b: 250).

However, Rosanvallon does not content himself with the ironic praise of the unfinished and agonistic nature of things that is common with more postmodernist authors. His way of writing history is also strongly impregnated with specifically republican ideals. For instance, Rosanvallon has a positive, affirmative view of social 'progress', thereby opposing the postmodernist account of modern history as a mere process of refinement of the tools of oppression. Progress, as Rosanvallon understands it, does not only encompass the approximation towards a fixed ideal, but rather the attempt to overcome the separation between theory and practice as such (Rosanvallon 1995: 34). The basic idea even comes close to the famous 'Theses on Feuerbach' authored by the young Karl Marx. In opposition to Marxism, however, Rosanvallon does not assume that there is any epistemologically privileged class, party or other group, leading or embodying this progress. Rather, progress is a republican project that every citizen takes part in. From this it follows that the task of the historian or the philosopher cannot be strictly separated from the actual practice of democracy (Rosanvallon 1998: 363). Democracy not only *has* a history, it *is* itself a story that is constantly told and retold and to which everyone who produces knowledge about society contributes, be it by writing scientific books, novels or by lecturing (Rosanvallon 2006b: 38). It is precisely in this sense that Rosanvallon (2006b: 57) intends "to enrol […] in the line of all of the scholars who were the most indefatigable citizens, precisely through their works". For if shared experience allows us to understand democracy's past presents, as Rosanvallon assumes, then our own present thinking and writing, when trying to come to grips with these experiences of the past, is nothing less than another small step in the big endeavor initiated by the original promise of freedom (Rosanvallon 2006a: 32).

This is not to be confused with the posture of the intellectual activist, lending public authority to a particular ideology by means of his scientific reputation (Rosanvallon 1995: 36). Rather, for Rosanvallon, academic debates can be seen as a contribution to the general task of collectively deciphering and making sense of our shared world. At this point, another specific component of Rosanvallon's understanding of the political surfaces. He considers it essential to find forms of perceptions and representation of government and society that make the latter 'readable' to citizens. Rosanvallon (2006a: 313) explicitly speaks of a 'cognitive' dimension of the political. This aspect is also explored at large in the project *Rac-*

onter la vie, an initiative by Rosanvallon himself to collect autobiographical narratives in order to generate shared knowledge about society, and to counteract the speechless fragmentation that has taken hold of the republic (Rosanvallon 2014). While the general republican intention, keeping alive a 'concern for the world' (Hannah Arendt) as its deeper motivation for research, is certainly honorable, this specifically cognitive turn proposed by Rosanvallon is not without problems. While it is true that the ability to cognitively appropriate the social world surrounding them is a precondition for the practical and political empowerment of citizens, in my view, one should take care not to reduce the political itself primarily to a problem of proper knowledge or epistemology, thereby involuntarily obscuring the more down-to-earth issues of actual distribution of political power – a tendency that, here and there, surfaces in Rosanvallon's books.

5. CONCLUSION. FRANCE AS THE LABORATORY OF MODERN DEMOCRACY?

The artful combination of social and constitutional history, political theory and the history of concepts offered by Rosanvallon is highly innovative. His various case studies contribute to an enriching rediscovery and reassessment of the past as well as the present of political concepts. This is acknowledged also by scholars who, like myself, do not go along with all of Rosanvallon's conclusions. Influenced by Claude Lefort, Rosanvallon's perspective on democracy is firmly grounded in Political Theory, in contrast to the approach of more conventional historians. To the meticulous, empiricist historian, the notion of a sphere of 'the' political that can be analyzed through its constitutive ambiguities and tensions might appear somewhat speculative. The same goes for the important assumption that there exists a continuum of experiences of freedom, opened up by the democratic revolution, which links past and present. But the Political Theorist, in contrast, is trained to operate with such theoretical and epistemological assumptions, and to think of ambiguities not as the result of inaccurate definitions, but as subjects of research and further exploration. Rosanvallon applies this more philosophical kind of scrutiny and argument to the field of the history. In my view, this makes his approach especially attractive and fruitful for Political Theorists, when compared to Koselleck's more semantic orientation or Skinner's strictly historicizing research centered on the intentions and contexts of single authors.

But is it really possible to separate a Rosanvallonian 'method' from his specific object of research? There is no denying that Rosanvallon's books focus not on modern democracy in general, but mostly on French democracy in particular.

To be sure, he is quite aware of the danger of a national bias, requiring of himself a 'comparative curiosity' in order to complement the openness for internal tensions of democracy with an openness for the peculiarities of democratic experiences in different countries (Rosanvallon 1995: 35; cf. Rosanvallon 2008). In this vein, Rosanvallon's more recent studies regularly bring the United States, England and sporadically the German experience into the picture. Nevertheless, a good part of his studies, and especially the passages pertaining to the 19th century, still very strongly focus on the French case. This raises a question: could it be that Rosanvallon's method simply mirrors the particular French experience? Or to phrase the same question in a different way: Is it possible that *only* French democracy is characterized by inherent tensions, antinomies and ambiguities, resulting from its twofold heritage of absolutism and violent revolution, which for decades prevented a stable, consensual evolution? Should this be true, then Rosanvallon's approach of unfolding democracy's internal oppositions and contradictions could of course not be extended to other cases and would be pretty much worthless outside France.

Rosanvallon is fully aware of this problem. But he firmly insists that it is indeed France's particularly tormented historical experience which renders it a veritable laboratory of political modernity as such – not regarding the 'solutions', but the problems. He concedes that the French democratic experience is more contradictory and fragmented than, for instance, the development in England, the country of slow and pragmatic transition; but it is precisely for this reason that, according to Rosanvallon, the French experience encompasses the whole range of democracy's universal problems in their clearest and most concentrated form (Rosanvallon 1992: 48; Rosanvallon 2000: 36). Put this way, the French case is merely an extraordinary radical and chaotic instance of the universal 'riddle' of democracy – and therefore also of extraordinary interest to the researcher (cf. Mélonio 2015: 90f.).

The generalizability of Rosanvallon's historical approach ultimately rests on these premises, which I largely tend to share. But probably some critics will dismiss such reasoning as typically French arrogance and overestimation of one's own significance. In the end, this must be understood as yet another heuristic anticipation, the truth of which cannot be proven a priori, but which has to prove itself useful in practical research. Everything depends on whether a Rosanvallonian 'democratic universalism of problems' (Rosanvallon 2008: 120) can fruitfully be pursued and substantiated outside the French context in actual research.[12] Can his approach help us find historically sound explanations and interpretations for the evolution of democracy outside France? I believe so; but admittedly, we cannot tell for sure at the moment. However, at a time when conventional history of ideas is pretty much dead academically and in desperate need of new impulses and paradigms, it seems more than worthwhile to give a Rosanvallonian history of the political a fair try.

BIBLIOGRAPHY

Bedorf, Thomas/Röttgers, Kurt (eds.) (2010): Das Politische und die Politik, Berlin: Suhrkamp.

Bernardi, Bruno (2015): "Pour une histoire conceptuelle du politique. Questions de méthode." In: Sarah Al-Matary/Florent Guénard (eds.), La démocratie à l'œuvre. Autour de Pierre Rosanvallon, Paris: Seuil, pp. 31-48.

Busen, Andreas/Weiß, Alexander (2013): "Ansätze und Methoden zur Erforschung politischen Denkens: The State of the Art?" In: Andreas Busen/Alexander Weiß (eds.), Ansätze und Methoden zur Erforschung politischen Denkens, Baden-Baden: Nomos, pp. 15-40.

Dormal, Michel (2016): "Ein demokratischer Fürstenspiegel." August 11, 2016, (http://www.soziopolis.de/lesen/buecher/artikel/ein-demokratischer-fuerstenspiegel/).

Dormal, Michel (2017): Politische Repräsentation und vorgestellte Gemeinschaft. Der Beitrag der Demokratisierung zur Nationsbildung in Luxemburg (1789-1940), Frankfurt am Main: Peter Lang GmbH.

Eberl, Oliver/Marciniak, Angela (2011): "Ideengeschichte in der Vielfalt der Disziplinen. Anmerkungen aus politikwissenschaftlicher Sicht." In: Neue Politische Literatur 56, pp. 367-388.

Egner, David (2013): "Begriffsgeschichte und Begriffssoziologie. Zur Methodik und Historik Carl Schmitts und Reinhart Kosellecks." In: Andreas Busen/Alexander Weiß (eds.), Ansätze und Methoden zur Erforschung politischen Denkens, Baden-Baden: Nomos, pp. 81-102.

---

12 I myself have made such an attempt with regard to the history of democracy in Luxembourg – a country nevertheless still very strongly influenced by its neighbor France (cp. Dormal 2017).

Huhnholz, Sebastian (2015): "Bielefeld, Paris & Cambridge? Wissenschaftsgeschichtliche Ursprünge und theoriepolitische Konvergenzen der diskurshistoriographischen Methodologien Kosellecks, Foucaults und Skinners." In: Ludwig Gasteiger/Marc Grimm/Barbara Umrath (eds.), Theorie und Kritik: Dialoge zwischen differenten Denkstilen und Disziplinen, Bielefeld: transcript, pp. 157-182.

Jennings, Jeremy (2001): "'Le retour des émigrés'? The Study of the History of Political Ideas in Contemporary France." In: Dario Castiglione/Iain Hampsher-Monk (eds.), The History of Political Thought in National Context, Cambridge: Cambridge University Press, 204-227.

Koselleck, Reinhart (1989): "Social History and Conceptual History." In: International Journal of Politics, Culture and Society 2, pp. 308-325.

Koselleck, Reinhart (2011): "Basic Concepts in History: A Historical Dictionary of Political and Social Language in Germany. Introduction." Translated by Michaela Richter. In: Contributions to the History of Concepts 6, pp. 1-37.

Lane, Melissa (2012): "Doing Our Own Thinking for Ourselves: On Quentin Skinner's Genealogical Turn." In: Journal of the History of Ideas 73, pp. 71-82.

Lefort, Claude (2001): Essais sur le politique (XIXe-XXe siècles), Paris: Seuil.

Luhmann, Niklas (2000): Die Politik der Gesellschaft, Frankfurt am Main: Suhrkamp.

Al-Matary, Sarah/Guénard, Florent (eds.). (2015): La démocratie à l'œuvre. Autour de Pierre Rosanvallon, Paris: Seuil.

Mélonio, Françoise (2015): "La démocratie française et les apories de la modernité politique." In: Sarah Al-Matary/Florent Guénard (eds.), La démocratie à l'œuvre. Autour de Pierre Rosanvallon, Paris: Seuil, pp. 81-96.

Mouffe, Chantal, 2005: On the Political. London: Routledge.

Palonen, Kari (2002): "The History of Concepts as a Style of Political Theorizing: Quentin Skinner's and Reinhart Koselleck's Subversion of Normative Political Theory." In: European Journal of Political Theory 1, pp. 91-106.

Podlech, Adalbert (1984): "Repräsentation." In: Otto Brunner/Werner Conze/Reinhart Koselleck (eds.), Geschichtliche Grundbegriffe. Volume 5, Stuttgart: Klett-Cotta, pp. 509-547.

Raphael, Lutz (2013): „Demokratiegeschichte als Problemgeschichte und Gegenwartsanalyse. Das Werk Pierre Rosanvallons." In: Neue Politische Literatur 58, pp. 7-20.

Rosanvallon, Pierre (1986): "Pour une histoire conceptuelle du politique (note de travail)." In: Revue de synthèse 107/1-2, pp. 93-105.

Rosanvallon, Pierre (1990): L'État en France. De 1789 à nos jours, Paris: Seuil.

Rosanvallon, Pierre (1992): Le sacre du citoyen. Histoire du suffrage universel en France, Paris: Gallimard.

Rosanvallon, Pierre (1995): "Faire l'histoire du politique: Entretien avec Pierre Rosanvallon." In: Esprit 209, pp. 25-42.

Rosanvallon, Pierre (1998): Le peuple introuvable. Histoire de la représentation démocratique en France, Paris: Gallimard.

Rosanvallon, Pierre (2000): La démocratie inachevée. Histoire de la souveraineté du peuple en France, Paris: Gallimard.

Rosanvallon, Pierre (2001): "Towards a Philosophical History of the Political." In: Dario Castiglione/Iain Hampsher-Monk (eds.), The History of Political Thought in National Context, Cambridge: Cambridge University Press, pp. 189-203.

Rosanvallon, Pierre (2003): Pour une histoire conceptuelle du politique. Leçon inaugurale au Collège de France faite le jeudi 28 mars 2002, Paris: Seuil.

Rosanvallon, Pierre (2006a): La contre-démocratie. La politique à l'âge de la défiance, Paris: Seuil.

Rosanvallon, Pierre (2006b): "Inaugural Lecture, Collège de France." In: Samuel Moyn (ed.), Democracy Past and Future, New York: Columbia University Press, pp. 31-58.

Rosanvallon, Pierre (2007): "Intellectual History and Democracy: An Interview with Pierre Rosanvallon." In: Journal of the History of Ideas 68, pp. 703-715.

Rosanvallon, Pierre (2008): "L'universalisme démocratique: histoire et problèmes." In: Esprit 341, pp. 104-120.

Rosanvallon, Pierre, (2011a): "'Écrire une histoire générale de la démocratie.' Entretien avec Pierre Rosanvallon." In: Participations 1, pp. 335-347.

Rosanvallon, Pierre (2011b): "Entretien avec Pierre Rosanvallon." In: Raisons politiques 44, pp. 173-199.

Rosanvallon, Pierre (2014): Le parlement des invisibles, Paris: Seuil.

Rosanvallon, Pierre (2015a): Le bon gouvernement, Paris: Seuil.

Rosanvallon, Pierre (2015b): "Bref retour sur mon travail." In: Sarah Al-Matary/Florent Guénard (eds.). La démocratie à l'œuvre. Autour de Pierre Rosanvallon, Paris: Seuil, pp. 229-250.

Rosanvallon, Pierre/Schulz, Daniel (2016): "'Die Unbestimmtheit der Demokratie' – ein Gespräch mit Pierre Rosanvallon." In: Zeitschrift für Politische Theorie 7, pp. 105-119.

Schulz, Daniel (2015): Die Krise des Republikanismus, Baden-Baden: Nomos.

Skinner, Quentin (1969): "Meaning and Understanding in the History of Ideas." In: History and Theory 8, pp. 3-53.

Skinner, Quentin (2002): "Interpretation and the Understanding of Speech Acts." In: Quentin Skinner, Visions of Politics, Cambridge: Cambridge University Press, pp. 103-127.

Skinner, Quentin (2005): "Hobbes on Representation." In: European Journal of Philosophy 13, pp. 155-184.

Skinner, Quentin (2012): Die drei Körper des Staates, Göttingen: Wallstein.

Straßenberger, Grit/Münkler, Herfried (2007): "Was das Fach zusammenhält. Die Bedeutung der Politischen Theorie und Ideengeschichte für die Politik-wissenschaft." In: Hubertus Buchstein/Gerhard Göhler (eds.), Politische Theorie und Politikwissenschaft, Wiesbaden: Springer VS, pp. 45-78.

Tully, James (1988): "The pen is a mighty sword: Quentin Skinner's analysis of politics." In: James Tully (ed.), Meaning and context: Quentin Skinner and his critics, Cambridge: Polity Press, pp. 7-25.

Urbinati, Nadia (2006): Representative Democracy. Principles and Genealogy, Chicago: University of Chicago Press.

Verdo, Geneviève (2002): "Pierre Rosanvallon, archéologue de la démocratie." In: Revue Historique 623, pp. 693-720.

Weymans, Wim (2007): "Understanding the Present through the Past? Quentin Skinner and Pierre Rosanvallon on the Crisis of Political Representation." In: Redescriptions 11, pp. 45-60.

6 On the Critical Potential of Rosanvallon's Wide Definition of Democracy[1]

Wim Weymans

In well over twenty books and many essays and journal-articles published over the past 35 years, Pierre Rosanvallon has analyzed many aspects of democracy's past and present. In what follows, I argue that the originality of Rosanvallon's contribution to political theory not only lies in the wide scope of his definition of democracy but also in its critical nature. Democracy for him does not merely refer to a legal or political system but also to democratic societies in their totality, or what he calls a democracy as a 'social form' [forme de société] and the many different contexts in the past and present in which it took shape. Initially, – when he began his scholarly career at the Parisian Ecole des Hautes Etudes en Sciences Sociales (EHESS) at the beginning of the 1980s – he mostly limited the application of his broad conceptual and temporal definition of democracy to France, with occasional comparisons, primarily with the UK and the US. Yet since his appointment to the prestigious Collège de France in 2002 he widened this geographical scope, which now includes many other countries. Today he even strives for 'as thorough as possible a definition of democracy – one that includes all its dimensions and forms' (Rosanvallon 2011a: 226). The fact that Rosanvallon expands democracy beyond the traditional narrow definition used in mainstream political theory may explain in part why the scholarly reception of his work has been comparably limited. The quasi-absence, until a decade ago, of translations of his works in English did not help either. In what follows, I will show how this broad definition of democracy allows him to write its history while also offering a critical perspective that allows us to differentiate between proper and improper views of

---

1 An earlier version of this chapter already appeared in German as Weymans 2015. I thank Stephen W. Sawyer for his comments on earlier versions of this chapter.

democracy and give a diagnosis and remedies for its current crisis. At the end of this essay, I will argue that the scope of his critical definition may perhaps be, paradoxically, at once too wide and not wide enough.

THE ORIGINS OF A BROAD DEFINITION

Within Rosanvallon's definition of democracy modern democratic societies are "those in which the conditions of life in common are not defined *a priori*, engraved in a tradition, or imposed by an authority" (Rosanvallon 2006: 36). Since democratic societies are by definition no longer seen as determined by a tradition or by God, they need a different foundation. Once sovereignty no longer lies in a special caste or group that rules in the name of a predetermined social order, it instead tends to be claimed by the people, and seen as a collection of free and equal individuals. But why should people be treated equally? In pre-democratic traditional societies, inequalities could still be legitimized by referring to a divine or traditional foundation. Yet once – with the dawn of political modernity – the a priori consensus on a stratified or hierarchical society disappears, the only remaining option is to consider all individuals as formally equal before the law, abstracting from their particular background, class or group. As Rosanvallon explains:

"The development of juridical conventions and fictions is […] driven by the concern to achieve an equality of treatment and to institute a common space among men and women who are very different from one another. Such abstraction is in this sense a condition of social integration in a world of individuals (whereas in traditional society concrete differences were a factor of insertion, the hierarchical order basing itself on the principle that differences were to interlock with and complement one another)." (Ibid: 42)

In democracies the people are seen as a unified fiction consisting of equals, despite all of their factual differences. This becomes visible in universal suffrage, a key element in the history of democracy. Rosanvallon explains its role in democratic societies as follows:

"The ballot […] couches heterogeneous expressions in a common language and radically simplifies the social world. […] Equality thus arises from the fact that the votes are counted rather than weighed (the opposite of what suffrage, limited by property qualification, achieved). The citizen, endowed with one vote, is seen as a pure individual, symmetrical with all other individuals and stripped of all specific characteristics. […] Abstraction is thus the quality that constitutes him socially and drives the development of the idea of political equality. That is why this form of equality is so radical and exemplary. It emancipates the individual from all the distinctions by which men are usually ordered and classified." (Rosanvallon 2013: 34-35)

For many theorists, the juridical idea of free and equal individuals (as expressed in elections) is sufficient to organize democratic societies. Some argue that society is based on a contract between free individuals who abstract from their particular background. Others believe that the regulation by the market is the basis of society through a spontaneous cooperation between self-interested individuals. In both approaches, free and formally equal individuals are seen as the basis for a harmonious democratic society, be it through a social contract or an invisible hand. If one adopts such a limited view of democracy based on formal equality and free individuals, then equality between rights-bearing individuals can be seen as a sufficient basis for a legitimate social order. Yet once one takes a broader view of democracy, Rosanvallon suggests, it becomes clear that formal equality or individual rights are not merely a solution but also a problem.

Indeed, because of its abstract foundations – such as the idea of formal equality –, modern societies no longer experience themselves as an organic hierarchical unity but rather as a diverse, fragmented and conflictual whole (cf. e.g. Rosanvallon 1998: 12-19). As Rosanvallon explains:

"If in democracy this formalism is thus a positive principle of social construction, it makes the construction of a tangible people more uncertain at the same time. Accordingly, a contradiction arises between the *political principle* of democracy and its *sociological principle*: the political principle consecrates the power of the very collective subject that the sociological principle tends to make less coherent and whose visibility it tends to reduce." (Rosanvallon 2006: 42-43)

Although formal equality and juridical abstractions form society's political foundation, for Rosanvallon they at the same time create a lack of social order. The fact that it is now politically or formally clear who is the sovereign author of society (the people), also implies that at a sociological level society's form becomes unclear to itself. As a result, the new sovereign – the people – is as powerful as it is indeterminate. While no one doubts politically or juridically that sovereignty in democratic societies lies in the people, few know what the people exactly wants or looks like. According to Rosanvallon, "The people is a master at once imperious and impossible to find. 'We the people' can take only debatable form. Its definition is at once a problem and a challenge" (2006: 37).

Moreover, this tension between the political power of the people and its sociological lack of definition, tends to increase over time: as formal democratic principles become gradually more successful at a political or juridical level (through expansion of elections and formal equality), these democratic societies are allowed to become more pluralistic and individualized and therefore become harder to decipher, know, predict and represent. Rosanvallon himself talks about "the gap between the progress of democracy as regime and the regression of democracy as social form" (2013: 3). Elsewhere he explains: "the 'people,' understood in a political sense as a collective entity that ever more powerfully imposes its will, is less and less a 'social body.' Political citizenship has progressed, while social citizenship has regressed." (ibid: 1)

How, then, to 'solve' this problematic tension? Unlike Marxists, Rosanvallon – and this is important – does not want to do away entirely with this tension, since it is a precondition for freedom and equality and social integration in democratic societies. The abstract and formalistic rules and the general and vague language that politicians have to use are indeed necessary to guarantee freedom and equality before the law (Rosanvallon 1988a: 159-160; Rosanvallon 1998: 92). Politicians are supposed to speak in the name of everyone and the common good, and not in the name of a particular group, class or interest. This also means that people will always feel that their representatives do not fully represent them or their group, and there will thus always remain a gap between politics and society.

Political representation is thus inevitable because a society will always depend on external institutions that represent its generality and that partly escape its control. Like his mentor Lefort, Rosanvallon believes "that collective expression is practically inconceivable without the intervention of a certain exteriority" (Rosanvallon 2006: 47). Rosanvallon therefore contrasts the idea of mediation to the illusion of immediacy, whereby a collection of individuals can allegedly fully and immediately organize themselves harmoniously without depending on any external power or representative institutions.

Although that structural gap between the people and their rulers is inevitable, one can still imagine solutions that diminish the distance between society and its representative institutions without abolishing it. Yet such remedies presuppose a broad perspective on democracy as a form of society, as it enables us to see solutions that one would miss if one adopts a narrow definition of democracy. Seen from a broader perspective, the tension caused by the formal and abstract nature of democratic politics does not require us to do away with these abstractions, but rather to *compensate* for them through often-neglected practices and features of democratic societies that *complement* these abstractions. Rosanvallon emphasizes the importance of making social conflict and tensions visible, of mediating institutions and the need to consider democracy's historicity. As will become clear in what follows, these three features allow him not only to conceptualize democracy in a wider sense but also to write a *critical* history of democracy that allows him to differentiate between democratic practices and ideas and their undemocratic counterparts. In so doing, I will try to refute the criticism by some scholars that Rosanvallon's broad approach is insufficiently critical (cf. e.g. Conti/Selinger 2016: 556-557).

THE VISIBILITY OF CONFLICT

A first feature that Rosanvallon emphasizes as a way to overcome abstractions and to criticize undemocratic representations, concerns the inevitability of conflict. If a social form in democratic societies is no longer a priori given, then it will naturally become subject to political and societal debate. Yet, those who look at democracy in a narrower sense often tend to forget that formal or legal principles such as formal equality, justice or rights cannot in themselves be a sufficient basis for social order, as they remain subject to political debate rather than transcending it. Take for example the fundamental principle of equality. Those who look at democracy in a narrower sense often tend to forget that formal equality and other formal or legal principles such as justice or rights cannot in themselves be a sufficient apolitical basis for social order, since they too may be debated politically. Even though formal equality can be used as a foundation for democratic societies, its formal and abstract nature at the same time also means that it will indeed always be subject to conflict and discussion, both in theory and in practice (Rosanvallon 1992b: 127; Rosanvallon 1988b: 212). As Rosanvallon puts it: "a society of equals [...] defines a horizon; it is an objective, a goal whose precise contest is continually subject to public debate and criticism. It is part of a permanent democratic debate concerning the notions of justice and equality." (2013: 121-122) This is why equality has been interpreted in so many different ways in its relatively short history (cf. Rosanvallon 2013). Or has he writes about "democratic values" such as "liberty, equality, justice":

"When it comes to putting them into practice, these values turn out to be less obvious than they at first appeared. Equality? Very well, but what equality? And what, in fact, is equality? 'Equal pay or the 'reduction' of inequalities? A 'just' distribution of the fruits of growth? Fine, but how does one define 'justice' in this case?" (Rosanvallon 1988b: 212)

This also explains why election procedures vary according to time and place and thus have a history of their own (see Rosanvallon 1992a).

Conflicts are not just legitimate and unavoidable, they also help social integration, as people feel involved in society when its underlying problems and challenges – on issues such as health care, immigration, pension reform, etc. – are subject to debate. As Rosanvallon writes:

"Conflict and society are inseparable terms. The acceptance of conflict lies at the heart of the process of the self-production of the social. Far from denying or ignoring conflict under the guise of an improbable 'consensus', the democratic ideal makes such conflict productive and constructive." (Rosanvallon 1988b: 211)

This is for example why Rosanvallon argues that the welfare state's legitimacy increases if its underlying solidarity mechanisms become visible, so that people know what and why they contribute. As he writes: "the only way for the welfare state to become better accepted is to make its machinery operate explicitly for everyone" (ibid: 211). Therefore, in a democracy, conflicts and inequalities need to be made visible and discussed openly (cf. e.g. Rosanvallon 1992b: 104; Rosanvallon 2000: 34, 40). Politics and sovereignty today still have a role to play for Rosanvallon, then only if they take into account conflict and societal struggles:

"If politics is to be made more visible, we need to remind ourselves constantly of the purpose it is meant to accomplish: to take a people that is nowhere to be found and transform it into a vibrant political community. Symbolization is a collective reflection. […] It is the history and memory of the struggles of men and women to institute a society of equals, despite all the difficulties. The resymbolization of politics is thus part of a permanent questioning of social differences." (Rosanvallon 2008: 312)

MEDIATION AND REPRESENTATION VERSUS IMMEDIACY

Seen from Rosanvallon's broad perspective, democratic societies can, secondly, compensate for their lack of natural social order through mediating institutions and practices. Think of unions, political parties, associations or an independent bureaucracy but also social sciences that try to understand and give meaning to an individualized society, which lacks an a priori form. As the majority of political theorists stick to traditional narrow theories of democratic legitimation through elections, they often neglect these (often unelected or unpolitical) mediating institutions, in favor of parliaments, elections and citizenship.[2]

So, what does mediation or representation consist of? Admittedly, at first sight Rosanvallon's answer appears ambiguous, as he appears to vacillate between a descriptive and constructivist position (cf. Conti/Selinger 2016). On the one hand he wants social scientists to mirror society "as it is." In a postmodern era where society, knowledge and the people are often said to be constructions and fictions, Rosanvallon argues that society consists of realities, voices, opinions and groups with concrete voices that need to be heard and "adequately" represented or described. His "realist" position thus asks social scientists to give a "truer" account of society to compensate for the limited image that elections can offer us. This realism also implies a yardstick to distinguish correct representations from wrong ones. In this view, a complex social reality can be hidden or made visible, be properly represented or – in the case of ideology – misrepresented (cf. e.g. Rosanvallon 2014: 12-15), for example by denying its conflictual nature.

Yet for Rosanvallon this is only part of the story. If the task were to simply "mirror" or "express" a given social structure, then one would not need politics or other mediating institutions. This is why Rosanvallon's realism is compensated by a more "constructivist" view of representation. On the one hand, constructivist means that, although democratic societies still consist of distinct social realities, their overall form is no longer given. This implies that in democracies no final description of society can be offered (which doesn't mean that one cannot strive to improve existing descriptions in order to make them more in tune with new social realities). Different parts of society do exist, but what keeps them together still needs to be "constructed."[3] On the other hand, constructivism also means that representing democratic societies cannot just mean passively mirroring what is already there as it also involves creating new realities – compromises, debates, reflections, images, concepts and institutions, etc. – that were not there before and that need to be constructed. Put differently: once they are given a voice, different groups, interests and positions still need to create compromises and stage debates. In short, representation implies both a "realist" or "descriptive" element (where

---

2   Although Rosanvallon offered an original analysis of the essential role that political parties play in democratic societies (cp. Rosanvallon 1998), in his more recent work (cp. Rosanvallon 2008: 170; Rosanvallon 2018: 13-14) he no longer appears to believe in the role that they can play today. Cp. on this also Weymans 2019.

3   This explains why he declares (cp. Rosanvallon 1998: 18) that the people does not exist before the act of their invocation and why the people therefore needs to be constructed ("il est à construire"). Cp. also Rosanvallon 1998: 91 and Rosanvallon 2014: 12.

society in its variety needs to be taken into account) as well as a "constructivist" creative, abstract, political dimension (where mediating instances or writers actively allow society to get a voice by developing new categories that correspond to new social realities and that thus contribute to making society as a whole "legible").

Some have criticized Rosanvallon for the ostensible tensions and inconsistencies between his realist (or descriptive) theory of representation and his constructivist theory (Conti/Selinger 2016). Yet, I believe that Rosanvallon's theory of representation is still largely coherent in so far as it is precisely a lack of a natural a priori order (the premise of "constructivism") which invites everyone to strive for an adequate description of that society ("realism") without ever reaching that goal (in line with "constructivism"). Just as we still strive for a more equal society and denounce new inequalities without ever pretending to reach "full equality," we likewise strive for an adequate description of society, trying to include forgotten voices, without ever pretending that any description coincides with society as such. It is precisely the structural indeterminacy of society (or of equality) that drives towards offering more adequate descriptions (or to strive for more equality and denounce inequalities) in an open-ended process. Moreover, when striving for an adequate description of social reality ("realism") we cannot just mirror what is given but we also need to develop ("construct") adequate tools in order to do justice to social change.

Rosanvallon's combination of a realist and constructivist theory of representation allows him to distinguish his theory from rival ones. By emphasizing that society needs to be seen "as it really is" he can criticize "constructivist" (Jacobin) theories that see individuals just as abstract citizens represented through elections, thus refusing to consider a broader pluralist social reality (Rosanvallon 1988a: 167). Conversely, the constructivist dimension of his theory allows him to criticize purely realist views that see representation as merely mirroring society "as it is," without political mediation, whereby there is no difference between the representative and the represented, which was a view that was for example defended by a part of the French labor movement of the nineteenth century (ibid: 173-175; Rosanvallon 1998: 67-86).

"DEMOCRACY *IS* A HISTORY"

Just as democratic societies need to compensate for their abstract nature through various forms of mediation and conflict, so theorists of democracy likewise need to contextualize a priori formal definitions of democracy including their various historical embodiments. The fact that democratic societies no longer correspond to a stable definition thus also implies theoretical indeterminacy. As Rosanvallon puts it:

"Far from corresponding [...] to a simple practical uncertainty as to how to bring it about, democracy's unmoored meaning is due quite fundamentally to its essence. It implies a type of regime that resists any attempt at unequivocal classification." (2006: 36-37)

Ahistorical normative a priori definitions of democracy that can be used as a yardstick to judge imperfect historical realizations are thus meaningless for Rosanvallon. All this is, again, the result of taking a wider view of democracy beyond its juridical or strictly political role. As a result, any theory of democracy must also explore its history, which explains why most of Rosanvallon's works are historical in nature. As Rosanvallon explains:

"It has been my ambition, therefore, to rethink democracy by following the thread of its history as it has been spun. But note that it is not simply a matter of saying that democracy *has* a history. More radically, one must see that democracy *is* a history. It has been a work irreducibly involving exploration and experimentation, in its attempt to understand and elaborate itself." (2006: 38, original emphasis)

As a result, many see Rosanvallon as a historian, thus ignoring the underlying importance of his work for political theory, which may be one explanation for the limited reception of his work amongst theorists. This is regrettable since historicity hardly excludes a critical program.

A CRITICAL AND NEGATIVE HISTORY OF DEMOCRACY

Indeed, the fact that democratic theories and societies are embedded in specific contexts that vary over time, does not imply relativism or a lack of a standard that allows us to adjudicate between different representative claims (as is claimed by Conti/Selinger 2016: 556-558). On the contrary, despite his emphasis on the indeterminate nature of the people or of an ideal such as "equality," Rosanvallon still uses an implicit normative and critical yardstick to judge what counts as proper forms of democracy and what does not. As we have just seen, a proper definition of democracy implies an acceptance of the inevitability of conflict, the need for mediation, and of democracies' various national and historical contexts. Whoever denies democracy's mediation, conflict or historicity by replacing mediation with the illusion of immediacy, conflict with harmony and historicity with a priori definitions becomes, for Rosanvallon, ideological or even potentially undemocratic. As he writes: "An ideology is a system of representations that parries all critiques of a social order by making it seem that the principles on which it is based are self-evidently just." (Rosanvallon 2013: 319, n. 44) Rosanvallon's broad definition and its implicit criterion allows him to write a critical history of democracy in which he shows which ideas have undermined or supported democracy. As it turns out, in its young history democracy has often been misunderstood.

In the past Rosanvallon identified at least three different strands of undemocratic thought. First there is the French political culture that saw elections as the only legitimate expression of the people's will, which was based on "the idea that popular sovereignty was structurally linked to the radical project of a self-instituted society" (Rosanvallon 2011a: 124). The state is allowed to act in the people's name, but any autonomy or mediation by the state – e.g. in the form of an independent bureaucracy – is rejected. As a result, "any intermediary structure that stood in the way of direct communication between the nation and its elected representatives was a priori suspect of impeding the expression of the national will and conspiring against liberty" (ibid: 33-34).

Secondly and conversely there is the liberal belief that society is not derived from a social contract between equal individuals, but rather from the "invisible hand" whereby it is produced quasi automatically by self-interested individuals. As a result, a society no longer needs politics or other forms of mediation, as the invisible hand produces immediate sociability. For Smith "the market" therefore replaces politics, as Rosanvallon explains:

"The concept of the market [...] was understood at the time to refer to a general form of social organization. As conceived by [...] Adam Smith [...] the market represented the self-organization of a nascent civil society [...]. It thus stood in opposition to the idea of contract and to the political concepts of the social bond. Smith was therefore the first theorist of the withering away of politics, just as he was the founder of modern economics." (2013: 234-235)

Interestingly, for Rosanvallon, even Marx ultimately subscribes to this ideal of a harmonious society liberated from the state or other forms of mediation. In Rosanvallon's own words:

"Communist society thus aimed to achieve *natural harmony among men*. [...] Communism was rooted in the idea of a pure social bond, of a society in which relations among men would not be mediated by economics or politics. [...] Communism as a society of pure commerce among men thus paralleled the liberal utopia." (2013: 127-128).

He explains how this reasoning could already be found in Marx:

"Marx does nothing else than return to the classical theories of the eighteenth century of sympathy and the natural harmony of men. [...] For Marx it is the fault of bourgeois society that the individual is corrupted, for having reduced him to living in society only through the manifestation of his economic interest. In another context than bourgeois society, however, the arithmetic of the passions could produce spontaneous harmony and would no longer need the crutch of interest to produce it. [...] Marx thus fully consummates the modern illusion of social transparency." (Rosanvallon 2006: 181-182)

This not only means that Marxism is more "liberal" than it may care to admit, but also that neo-liberal ideals of minimal government share the same quasi-totalitarian anti-political view of society as their Marxist enemies (see also Rosanvallon 1999 [1979]). In sum, these "republican", "liberal" and "Marxist" solutions all presuppose that society can institute itself beyond mediation, that harmony can be achieved and conflict overcome.

Democracy's history shows that anti-democratic ideas were de facto refuted by events and practices. If historians look not just at ideas but also at practices and institutions at the grassroots, they can see that reality proves how and why anti-democratic theories were in fact inadequate (and why Rosanvallon's analysis was right). The French republican tradition, for example, denied in theory the importance of mediating institutions and even prohibited certain associations. Yet like his mentor Lefort (cf. Lefort 1986: 248-251), Rosanvallon emphasizes that practices diverge from ideologies and that it would be wrong to think that these theories or prohibitions did in fact correspond to the social reality they sought to master and repress. Rosanvallon emphasizes that there is "another history that needs to be taken into account if we wish to achieve a fuller portrait, namely, the history of the powerful forms that resistance to this very Jacobinism has taken" (2007: 2; see also Rosanvallon 1990). This is also why he partly criticizes Foucault for believing that the utopian statist project of rationalisation actually corresponds to reality, thus overlooking forms of resistance (ibid: 126). If one looks at the archives one can see how the French *de facto* still had to allow, implicitly, mediating institutions and associations in order to compensate for the lack of organic social order in democratic societies. Even though they were often not properly acknowledged or criticized, even France, like other democracies, needed political parties, unions, associations and an independent bureaucracy to actively structure and build a society that went beyond individuals (Rosanvallon 2007; Rosanvallon 1995: 104; Rosanvallon 1998: 167-169). Likewise, the opposite liberal dream of an anti-regulatory society can be refuted by simply pointing out that the modern bureaucratic welfare state is the *de facto* result of a society of individuals. More individuals and more equality in reality means more state, not less (Rosanvallon 1992b: 78). This is also why he states that more rule of law (*État de droit*) automatically implies more bureaucracy (Rosanvallon 1990: 277) and that for him "the liberal individual and the administrative state go hand in hand" (Rosanvallon 1988b: 203).

ON HOW NOT TO SOLVE DEMOCRACY'S PROBLEM

We have seen that in democratic societies citizens often feel that politicians only speak in abstract, general terms and do not listen to their particular stories or needs. Although this discontent or disappointment is a structural part of democracies, for a long time election-based politics seemed able to adequately represent a class-based society. Yet since the 1970s this structural disappointment has resurfaced and increased, thus showing the limits of "the electoral-representative democracy [...] based on the axiom that the general will is fully and directly expressed through the electoral process" (Rosanvallon 2011a: 123). Rosanvallon discusses many causes of this increasing discontent: some general and some only applicable to France; some economic – the changing nature of capitalism that undermined a clearly identifiable class-based structure – and some either social or political. As a result of these changes, society has "become more opaque [...] and therefore less easily represented than the old class society with its well-defined gradations and boundaries" (Rosanvallon 2018: 13).

Whatever the causes, the underlying problem remains the tension between democracy as a political system and as a social form. A broad view of democracy not only allows this tension to become visible but also offers ways of mitigating it. Those who instead start from a narrow legal theory of democracy argue that this crisis can only be solved through legal or political means such as more political representation, more procedures, more citizenship, more (human) rights and so on. Yet as the problem is caused by the limits of a traditional juridical model based on elections, procedures and rights, more procedures or rights will not alleviate these challenges. Rosanvallon therefore thinks that it is naive to believe that politics can be based on individual rights alone (Rosanvallon 1988a: 145), or that it can be seen in purely normative or abstract terms, as neo-Kantian theorists like Rawls or Habermas tend to believe. Although they are right that democracy has a formal, abstract dimension, they wrongly think that it is sufficient. This is why Rosanvallon writes:

"It is necessary to come to grips [...] with the problematic character of the modern political regime [...] and not hope to dissipate its enigma through an imposition of normativity, as if a pure science of language or law could provide men with the reasonable solution to which they would have nothing to add but conformity." (2006: 44)

In fact, such "solutions" ultimately make the problem worse. Rawls' original position for example attempts to reduce the visibility of social conflicts and social diversity, but for Rosanvallon making social diversity less visible precisely increases the problem of society's lack of form (Rosanvallon 1992b: 102; Rosanvallon 1998: 338-340). For him social conflict instead needs to be made more visible rather than hiding it behind abstract legal categories such as justice, rights or equality.

Rosanvallon also rejects ideas that, conversely, want to solve the problem by simply overcoming the gap between abstract politics and society: for example, by suggesting that the people's voice is given and simply needs to be directly expressed (such as in opinion polls or referenda), beyond the mediation of "traditional politics." Or through so-called identity politics which runs the danger of seeing politics as nothing more than the expression of allegedly preexisting identities. In this context, he especially rejects populist ideas that exploit the democratic disappointment and play on people's fears by proposing a unified preexisting nation and excluding its "others" (Rosanvallon 1998: 340-354). In all these examples, the problem of the lack of social consistency is solved by assuming that society has a clear substance or will, that simply needs to be adequately expressed rather than distorted by politics.

If direct democracy's ideals and their procedural counterpart are both inadequate, how, then, may we solve today's problems? One way to decrease the disappointment consists in showing the limits of the traditional ideals of democracy. Once people expect less from traditional forms of democracy (procedures or elections) and realize that society needs external mediating instances (rather than direct democracy) and has to accept conflict (rather than believing in unity and harmony), they will be less disappointed when they are confronted with democracy's supposed "limits." In that sense Rosanvallon's work can be seen as an attempt to diminish democratic disappointment (cf. Rosanvallon 1995: 117).

Yet throughout his work Rosanvallon has also consistently defended a more structural solution to the crisis, namely to expand democracy beyond elections. Juridical fictions, elections and traditional forms of legitimation and citizenship, should, in other words, be complemented or compensated *for* by other forms of generality, representation, legitimacy or citizenship. In this, Rosanvallon follows Condorcet for whom "'the people' [...] was too various to be 'represented' adequately by just one of its manifestations" (Rosanvallon 2011a: 129). This is why Rosanvallon's approach shows "that there is more than one way to act or speak 'on behalf of society' and to be representative" (ibid: 8). Rosanvallon proposes at least three different ways to expand democracy beyond elections in order to make people feel represented again and diminish the gap between society and its representative institutions.

First, there are radical "leftist" alternatives, which he has defended throughout his career. In the 1970s, he actively propagated self-management (*autogestion*) or democracy at the grass-roots in companies and at a community-level beyond the state and the market. In the 1980s, he became one of the first defenders in France of deliberative democracy and later participatory democracy (on this see Rosanvallon 2011b). Less radically, perhaps, he also, in the late 1980s, briefly defended "third way" or "new labour" solutions to include citizens in society through work and a "new social contract," "active citizenship," "positive obligations" and "moral imperatives" (Rosanvallon 2000: 65-67, 88-89).[4] In all these alternatives, traditional parliamentary representation is complemented by more substantial forms of representation and civic involvement such as self-management or new forms of participation or work.

Apart from these "participatory" options, Rosanvallon also, secondly, proposes more "institutional" and "traditional" ways to complement elections. As he explains: "democratic politics became something more than merely electing representatives. There are now many more ways in which a regime can be recognized as democratic, some of which complement the consecration of the polling booth while others compete with it" (Rosanvallon 2011a: 7). In the archives he discovers alternative forms of representation, citizenship or legitimacy that were developed alongside traditional electoral practices. Examples of such alternative institutions or practices, that are rarely acknowledged yet no less effective, include unelected state-institutions, unelected independent watch-dogs or regulators, constitutional courts or new "negative" forms of citizenship, whereby citizens constantly oversee and control their rulers (cf. Rosanvallon 2008; Rosanvallon 2011a). For Rosanvallon, some of these alternatives, institutions and practices could help to complement the waning legitimacy of elections, thus overcoming citizens' disappoint-

---

4   For a critical assessment of Rosanvallon's views of "the social question" cp. Duvoux 2015.

ment. As he writes, "on this basis it may be possible to construct a theory of indirect democracy to compensate for the deficiencies of electoral-representative democracy" (Rosanvallon 2011a: 11). Rather than turning to populist fantasies of a unified popular will one should instead turn to these alternative democratic forms of legitimacy and representation.

Rosanvallon's third solution of moving beyond elections is probably the most original. As we have seen, procedures, elections, formal equality and the rule of law aim at treating everyone equally, thus simultaneously generating abstractions out of particular groups and circumstances. People are then disappointed because they feel that their particular problems are not taken into account. The everyday life of a large part of the population indeed remains in the dark and is not given a voice. Instead of more deliberation, procedures or traditional forms of representation, people simply want their voices to be heard and recognized. Representation not only means that someone acts or deliberates for someone else while looking for the common good, but also that someone's particular story or situation is expressed and recognized (for this diagnosis see Rosanvallon 2014: 9-11, 24-26; Rosanvallon 1988a: 139-140).

In what are perhaps some of the most interesting parts of his work, Rosanvallon shows how in the period before the breakthrough of universal suffrage, many attempts were made to give people and society a voice outside politics. Nineteenth-century writers such as Balzac, Zola or Hugo but also many journalists used literature, often based on extensive research, as a tool to bring to light hidden lives. Similarly, the social sciences for Rosanvallon emerged as an attempt to help society understand and represent itself. Using the term of a nineteenth-century novelist, Rosanvallon calls this "poetic representation" and stresses that "representation" is also a cognitive process (Rosanvallon 2014: 35-47, 56-57; Rosanvallon 1998: 279-301; Rosanvallon 1995: 123). He emphasizes that especially today we need much more such poetic or cognitive representation, as the changing socio-economic context has created more individualized life-trajectories and professions that need to be understood, shown and recognized, by using more individualized "narrative" categories and approaches. Traditional class-identities that could still be easily represented have indeed been gradually replaced by complex individualized identities that are harder to represent. Yet precisely because these individuals are no longer part of a clearly visible class, they all the more need to make their stories heard, so that they can still feel part of a larger group and feel that their life-stories are recognized. Social exclusion or poverty is for example not just related to class, but also to certain life events (e.g. a divorce) which means that such events need to be narrated in order to become visible and acknowledged.

Social scientists but also – in the wake of Orwell for example – writers and journalists, can show, map and analyze these new forms of exclusion, life-trajectories or hidden groups and practices in society. They can, for example, tell what challenges a divorced parent has to face or what it means to work in a factory today. Such cognitive or poetic representation not only helps people to feel heard again and allow them to become part of a larger group, but also helps society as a whole to better understand itself (Rosanvallon 1998: 354-361; Rosanvallon 2000: 96-102; Rosanvallon 2014: 23-31).

This illustrates Rosanvallon's ambiguous view on representation, which, as we have seen, both means "truly" reflecting a "hidden" social reality "as it is" (in that sense "realist") and actively making that reality visible, through narratives, social sciences, websites etc. (and in that sense "constructivist," as the reality and identities can only appear through the activity and tools of the one representing it).[5] Given that "the 'people' can no longer be apprehended as a homogenous mass" but instead "is felt to be rather a series of separate histories, an accumulation of specific situations" (Rosanvallon 2011a: 4), a representation of life trajectories, can even be seen as a more adequate way of representing the people than elections.

Rosanvallon has also put his "constructivist" theory into practice. Whereas other solutions still depend on activists or politicians to turn them into reality, in the case of poetic and cognitive representation social scientists themselves can make a difference. Contrary to many other political theorists who limit themselves to publishing specialized academic books and articles, Rosanvallon has contributed to cognitive and poetic representation. For example, in 2014 he launched a book-series and a website that published hitherto invisible life-stories and analyses of hidden parts of society, thus constituting a "parliament of the invisible" (*parlement des invisibles*) (Rosanvallon 2014: 59-63). Cognitive representation, for Rosanvallon, not only means showing social reality, but also reflecting and debating about it. This is why he stresses the importance of *think-tanks* to foster debate, and participated in an important example in the 1980s (*The Fondation Saint-Simon* that also included François Furet). Since 2002 he has tried to improve the quality of public debate through a book-series (*La République des Idées*) where social scientists present new analyses and ideas or methods that often look at social and political problems differently through small, accessible books. By analyzing social reality, researchers can highlight hidden conflicts and stimulate intellectual discussion (which is what Rosanvallon mainly means by "deliberation") (cf. Rosanvallon 1988a: 180-181). And in 2007 he launched a free bi-lingual online journal and website (called *La Vie des Idées* and its English counterpart *Books & Ideas*).

---

5 For the "constructivist" reading cp. for example Rosanvallon 1998: 356-361.

In so doing, he has combatted academic compartmentalization and stimulated public debate (cf. for all this e.g. Rosanvallon 2011b: 347).

ROSANVALLON'S DEFINITION OF DEMOCRACY: INTELLECTUALLY BROAD YET POLITICALLY NARROW?

We have seen that Rosanvallon's broad theory of democracy allows him to rethink democracy's past, present and future. Yet, paradoxically, it is perhaps precisely the wide scope of his theory that may also pose a certain problem. This has to do with Rosanvallon's double vocation. For Rosanvallon the work of the scholar and that of the citizen engaged in public debate should reinforce each other. He writes:

"For the modern and contemporary history of the political, there is (...) no hope of discovering a zone of inquiry protected, thanks to some means of inaccessibility, from the movements of life. Its ambition, rather, is to descend in the civic arena to offer it a supplement of intelligibility and a dose of lucidity." (Rosanvallon 2006: 57)

Yet one wonders if the combination of the scholar and that of a partisan citizen is indeed as easy as Rosanvallon seems to suggest. As a scholar Rosanvallon wants to offer a broad comprehensive theory (and thus also a history) of modern democratic societies. Yet as a leftist intellectual who is engaged in (mainly) French debates, he clearly wants to foster a more tightly defined set of socialist ideals. For him democracy would seem to imply some form of socialism, which explains the following statement: "The time has come to fight for integral democracy, which will come about through the mutual interaction [interpénétration] of two ideas that have been kept apart for too long: namely socialism and democracy." (Rosanvallon 2013: 11)[6] This statement has two possible meanings. Either it means that only a socialist leftist interpretation of democracy is a properly democratic one, which is to suggest that "the right" does not have a proper view of democracy. Or else it means that there is something like a specifically socialist reading of democracy alongside a conservative one. But if that is the case, then Rosanvallon no longer

---

6 It is worth pointing out that in the 1970s, before he became an academic, Rosanvallon was working for the CFDT, a reformist new left union which defended democracy at a time when it was not fashionable to do so (hence its name, in translation: "the French *Democratic* Confederation of Workers"). So, from the start democracy, for Rosanvallon, was seen as a project that he associated with the left. Moreover, at that time he was also part of the Michel-Rocard wing in the French socialist party.

offers a broad general theory of democracy. While this makes his rather partial interpretation of democracy appealing to the left, it also limits its scope. Stronger still, Rosanvallon's theory can in that sense perhaps even be regarded as ideological, to the extent that he legitimizes particular values (a leftist worldview) by depicting them as universal (i.e. representing a broad theory of democracy).

There is, moreover, an implicit tendency in Rosanvallon's work to suggest that the left acknowledges social conflict, while the democratic right denies it. He thus implicitly suggests that by accepting social conflict, the left is more democratic than the right. In so doing, Rosanvallon implies that a truly democratic society that acknowledges its social conflict is leftist. Yet, if this is so, then a political system that truly acknowledges societal conflict should paradoxically first overcome its own left/right divisions. A proper acknowledgment of societal conflict would then *à la limite* imply an abolishment of the undemocratic right and thus of political conflict. Although Rosanvallon of course never argues for abolishing conflict or the democratic right (and although he often discusses thinkers that are not part of the leftist tradition such as Guizot or Schmitt), it would still be the logical outcome of a theory that does not really account for a democratic role of right-of-center parties, ideologies and ideas.

When expanding the scope of his work even further, Rosanvallon may thus have to make a choice: either make his theory of democracy truly comprehensive and thus also offer democratic practices that are right of center a legitimate place in his theory. Or else openly acknowledge his partisan socialist interpretation of democracy. In that case, however, he may no longer claim to defend a truly broad theory of democracy.

BIBLIOGRAPHY

Conti, Gregory/Selinger, William (2016): "The Other side of Representation: The History and Theory of Representative Government in Pierre Rosanvallon." In: Constellations 23/4, pp. 548-562.

Duvoux, Nicolas (2015): "Les métamorphoses de la responsabilité." In: Sarah Al-Matary/Florent Guénard (eds.), La démocratie à l'oeuvre. Autour de Pierre Rosanvallon, Paris: Seuil, pp. 197-210.

Jainchill, Andrew/Moyn, Samuel (2004): "French Democracy between Totalitarianism and Solidarity: Pierre Rosanvallon and Revisionist Historiography." In: Journal of Modern History 76, pp. 107-154.

Lefort, Claude (1986): The political forms of modern society, Cambridge: Polity Press.

Rosanvallon, Pierre (1988a): "Malaise dans la représentation." In: François Furet/Jacques Julliard/Pierre Rosanvallon (eds.), La république du centre. La fin de l'exception française, Paris: Calmann-Lévy, pp. 131-182.

Rosanvallon, Pierre, (1988b): "The Decline of Social Visibility." In: John Keane, (ed.), Civil Society and the State, London/New York: Verso, pp. 199-220.

Rosanvallon, Pierre, (1990): L'état en France. De 1789 à nos jours, Paris: Seuil.

Rosanvallon, Pierre (1992a): Le sacre du citoyen, Paris: Gallimard.

Rosanvallon, Pierre (1992b): La crise de l'Etat-providence, Paris: Seuil.

Rosanvallon, Pierre (1995): "Esquisse d'une histoire de la déception démocratique." In: Alexandru Dutu/Norbert Dodille (eds.), Culture et politique, Paris: L'Harmattan, pp. 103-124.

Rosanvallon, Pierre (1998): Le peuple introuvable. Histoire de la représentation démocratique en France, Paris: Gallimard.

Rosanvallon, Pierre (1999): Le capitalisme utopique. Histoire de l'idée de marché, Paris: Seuil.

Rosanvallon, Pierre (2000): The New Social Question. Rethinking the Welfare State, Barbara Harshav (trans.), Princeton, NJ: Princeton University Press.

Rosanvallon, Pierre (2006): Democracy Past and Future, Samuel Moyn (ed.), New York: Columbia University Press.

Rosanvallon, Pierre (2007): The Demands of Liberty. Civil society in France since the Revolution, Arthur Goldhammer (trans.), Cambridge, MA: Harvard University Press.

Rosanvallon, Pierre (2008): Counter-democracy. Politics in an age of distrust, Arthur Goldhammer (trans.), Cambridge: Cambridge University Press.

Rosanvallon, Pierre (2011a): Democratic Legitimacy. Impartiality, Reflexivity, Proximity, Arthur Goldhammer (trans.), Princeton/Oxford: Princeton University Press.

Rosanvallon, Pierre (2011b): "Ecrire une histoire générale de la démocratie. Entretien avec Pierre Rosanvallon." In: Participations 1/1, pp. 335-347.

Rosanvallon, Pierre (2013): The Society of Equals, Arthur Goldhammer (trans.), Cambridge, MA/London: Harvard University Press.

Rosanvallon, Pierre (2014): Le parlement des invisibles, Paris: Seuil.

Rosanvallon, Pierre (2018): Good Government. Democracy beyond Elections, Malcolm DeBevoise (trans.), Cambridge, MA: Harvard University Press.

Weymans, Wim (2004): "Pierre Rosanvallon und das Problem der politischen Repräsentation." In: Oliver Flügel/Reinhard Heil/Andreas Hetzel (eds.), Die Rückkehr des Politischen: Demokratietheorien heute, Darmstadt: Wissenschaftliche Buchgesellschaft, pp. 87-112.

Weymans, Wim (2005): "Freedom through Political Representation? Lefort, Gauchet and Rosanvallon on the relationship between state and society." In: European Journal of Political Theory 4/3, pp. 263-282.

Weymans, Wim (2007): "Understanding the Present through the Past? Quentin Skinner and Pierre Rosanvallon on the Crisis of Political Representation." In: Redescriptions. Yearbook of Political Thought and Conceptual History 11, pp. 45-60.

Weymans, Wim (2015): "Demokratie als Gesellschaftsform: Pierre Rosanvallon und die vielfältigen Stimmen des Volkes." In: Oliver Flügel/Franziska Martinsen (eds.), Aktuelle Staatskritik und Demokratietheorie aus Frankreich, Stuttgart: Steiner, pp. 167-185.

Weymans, Wim (2016): "Radical Democracy's Past and Future: Histories of the Symbolic." In: Modern Intellectual History 13/3, pp. 841-851.

Weymans, Wim (2019): "From Marianne to Louise. Three Ways to Represent the (European) People in Democratic Societies." In: Anna Schober (ed.), Popularization and Populism in the Visual Arts: Attraction Images, London/New York: Routledge (in press).

7 Restocking the Storehouse of Democratic Ideas

Pierre Rosanvallon at the Collège de France (2002-2018)*

Alain Chatriot

> "I can recognize myself quite well in one of the more famous expressions of this author [Edgar Quinet] of *The Revolution*: 'French democracy has exhausted its storehouse of ideas, which has to be stocked up again.' I eagerly adopt Quinet's program myself, and I feel myself close to his concern to help prepare for the future by rooting reflection on the present in the comprehension of the ordeals of the past."
> *(Rosanvallon 2006a: 34)*

Such were Pierre Rosanvallon's words on March 28, 2002 during his inaugural lecture at the Collège de France. Beyond the reference to a former member of the illustrious institution, he offered a clear summary of his research and teaching program. A program that he largely completed in his almost two decades at the College de France. We propose here to explore this period of Pierre Rosanvallon's intellectual production, since it is undoubtedly the part which has been the least studied in examinations of his work (Verdo 2002; Jainchill/Moyn 2004; Godmer/Smadja 2011a).

---

* This article was translated from the original French by Stephen W. Sawyer.

Without a doubt, the four volumes (the "tetralogy") published between 2006 and 2015 (Rosanvallon 2006b, 2008b, 2011b, 2015a) have enjoyed a wide reception, but they have not necessarily been placed within the perspective of the Rosanvallon's previous work and in particular his "trilogy" on modern French democracy (Rosanvallon 1992, 1998, 2000). Moreover, while they sat at the center of his intellectual production they do not in themselves sufficiently capture the entirety of his engagements during this period. The conference "La démocratie en travail" held at Cerisy in September 2014 (Al Matary/Guénard 2015) provided a moment of reflection on this larger body of work, but it seems to me that one may usefully complement this study by retracing the construction of his oeuvre since his entrance into the Collège de France. Furthermore, it seems that this moment was for Rosanvallon, first, the culmination of a reflection on the history of French democracy; second a period for the development of a new approach to a theory of democracy, which gave rise to the publication of the tetralogy; and, finally, a period of civic engagement pursued in a variety of forms. We seek here to explore this path and thus to provide some insights for interpreting Rosanvallon's work.

THE PERSISTENCE OF AN INTELLECTUAL PROJECT

Several texts have already been published on the intellectual trajectory of Pierre Rosanvallon before his entry into the Collège de France (Gaubert 2009; Rosanvallon 1995b; Rosanvallon 2015b). Moreover, Pierre Rosanvallon has also provided his own interpretation of his trajectory in the 2017 and 2018 lectures at the Collège de France, where he outlined his perspective on the intellectual history of the period 1968-2018 (Rosanvallon 2018c). This was not an entirely new enterprise for him, for already in 2002, his inaugural lecture testified to the pursuit of a particular form of political history, defined as a "conceptual history of the political," which he had explained previously and illustrated in his books (Rosanvallon 1986, 1995a, 1996a, 2001b).

Responding to more "traditional" approaches centered on the history of political life, he clarified his method and object of study:

"In speaking of 'the political' as a noun, I thus mean as much a modality of existence of life in common as a form of collective action that is implicitly distinct from the functioning of politics. To refer to 'the political' rather than to 'politics' is to speak of power and law, state and nation, equality and justice, identity and difference, citizenship and civility – in sum, of everything that constitutes political life beyond the immediate field of partisan competition for political power, everyday governmental action, and the ordinary function of institutions." (Rosanvallon 2006a: 36)

At the same time, he insisted on the importance of a historical approach for understanding contemporary political questions:

"Such a conception of the political makes a historical approach the condition of its thorough study. [...] It has been my ambition, therefore, to rethink democracy by following the thread of its history as it has been spun. But note that is not simply a matter of saying that democracy *has* a history. More radically, one must see that democracy *is* a history. It has been a work irreducibly involving exploration and experimentation, in its attempts to understand and elaborate itself." (Ibid: 38, original emphasis)

It would seem, however, that Rosanvallon's methodological preoccupations nonetheless remained secondary to his ambition to study key political problems. He expressed this idea clearly in an interview in 2011:

"I am often asked to more thoroughly formalize 'my method.' This would no doubt be an important thing to do if I wanted to serve as the head of a school. It seems to me that the real problem in the social sciences is writing books about social facts. Of course, there are methodological requirements that I try to adhere to. But each book to be written requires a new research investment and not just a recipe that must be applied. It is clear that researchers who are content to 'apply' a given conceptualization are not those who are rebuilding a field of research." (Gaumer/Smadja 2011b: 193-194)

Within this framework, the first two years of courses were dedicated to an exploration of the role of intermediary bodies in democracy. It must be noted that the book that emerged from these lectures *The Demands of Liberty/Le Modèle politique français* (Rosanvallon 2004) constituted the companion volume to the history of the state in France that he had published more than a decade earlier (Rosanvallon 1990). Moreover, the two books had the same "open-ended" character (Rosanvallon 2007: 9). At the end of his introduction – which was not translated in the English edition – the author explains how the volume completed his previous work:

"In undertaking this research, the results of which are presented here, I have tried to give an answer to questions that I have been asking since the publication of *Pour une nouvelle culture politique* [Rosanvallon/Viveret 1977] and with which I was confronted anew while writing *L'État en France*. A reflection on the relevance of the notion of a 'French exception' also underpinned the two volumes dedicated to the singularity of French liberalism: *Le Moment Guizot* and *La Monarchie impossible*. With the trilogy more recently dedicated to the history of French democracy (*Le Sacre du citoyen; Le Peuple introuvable; La Démocratie inachevée*), this volume completes a whole series of works that had the ambition of presenting an overall framework for understanding the French model, situating it in a more general history of democratic modernity." (Rosanvallon 2004: 19)

The Demands of Liberty could also be situated in the continuation of subjects that had been previously explored: the place of trade unionism in France (Rosanvallon 1988), the relationship to old regime corporations (Rosanvallon 1989) and the complex and difficult path toward the recognition of political parties (Rosanvallon 1996b). More generally, the book developed an idea that was already clearly expressed in his more erudite work on the French constitutional monarchies from 1814-1848. As he explained:

"it is possible to write two diametrically opposed histories of French politics. On the one hand, a story that emphasizes the Jacobin tradition and centralization, and that emphasizes the permanence of the illiberal temptation related to the absolutization of the sovereignty of the people. On the other, there is a more peaceful history, that of the extension of the freedoms and progress of representative government. [...] The two approaches are not a mere opposition between distinct partisan assumptions. They correspond mainly to a separation between the history of representations and political cultures and the history of institutions. It is urgent to bring out the second story, too often neglected. [...] The examination of the Charters of 1814 and 1830 constitutes an ideal ground to explore the hidden side of the hexagonal political history. They embody in a way the 'English moment' that must be confronted with the 'Jacobin moment'." (Rosanvallon 1994: 7-8)

It has rarely been noted that it was during this period in the late 1990s that Rosanvallon began his explorations of "illiberalism," in particular though his interest in reexamining the Second Empire (Rosanvallon 2001a).

The volume resulting from these first two years of lectures ends with an observation which is important for understanding his later research: the ambition was not just to understand the specificity of the French context but to explore the broader question of democracy:

"The issue now is no longer one of an absolute or relative 'French exception' that must somehow be eliminated. Instead, what we see everywhere is a crisis of politics and a questioning of the real nature of democracy. [...] Fresh thinking about the overall architecture of democracy is urgently needed. People everywhere are searching for new definitions of sovereignty and legitimacy, new procedures of representation, and new forms of public expression. At issue is the very nature of the political. To be sure, the question is too vast even to be posed properly in the brief space of a conclusion. Hence a more thorough examination will have to be deferred to another work." (Rosanvallon 2007: 265)

Seminars at the Collège de France accompanied the evolution of this work on the history of political and democratic theory. Taking the opportunity to invite fellow scholars, the subjects discussed were oftentimes directly related to the subject of that year's lectures ("Intermediary bodies within democracy: case studies" in 2003; "Recent research on the question of inequality" in 2011; "Governing and Authority" in 2015), and in some cases they focused on specific themes ("The Culture of Political Will in France, 19th-20th centuries" in 2004; "The Notion of Political Responsibility" in 2006; "Elections and the Vote" in 2012; "Cosmopolitan Democracy" in 2013; "Democracy and Referendums" in 2014). And on some occasions they offered the opportunity to present work on political theory (2008, 2010, 2017).

When one examines the list of scholars invited to Rosanvallon's seminars, one notices a disciplinary eclecticism drawn from a variety of fields such as History, Law, Political Science, Sociology, Philosophy, Economics, Management and a diversity of profiles (from doctoral students to emeritus professors). Far from limiting his focus to modern history, Rosanvallon also invited specialists of the ancient world (Paul Demont on election by lots in ancient Greece; Virginie Hollard on the vote in ancient Rome; Clément Bur on infamy and citizenship in Rome, etc.) as well as the medieval and early periods (Olivier Christin on development of majoritarian decision-making; Patrick Boucheron on the fresco "The Allegory of Good and Bad Government"; Marie Dejoux on the investigations into the reparations of Louis IX; Antoine Lilti on celebrity in the Enlightenment, etc.). Some of the sessions were particularly memorable such as the dialogue with Bernard Manin (April 7, 2004) and the invitation of Claude Lefort (April 16, 2008).

On occasion, the seminar took place on one or two days. A symposium was co-organized with the Chair held by Mireille Delmas-Marty with the title "Law and Politics in the Construction of an International Order: The Current State of the Debate" in June 2006; a conference entitled "Challenges to Democratic Universalism: A New Paradigm?" took place in June 2007; and a conference on "Democracy in the Age of Post-Truth" closed the series in February 2018.

AND THE SECOND TRILOGY BECOMES A TETRALOGY

"Teaching at the Collège de France does not consist in descending a long calm river whose course has been traced in advance. First of all, because it is the rule that one must present each year the results of new research, or at least explain the objectives, the hypotheses and the first lineaments, with all that this implies in terms of prior documentation and conceptualization. But also because any research project can lead to a dead end, be less successful than expected or involve additional research that runs further afield than expected, and which necessarily requires one to pause, turn back, or take a new direction." (Annuaire du Collège de France 2015: 789)

Thus opened the course synopsis [*résumé de cours*] for 2014 that developed the beginning of his lecture on January 22 of that year.

This declaration provides a relatively clear picture of the progressive development of his work at the Collège de France, which emerged in the form of four volumes on the history of democracy. If we look back on the chronology of the lectures, one sees that this oeuvre did not develop in a linear fashion. It advanced instead piece by piece. In 2004, the lectures explored "the disenchantment of democracy: history and forms of a sentiment." While these lectures remained relatively focused on the history of nineteenth-century France, the course was never published as a book, even if it informed later publications. In 2005, the lecture entitled "Democratic Dilemmas" was given in Cambridge Massachusetts, offering a comparison between the history of democracy in France and the United States. In 2006, the lectures focused on "new paths of popular sovereignty" and led to the publication of *La contre-démocratie* (Rosanvallon 2006b). There are a number of elements in this book that develop points he had already explored, for example, his analysis of the political thought of Pierre Mendès France on "generalized democracy" (Rosanvallon 2005). The 2007 lectures ("Institutions of General Interest") and of 2008 ("Metamophoses of Legitimacy") laid the foundation for the volume *La légitimité démocratique* (Rosanvallon 2008b). After a sabbatical leave in 2009, the courses of 2010 and 2011 entitled "What is a Democratic Society? I and II" provided the cornerstone for *La société des égaux* (Rosanvallon 2011b).

At the moment of its publication, Rosanvallon presented *The Society of Equals* as the completion of a second trilogy and announced his future ambition to offer a more theoretical approach to democracy (Rosanvallon 2011c). The 2012 and 2013 lectures under the title "Democracy: Outline of a General Theory, I and II" continued in this direction. The first year he focused in particular on the question of "democratic indetermination" (drawn from Claude Lefort, but developed in a different direction). In 2013, he insisted upon the variation of the definitions of democracy, the fragility of such regimes, their disenchantment and finally their pathologies, which he attempted to bring together into a "general theory." If these courses did not lead to a specific publication, it is in part because Rosanvallon decided to take a detour by studying the question of executive power.

"Indeed, I realized that there was a dimension of democratic life that I had never addressed in my work and that it was essential to attempt to do so before providing a synthesis: that of executive power. I had only touched upon the latter in my analysis of counter-democracy. But without digging into it thoroughly, even though it has become for all citizens and all individuals the central figure of 'power' as they experience, confront or challenge it daily." (Annuaire du Collège de France 2015: 790)

The book that came out of these lectures, *Le bon gouvernement* (Rosanvallon 2015a), is indicative of an approach that privileges a longer analytical timeframe – one that spreads beyond the chronology of the first trilogy that began with the eighteenth century and the French and American Revolutions – and an ambition to compare relatively distant historical experiences (Rosanvallon 2003b).

It is obviously beyond the scope of this chapter to present this work in greater detail, but it is important to highlight that all of these works found their raison d'être in what is presented as a certain crisis of the present. Two passages, written 10 years apart reveal this constant concern: "The democratic ideal now reigns unchallenged, but regimes claiming to be democratic come in for vigorous criticism almost everywhere. In this paradox resides the major political problem of our time," wrote Rosanvallon in 2008 (2008a: 1). And then, again in 2018:

"There are many more books yet to be written if we are to understand the history of democracy and how it has changed. But I may at least hope to have provided others scholars with a set of tools they will find useful in carrying on with the whole that remains to be done. History is now breathing down our necks. Perhaps never before has it been a more urgent necessity that we try to make sense of it. Rushing headlong into the future, the present is in danger of losing its balance. Beneath lies the abyss." (Rosanvallon 2018a: 18-19)

This political preoccupation is overwhelmingly present in *The Society of Equals*. He expresses this idea in the opening lines of the book:

"Democracy is manifesting its vitality as a regime even as it withers as a social form. The sovereign citizenry has steadily increased its ability to intervene in government and magnify its presence. [...] But the 'people', understood in a political sense as a collective entity that ever more powerfully imposes its will, is less and less a 'social body'. Political citizenship has progressed, while social citizenship has regressed. This rending of democracy is the major phenomenon of our time, and an ominous threat to our well-being. If it continues, the democratic regime itself might ultimately be in danger." (Rosanvallon 2013a: 1-2)

These volumes also provided opportunities for Rosanvallon to take stock of his role as a public intellectual. At the end of the first volume of the tetralogy, Rosanvallon allowed himself to define his role as an intellectual by comparing himself to two of his predecessors:

"This book was written in 2005, the centenary of the birth of Jean-Paul Sartre and Raymond Aron. Sartre was the apostle of the twentieth century's culpable utopian dreams, the headstrong fellow traveler of a radical adventure that remained beyond the pale of his critique. Aron was a professor of disillusionment, a model of melancholy lucidity. Expressing the contrary logics of their generation to perfection, each embodied a form of intellectual grandeur. Yet each succumbed to an unfortunate temptation, that of icy reason on the one hand and blind commitment on the other, and in their opposite ways each thus fostered a form of impotence. The author of these lines has sought to escape this impasse by formulating a theory of democracy that is no longer cut off from the action intended to breathe new life into democracy." (Rosanvallon 2008a: 318)

As a result, Rosanvallon has consistently attempted to explore the multi-dimensional character of democracy. In the conclusion to *Democratic Legitimacy*, he explains:

"Indeed, both the abuse of the term and the confusion about its meaning stew from the diversity of approaches to the subject. For example, it is common to see a contrast between democracy defined as an exercise of collective power and democracy defined in terms of guaranteed individual freedoms. If we are to overcome this kind of ambiguity, we must grasp democracy in all its complexity. It can be separately, concurrently, simultaneously a civic activity, a regime, a form of society, and a mode of government." (Rosanvallon 2011a: 225)

A CONSISTENT CIVIC ENGAGEMENT

Reading the entry on the Chair of the Modern and Contemporary History of the Political in the yearbooks of the College of France provides a better perspective on Pierre Rosanvallon's activity, which was not limited to his courses, seminars and books across these seventeen years. The juries of dissertation and habilitation defenses on which he served as well as the book prefaces are mentioned in these documents. Two other specific areas of intellectual engagement also merit mention: the editorial activity around the *Republic of Ideas* as well as the online journal *Books and Ideas* (*La vie des idées*) and the participation in numerous scientific, media and political forums.

Created in 2002, the *Republic of Ideas* was an essential part of Pierre Rosanvallon's intellectual ambition. A collection of books presenting social science research to a wider audience, some volumes have been very successful (Castel 2003) while others have been controversial (Lindenberg 2002). With no clear disciplinary boundaries (from Geography to Sociology, Economics, Political Science and History), the works have sometimes accompanied broader public debates (on the middle classes, tax havens, solidarity, etc.). The *Republic of Ideas* also participated in two large public conferences in Grenoble in May 2006 on "the new social criticism" and in May 2009 in the context of the forum "reinventing democracy."

From the winter of 2002 to the summer of 2007, 24 issues of *La Vie des Idées* appeared, a paper journal intended to serve as a newsletter for the *Republic of Ideas*. Moving to a digital format in autumn 2007, the site was organized under Rosanvallon's Chair at the Collège de France the following year. From then on Rosanvallon's team of successive assistants at the Collège de France were directly involved in the development and success of this project – such was the case for Florent Guénard, Ivan Jablonka, Nicolas Delalande, Pauline Peretz, Thomas Grillot, Emilie Frenkiel, Sarah Al-Matary, Lucie Campos, Cristelle Terroni, Marieke Louis, Ariel Suhamy, Ophelia Simeon; while it was not the case for first two assistants Alain Chatriot (2002-2004) and Geneviève Verdo (2004-2006).

Two other editorial activities also merit mention. The project *Raconter la vie* (*Life Stories*), which was launched in 2014 and came to an end in 2017. Rosanvallon introduced the project in a volume *Le Parlement des invisibles* in which he wrote: "the country does not feel represented" (Rosanvallon 2014a: 10). He then returned to the long history of attempts to correct this lack of representation that has plagued modern democratic societies. The second editorial project was the book series *Les livres du nouveau monde* (*Books of the New World*) that Rosanvallon directs at Seuil and where he has published a variety of works, including those of several of his colleagues at the Collège de France. It was also in this collection that he published the book by economist Thomas Piketty, which proved to be a huge best-seller (Piketty 2013).

He also participated in a series of conferences in France and abroad. At the Collège de France, Rosanvallon took part in the Ernest Renan fall symposium – delivering a text on Renan's ambiguous relationship to democracy (Rosanvallon 2013b) – and then organized a second one in 2013 on "science and democracy"

(Rosanvallon 2014b), which provided him with an opportunity to reflect on democratic institutions in the face of climate change and other scientific issues, in particular the management of long-term public problems. A recent conference held in Toulouse in December 2017 demonstrates his constant desire to present his thoughts to a wide audience and to engage in a pedagogical dialogue with the public (Rosanvallon 2018b). In addition to numerous conferences (in Argentina in 2001, China in 2003, Japan in 2004, Great Britain in 2006 – and the pace has increased in recent years), Rosanvallon on occasion gave his annual lectures abroad, for example in 2004-2005 when the course on "The Dilemmas of Democracy" was held at MIT and the seminar on "The Interpretation of the French Political Model" that took place at Harvard. He also gave lectures in French universities (Nantes and Sciences Po Grenoble in 2017, IEP Lille in 2016 to take the most recent examples). His lectures are widely available from the Collège de France website and via diffusion on the French public radio station, France Culture. Similarly, his books have been widely re-edited and are easily accessible. He also regularly publishes articles exploring the progress of his work in such journals as *Esprit* and accepts media requests on the radio, the press and news outlets.

Following upon his years of training in social scientific research at the EHESS with Claude Lefort and François Furet, the era of the Centre Raymond Aron (Sawyer/Stewart 2016) and his "trilogy," the years at the Collège de France have been for Pierre Rosanvallon a moment that has mixed the completion of some projects as well as the launching of new ones. Rosanvallon, it would seem, accomplished a rare feat in fulfilling the announcement he made in his inaugural lecture:

"It is an opportunity, at a time I hope to be the midpoint of my career, to invigorate my research with a new energy, by relocating them in a intellectual milieu unique thanks to the radical freedom it provides – shielded, as one is at the College of France, from the pressures of any agenda, freed from any obligation to evaluate and train students, and liberated from the need to present one's credentials in the face of the usual disciplinary barriers." (Rosanvallon 2006a: 31)

This distance from the disciplines, clearly expressed in the choice of his guests for his seminar, the content of his books and editorial projects and the wide-ranging institutional freedom of the Collège de France allowed him to pursue both his individual and collective work.

No doubt, the intellectual projects will continue beyond these honors. The last course at the Collège de France, on February 7, 2018 was thus an opportunity for Rosanvallon to announce "a future work program" around two main axes: the definition of "post-electoral democracy" – and in particular an analysis of populism

– and a "reconceptualization of the social question." In short, a new set of books that will respond as always to the challenges of the present and concerns about the future of democracies as intellectual lucidity refuses to give way to political pessimism.

BIBLIOGRAPHY

Annuaire du Collège de France (2015), Paris: Collège de France.

Castel, Robert (2003): L'insécurité sociale. Qu'est-ce qu'être protégé? Paris: Seuil, La République des idées.

Gaubert, Christophe (2009): "Genèse sociale de Pierre Rosanvallon en 'intellectuel de proposition'." In: Agone 41-42, pp. 123-147.

Godmer, Laurent/Smadja, David (2011a): "Pierre Rosanvallon un penseur critique paradoxal?" In: Raisons politiques 44, pp. 163-172.

Godmer, Laurent/Smadja, David (2011b): "Entretien avec Pierre Rosanvallon." In: Raisons politiques 44, pp. 173-199.

Jainchill, Andrew/Moyn, Samuel (2004): "French Democracy between Totalitarianism and Solidarity: Pierre Rosanvallon and Revisionist Historiography." In: The Journal of Modern History 76, pp. 107-154.

Lindenberg, Daniel (2002): Le rappel à l'ordre. Enquête sur les nouveaux réactionnaires, Paris: Seuil, La République des idées.

Al-Matary, Sarah/Guénard, Florent (eds.). (2015): La Démocratie à l'œuvre. Autour de Pierre Rosanvallon, Paris: Seuil.

Piketty, Thomas (2013): Le capital au XXIe siècle, Paris: Seuil.

Rosanvallon, Pierre (1986): "Pour une histoire conceptuelle du politique (note de travail)." In: Revue de synthèse 107/1-2, pp. 93-105.

Rosanvallon, Pierre (1988): La question syndicale, histoire et avenir d'une forme sociale, Paris: Calmann-Lévy.

Rosanvallon, Pierre (1989): "Corporations et corps intermédiaires." In: Le Débat 57, pp. 172-175.

Rosanvallon, Pierre (1990): L'Etat en France de 1789 à nos jours, Paris: Seuil.

Rosanvallon, Pierre (1992): Le sacre du citoyen. Histoire du suffrage universel en France, Paris: Gallimard.

Rosanvallon, Pierre (1994): La Monarchie impossible. Histoire des Chartes de 1814 et 1830, Paris: Fayard.

Rosanvallon, Pierre (1995a), "Faire l'Histoire du politique." In: Esprit, Février, pp. 25-42.

Rosanvallon, Pierre (1995b), "Témoignage." In: Revue française d'histoire des idées politiques, 2/2, pp. 361-376.

Rosanvallon, Pierre (1996a), "Le politique." In Jacques Revel/Nathan Wachtel (eds.), Une école pour les sciences sociales, Paris: Cerf, éditions de l'EHESS, pp. 299-311.

Rosanvallon, Pierre (1996b): "Partis. Partis et factions." In: Philippe Raynaud/Stéphane Rials (eds.), Dictionnaire de philosophie politique, Paris: PUF, pp. 449-453.

Rosanvallon, Pierre (1998): Le peuple introuvable. Histoire de la représentation démocratique en France, Paris: Gallimard.

Rosanvallon, Pierre (2000): La démocratie inachevée. Histoire de la souveraineté du peuple en France, Paris: Gallimard.

Rosanvallon, Pierre (2001a): "Fondements et problèmes de l''illibéralisme' français." In: Revue des sciences morales & politiques 1, pp. 21-40.

Rosanvallon, Pierre (2001b): "Entretien. Sur quelques chemins de traverse de la pensée du politique en France." In: Raisons politiques 1, pp. 49-62.

Rosanvallon, Pierre (2003a): Pour une histoire conceptuelle du politique. Leçon inaugurale faite au Collège de France le jeudi 28 mars 2002, Paris: Seuil.

Rosanvallon, Pierre (2003b): "Avant-propos. Les vertus d'un comparatisme dérangeant." In: Marcel Detienne (ed.), Qui veut prendre la parole? Le Genre humain 40-41. pp. 7-12.

Rosanvallon, Pierre (2004): Le modèle politique français. La société civile contre le jacobinisme de 1789 à nos jours, Paris: Seuil.

Rosanvallon, Pierre (2005): "Pierre Mendès France et la démocratie généralisée." In: Dominique Franche/Yves Léonard (eds.), Pierre Mendès France et la démocratie locale, Rennes: Presses universitaires de Rennes, pp. 23-31.

Rosanvallon, Pierre (2006a): Democracy Past and Future, Samuel Moyn (ed.), New York: Columbia University Press.

Rosanvallon, Pierre (2006b): La contre-démocratie: La politique à l'âge de la défiance, Paris: Seuil.

Rosanvallon, Pierre (2007): The Demands of Liberty: Civil Society in France since the Revolution, Cambridge: Harvard University Press.

Rosanvallon, Pierre (2008a): Counter-Democracy: Politics in an Age of Distrust, Cambridge: Cambridge University Press.

Rosanvallon, Pierre (2008b): La légitimité démocratique: Impartialité, réflexivité, proximité, Paris: Seuil.

Rosanvallon, Pierre (2011a): Democratic Legitimacy: Impartiality, Reflexivity, Proximity, Cambridge: Harvard University Press.

Rosanvallon, Pierre (2011b): La société des égaux, Paris: Seuil.

Rosanvallon Pierre (2011c): "Ecrire une histoire générale de la démocratie (entretien)." In: Participations 1, pp. 335-347.

Rosanvallon, Pierre (2013a): The Society of Equals, Cambridge: Harvard University Press.

Rosanvallon, Pierre (2013b): "Renan, père fondateur de la République?" In: Henry Laurens (ed.), Ernest Renan, la science, la religion, la République, Paris: Odile Jacob, pp. 357-367.

Rosanvallon, Pierre (2014a): Le Parlement des invisibles, Paris: Seuil, Raconter la vie.

Rosanvallon, Pierre (ed.). (2014b): Science et démocratie, Paris: Odile Jacob.

Rosanvallon, Pierre (2015a): Le bon gouvernement, Paris: Seuil.

Rosanvallon, Pierre (2015b): "Bref retour sur mon travail." In: Sarah Al-Matary/ Florent Guénard (eds.): La Démocratie à l'œuvre. Autour de Pierre Rosanvallon, Paris: Seuil, pp. 229-250.

Rosanvallon, Pierre (2018a): Good Government: Democracy beyond Elections, Cambridge: Harvard University Press.

Rosanvallon, Pierre (2018b): Refonder la démocratie pour le bien public? Toulouse: Privat.

Rosanvallon, Pierre (2018c): Notre histoire intellectuelle et politique: 1968-2018, Paris: Seuil.

Rosanvallon, Pierre/Viveret, Patrick (1977): Pour une nouvelle culture politique, Paris: Seuil.

Sawyer, Stephen W./Stewart, Iain (eds.). (2016): In Search of the Liberal Moment: Democracy, Anti-totalitarianism, and Intellectual Politics in France since 1950, Basingstoke/New York: Palgrave Macmillan.

Verdo, Geneviève (2002): "Pierre Rosanvallon, archéologue de la démocratie." In: Revue historique 623, pp. 693-720.

8 Democracy and the Press in Rosanvallon's Historiography[1]

Greg Conti

Pierre Rosanvallon has spent much of his career interrogating the tensions between *democracy* and *liberalism*, above all as they have arisen in the history and political theory of modern France. This chapter seeks to probe one such tension with regard to an issue that has received little attention in the Anglophone scholarship on Rosanvallon, despite flitting through nearly all of his works: the press. While the range of his accomplishments grows by the year, one of Rosanvallon's greatest talents remains *reconstructive*: he is among today's finest scholars when it comes to exposing the core political-philosophical problems underlying historical debates. For this reason, the best way to approach Rosanvallon's thought on the press is by turning to his reconstruction of past outlooks on the subject. In particular, his treatments of two nineteenth-century approaches to the press stand out both for their virtuosity as exercises in conceptual history and for the way they address some of the more permanent difficulties of theorizing the relationship between electoral democracy and a free press. These two are what we might call (a) the *doctrinaire* approach, which was best exemplified in the work of the historian-philosopher-statesman François Guizot and which experienced its heyday during the Restoration and July Monarchy; and (b) the *Bonapartist* or *Caesarist* approach of Napoleon III's Second Empire of 1852-70.

What these two outlooks share is that, in Rosanvallon's historiography, they are both pathological. Neither properly establishes the connection between a free press and democracy. Nevertheless, he does not present them as equally deficient.

---

[1] Wherever possible, I have cited from available English translations. However, many of Rosanvallon's texts, as well as of the nineteenth-century sources discussed, remain untranslated; for all titles given in French, the translations are my own.

While both cases are characterized by a split between democracy and the press, it is the Bonapartist viewpoint that he considers especially wrongheaded and pernicious. Exploring the reasons for this asymmetry in his treatment of Guizot and Napoleon III not only enlightens us about Rosanvallon, but raises a few provocative questions for democratic theory.

This chapter proceeds as follows: section one sketches Rosanvallon's reconstruction of the doctrinaire and Bonapartist theories of the press. The second section probes the similarities and differences between the two theories as Rosanvallon understands them. The final section then offers a critique of his interpretations; in a nutshell, I argue there that Rosanvallon goes too easy on Guizot but too hard on the Bonapartists. This failure to rightly judge the force of the two views points us to a lacuna in Rosanvallon's thinking about democracy: namely, that despite the breadth of his catalog he has not given a precise accounting of how elections under universal suffrage are related to other elements of a broadly speaking "modern democratic" system, such as a vibrant civil society, the rule of law, a degree of equality and welfare provision, or (what concerns us at present) a free press.

ROSANVALLON'S RECONSTRUCTIONS OF TWO NINETEENTH-CENTURY VIEWS

Although scholarship on Rosanvallon has not accorded the press a primary place, his depictions of the doctrinaire and Bonapartist conceptions of the press are minor masterpieces of conceptual history. Beyond being avenues into Rosanvallon's thinking about issues of the press, its freedom, and its relationship to democracy, these depictions are worth revisiting in their own right, for they examine moments in the history of political thought which are of intrinsic interest but which have gotten little play in English-speaking political theory.

In both doctrinairism and Bonapartism, a dissociation between democracy and a free press is present, although the dissociation arises in a very different manner. This tension is the aspect of Rosanvallon's surveys of these schools of thought that will be of most concern to us.

For Rosanvallon, the jumping-off point for understanding the doctrinaires on the press is the recognition that they saw it as an *instrument of representative government* itself: "The liberty of the press for them is not so much a safeguard [against misgovernment] or a means of exercising a fundamental liberty as it is a *means of government* and the expression of a social necessity." (Rosanvallon 1985a: 65) This conception of the press was part and parcel of what Rosanvallon believes to be a great breakthrough of doctrinaire theory, which was to have reconceived representation in an expansive manner, as an interactive, discursive process and not as simply an act of authorization or a transfer of sovereignty.[2] Perceived in this framework whereby representative government is a "process of a cognitive, not mechanical, type," the press fits right in alongside more traditional political institutions such as elections and parliaments as a factor of governance (Rosanvallon 2000: 15). The press, thus conceived, was essential to the construction of an intelligent and informed rather than an arbitrary sociopolitical order (such as the *ancien régime* had been).

"The liberty of the press, explain de Broglie, Guizot, Rémusat, and Royer-Collard, corresponds to a necessity, a *social need*. It is not only the exercise of a natural faculty, a fulfillment of an individual liberty; it is 'one of the elements of the new social state [*nouvel état des sociétés*].'" (Rosanvallon 1985a: 66 [the quote is from Rémusat])

The press is "the heart and the regulator of a *democratic society*," Rosanvallon's doctrinaires declare (Rosanvallon 1985a: 67). It followed that, in terms of their "fundamental intuition" about a politics in which the ruling force is "publicity," the "liberty of the press" was on par with (or even lexically prior to) other mechanisms of representative government; it was a "potent means of establishing a new type of *political communication* [...] of achieving a reciprocal *revelation* between power and the public" (ibid). In stark contrast to "liberalism" of the English/Benjamin Constant-variety, Guizot and his comrades laud the liberty of the press for allowing "'society to show itself to itself [*se faire spectacle à elle-même*]'" and for constituting an "essential means of interpenetration of government and society" (Rosanvallon 1995a: 67-68). Rosanvallon allows the statesman Charles de Rémusat the definitive word:

"Only through the press can citizens communicate among themselves and take note of their opinion; by it alone can authorities receive light from them and render it back to them; and this exchange is necessary if citizens and the authorities are to march in the same paths." (Rosanvallon 1995a: 68)

---

2   Guizot "highlights the archaic character of procedural approaches [to representation] in order to draw attention to the increasingly informational character of the relationship between power and society in the modern world." (Rosanvallon 2000: 114-5)

The doctrinaires, then, are the high-water mark of a tradition of French thought (which Rosanvallon tracks in other contexts as well[3]) in which the press is treated as something approximating an equal partner with official state institutions in the task of representative government. The press has a *representative function*, conveying the truth about society's condition to the organs of power and allowing the acts and debates of the latter to react back on the citizenry in a progressive and enlightening manner. A free press is, moreover, not just an important player in this expansive "notion of representation [...] [as] political communication," but is itself a kind of symbol of a politics that, in contrast to closed or fixed societies like the *ancien régime* (Rosanvallon 1985a), is conducted as a give-and-take amongst the public and its governors.

The theoretical upshot of such a view will occupy us in the remaining sections; for now, it is critical to spell out one implication, emphasized repeatedly by Rosanvallon. This is that the reorientation of representative government around publicity, public discussion, the interaction of ideas and the intimacy between state and society – all mediated through a free press – lead to the marginalization of elections and of *political* democracy. Rosanvallon is clear that elections as such are not very meaningful from the doctrinaire perspective: "In this optic of political communication, the mechanisms of election ultimately play only a secondary role." (Rosanvallon 1985a: 69; Rosanvallon 2000: 116) From the "basic intuition [...] to consider the press as a means of government and not simply a liberty," the doctrinaires drew very "conservative" conclusions (Rosanvallon 2011: 211). If "every individual" was represented and given a "consultative voice" through the press, if elections were just "one element of a much larger system for the generation and circulation of information and opinion," then an equal vote could be seen as something other than an urgent democratic right (Rosanvallon 2011: 212).[4] And

---

[3] On the revolutionary era, cp. e.g. *La démocratie inachevée*, 50-1. On the importance for incipient nineteenth-century working-class movements of this notion of journalism and publicity as continuous with political representation, cp. Rosanvallon (2014: part II; 1988: 134-8).

[4] As Rémusat would say, even in a moment of resigned acceptance of a democratic franchise, "universal suffrage is only a legal means of getting the people to take part in their government. Whether it is the best means for all times and places, how could one claim this?" Even when doctrinaires expressed a more open attitude toward universal suffrage, they did so in a way that was strictly limited to instrumental considerations, and never came close to articulating any of the views which see universal suffrage as a democratic first principle (Rémusat 1863).

the doctrinaires – the most steadfast enemies of universal suffrage in French politics, who endorsed a very restrictive property requirement for the vote in order to screen those lacking "political capacity" out of the electoral system[5] – were not hesitant to deploy their *representativization* of the press not only against a specific set of policies for extending the franchise, but even against the very idea that possessing the suffrage could be seen as an index of whether the citizen was included in the civic life of the country (Rosanvallon 2011: 211-2).[6]

A curious consequence followed from this downgrading of elections and opposition to universal suffrage: to wit, that it reacted back on their own conceptual language and rendered it unstable. For Guizot and his ilk the value of the vote could be minimized because the realm of representation was so much wider than the electoral domain (Rosanvallon 2000: 118). But the concept of representation being employed here was counterintuitive; if it now meant the "circulation" or "distribution" or "interaction" of ideas rather than the reflection or transmission of "wills," then *what exactly was* being represented? (ibid: 116) The aim of *representing the people* has been transformed into something quite nebulous: the promise of a sort of ongoing conversation between government and society, or (in more modern terms) the assurance of the imbrication of the social and the political. Indeed, the connection between what the population wants as declared via some regular procedure and what the government does was severed so brusquely by the doctrinaires that even they, according to Rosanvallon, could not consistently maintain their preferred vocabulary of representation; instead, "Guizot makes of the reign of publicity the condition of the coming of a 'post-representative' politics" (ibid: 115, 199). The oscillation between the doctrinaires' promulgating an enlarged, improved notion of representation versus their aspiring to surpass representation altogether into some new "informational" or "interactive" dynamic is, indeed, characteristic of the structure of Rosanvallon's own political theory (Conti/Selinger 2016).

---

5 On the doctrinaires' capacitarian philosophy of the suffrage cp. Craiutu (2003). Similar to Disraeli's "Tory-democratic" lowering of the suffrage in England, the *ultra* and *legitimiste* right in France had moments of enthusiasm for a wider franchise which their principled commitment to a censitary requirement kept the doctrinaires from ever enjoying. For Rosanvallon's discussion of this point cp. Rosanvallon (1992: part II, ch. 2). As a general matter, an oft-ignored lesson of the history of modern political thought is that the traditionalist right is seldom the most hostile camp to democracy; after all, they tend to believe that their conservative values are well-ingrained in the population.

6 Guizot's theory was the diametric opposite from the "republican" view that the suffrage was a sacrament of social inclusion and belonging (cp. Rosanvallon 1994c).

If the crux of the doctrinaire view was to assimilate the press to more formal institutions and processes of representative government, then the crux of the Bonapartist position was the exact opposite. One result of the doctrinaires' elevation of the press as a means of government was to diminish the significance of elections and to marginalize electoral democracy. The Bonapartists, on the other hand, held that *only* democratic elections could confer public or representative standing and, hence, that an unfettered press posed a threat to democracy and popular sovereignty.

The core of their charge against a free press was that it permitted, and indeed fostered, *usurpation* (Granier de Cassagnac 1860: 21; Anon. 1864: 7) – that is, that it caused private entities to encroach illegitimately on the public business. This accusation was articulated in different ways depending on the rhetorical targets of the moment, but the core thought was constant. Two refrains stand out in Rosanvallon's gripping reconstruction of the Bonapartist defense of restrictions on the press. The first can be summed up with the question, *who elected the journalists*? For the Bonapartists:

"the press constituted a power of a political nature that was not properly representative, that had no democratic legitimacy. [...] The press, according to another particularly striking expression, is practically the 'rival of the public powers,' even though they were untethered by constraints of legitimacy and representativeness. If the press was not contained, [Granier de Cassagnac] continued, it would become 'a complete and flagrant usurpation of the public powers'. [...] A newspaper is thus a private institution that claims a political role. [...] Given that one could not elect journalists, there was no choice but to control them." (Rosanvallon 2000: 231-2; Rosanvallon 2008: 108)[7]

---

7   Rosanvallon quoted at length two other passages from Granier de Cassagnac that perfectly epitomize the Bonapartist conviction of newspapers as encroaching and usurpatory. (1) "The main characteristic of the influence of the press is the entire absence of delegation. To the contrary of all the regular powers, the least of which is rooted in and delegated by constitutional law, the press is a spontaneous and self-willed power, arising only from itself, from its interests, its caprices, and its ambitions. The number of public powers is limited; the number of newspapers is not. The remit of these powers is defined; the remit of newspapers is without either rule or measure." (2) "Without having the right to elect, [the press] seeks to direct the elections; without having the right to a place in the deliberative bodies, it seeks to influence the deliberations; without having the right to a seat in the councils of the sovereign, it seeks to provoke or to prevent acts of government; without having received a department, or an arrondissement, or a municipality, or even a hamlet, or any form of delegation whatsoever, it seeks to govern

In the words of Emile Ollivier, one of the great statesmen-theorists of the Second Empire (especially and intriguingly of its "liberal" phase), quoted by Rosanvallon: "In order to be a deputy, one has to be elected by the voters. The journalist bestows his powerful ministry upon himself." (Rosanvallon 2008: 109; Zeldin 1963) Appointed by and answerable to nothing but the money that founded the outlet, journalists nonetheless proceeded to substitute for the "absolute right of each citizen to form his own opinion and seek to make it prevail by the designation of the candidate who seems to merit his confidence," their own "abusive right, which they have arrogated to themselves [...] of directing the universal suffrage" (Anon. 1864: 5)

The second way in which the Bonapartists framed their objections was that the liberty of the press was an unleashing of capital upon politics. To fail to restrain the press was to accept the infiltration of private money upon public affairs. A newspaper was a "private institution [...] a 'capitalist corporation [that] buys itself a pack of talented writers'" (Rosanvallon 2008: 109; Rosanvallon 2000: 232). "Bonapartists," Rosanvallon remarks, "mercilessly attacked the press as the instrument of capital" (Rosanvallon 2008: 109). This understanding of the newspaper press as a "big-business," moneyed operation that was hence ineluctably tied to "private" and "partial" interests could also be couched in the conventional revolutionary-populist language of hostility toward the second estate:

"To put things differently, the newspaper could be seen as an aristocratic power in a democratic world. In this vein a brochure written by a friend of the regime tellingly bore the title *The Aristocracy of Newspapers and Universal Suffrage*. The Bonapartists judged from this that control of the press was entirely justified." (Rosanvallon 2000: 232; Granier de Cassagnac 1860: 24; Anon. 1864: 5)[8]

Un-elected, unconstitutional, unaccountable, capitalistic, aristocratic – such was, in outline, the Bonapartist take on the press. Two further features of the argument

---

the nation; in a word, it seeks to substitute its own action for the action of all the legal and established powers, without in reality being invested with a right properly so-called."

8   Although to my knowledge Rosanvallon does not address this, it is noteworthy that this charge of being "aristocratic" could be turned around in a direction supportive of "le journal," the idea being that in a democratic society the press provided an "intellectual" quality and a lever for minorities against majorities that were beneficial (cp. Dupont-White 1866: ch. 7). Not coincidentally, Dupont-White was a great translator of John Stuart Mill.

merit mention at this stage. First, Rosanvallon treats the Bonapartist dismissal of the freedom of the press as distinct from a traditional order- and stability-based argument against it. This is quite right. While the two could, of course, be jointly employed by defenders of the Second Empire's policy (Granier de Cassagnac 1860: 20-3), fear for "public order" or "civic peace" was a motivation for censorship and control quite separate from the principled convictions of Bonapartists about what constituted illegitimate incursions on the space of democratic politics; after all, throughout history most of those who would curtail the press for order's sake have not been democrats (Rosanvallon 1994a: 38), and newspapers "usurp[ing] the place of the ballot box and pretend[ing] to speak for public opinion" did not become wrong only if it eventuated in violence or a government's fall (Rosanvallon 2008: 109-10). What interests Rosanvallon – and what is truly the most theoretically powerful part of the view – is that Bonapartism rejected the liberty of the press on the grounds that doing so was *required by the commitment to democracy tout court*.

Second, because of this principled, democratic anchoring, the Second Empire's censorial and restrictive policy was more than an historical accident, the isolated decision of a few politicians. It was, instead, exemplary of a recurring and "pernicious" ideological "pathology of democracy" (Rosanvallon 2000: 234). For Rosanvallon, Louis-Napoleon's Caesarist version of democracy serves as the culmination (or nadir) of the "Jacobin" or "monist" tradition in France, a "fundamental political model of French democratic organization" (Rosanvallon 2006a: 140-1; Rosanvallon 2002). This insistence on seeing the Second Empire as the crest of a wave that rolls throughout French political history – that is, as a regime and constitutional theory that is continuous with other governments and ideologies while also going beyond them to some degree – shapes Rosanvallon's historiography in a way very relevant for our subject. It is because Rosanvallon is determined to have the Second Empire serve in the role of Jacobin democracy *par excellence* that he winds up focusing so heavily on the issue of the press.[9] So much of his message about the meaning of the mid-century Napoleonic experience has to hinge on their frontal attack against *la liberté des journaux* because in other regards it is very much arguable that the Second Empire was no more "illiberal," "narrowly legalistic," or "decisionist" than its predecessors (Rosanvallon 2008:

---

9   Both La démocratie inachevée, part I, ch. 5, and Counter-Democracy, ch. 4, give outsized attention to the press in order to convey the essence of the "Caesarian vision of politics." As Rosanvallon puts it, "Even though [the Empire] incontestably liberalizes from 1860 on by introducing non-negligible reforms, the regime remains inflexible on the issue of the liberty of the press."

111).[10] Whether or not the Bonapartist antagonism toward the press was really sufficient to support the thesis of its specialness as an ideology and mode of governance is a question to which we will return in the final section.

COMPARING DOCTRINAIRISM AND BONAPARTISM

Significantly, in the whole of Rosanvallon's capacious corpus these are the two most sustained discussions of the press. In light of this fact, it behooves us to consider what the two have in common, and to be precise about where the divergences come, rather than merely gesturing toward the divide between a (heterodox, admittedly) "liberal" view (Guizot) and an illiberal-Caesarist one (the Bonapartists).[11] This section takes up this task with respect to these views *as presented by Rosanvallon*; the next section does so with respect to elements of these schools of thought that were left out by Rosanvallon.

A first source of similarity is that they both eschew a grounding in individual rights. The gap between Guizot and Constant on this issue recurs throughout Rosanvallon's historiography, with the former standing for liberalism conceived of as a set of rights derivable from the value of the "liberty-autonomy of individuals," while the latter represents an alternative liberal school rooted in sociological and epistemological suppositions (Rosanvallon 1985: 88-9; Rosanvallon 1992: 301-3; Rosanvallon 2000: 104-10). Rosanvallon writes less often and less explicitly about the contrast between Bonapartism and Constantian liberal individualism, perhaps

---

10 Although its reputation is still very much contested, to believers in its essentially non-authoritarian character, the Second Empire's "liberalizing" credentials include the landmark legalization of trade-unions; the strengthening of the legislature and rebirth of parliamentarism; expansion of rights of association and meeting; and significant efforts at decentralization and expansion of civic participation (cp. Zeldin 1958; Price 1997; Hazareesingh 2004).

11 The question of whether to classify the doctrinaires as liberals is a vexed one. In an essay a decade after his major work on Guizot, Rosanvallon gave a negative answer, contrasting them with the "classical liberal universe" on a number of fronts (Rosanvallon 1994b). However, Rosanvallon's more considered verdict seems to be to accept the consensus – articulated best by scholars like Larry Siedentop and Lucien Jaume – that the doctrinaires are central to a specifically French liberal tradition that is much more equivocally related to concepts such as the free market, natural rights, or utility (cp. Rosanvallon 1985a; Siedentop 2012; Jaume 1997).

because the opposition is, he feels, too obvious to warrant much discussion. Nevertheless, Bonapartism's relationship to liberal individualism was more nuanced than simple rejection. At a general level, insofar as it understood itself to be the inheritor of Revolutionary principles, both Napoleon and his nephew believed in defending the natural *civil* rights of individuals, even if they sought to constrict *political* rights in various ways.[12] On our issue of the press's liberty, this distinction reappeared. It is not that Bonapartists completely wrote individual rights of expression out of the picture; they simply drew the boundary regarding the use of these rights so as to exclude newspapers – that is, organized, cheap, mass media. Though the Second Empire did, in reality, extend its punitive reach to books,[13] its publicists allowed that the publication of books was to be considered a matter of the exercise of personal liberty and therefore not inherently within the purview of government regulation. In an unexpected twist for a supposedly "absolutist" ideology, Bonapartists opposed in their essence the liberty to print a book, which is but a material extension of the individual right of expression, with the liberty of the press, which had for them a public dimension. The liberty to publish a book is a *means* of individual liberty, a perfectly neutral means. Journalism, on the contrary, in their judgment transformed the nature of the liberty in question. Journalism, insists for example Rouher, has its "existence as a collective being," it constitutes a "developed social power" (Rosanvallon 2000: 230-1).

The Bonapartists did not so much deny the reality of natural rights as assert their irrelevance when it came to addressing how the state should handle the considerable collective force that was the newspaper media.

That Rosanvallon should have fixed on two views that, by their different routes, refused to reduce the question of the liberty of the press to the championing of natural rights is not too surprising. The absence of this liberal tradition in the perspectives reconstructed mirrors Rosanvallon's own low regard for it. He has, throughout his career, demonstrated little attraction to this kind of liberalism.

---

12 Cp. e.g. Louis-Napoleon's portrayal of his uncle as the champion of "the rights of all" (1840). At this level the doctrinaires in fact mirrored the Bonapartists; even if, on Rosanvallon's telling, they had no truck with naturalism about rights, the separation of civil from political rights and the ascription of universality and equality only to the former, as well as the identification of this separation with the legacy of '89, were pivotal to their efforts to justify limitations on the suffrage (cp. Rosanvallon 1992: 321).

13 Among others, such great authors as Flaubert, Baudelaire, Montalembert, and Eugène Pelletan were prosecuted, and anti-clerical sentiments in literature could especially be made targets. On the regulation of the press in the Second Empire (cp. Furet 1992: 444-5; Soltau 1931: 170-2).

While much of his career has been devoted to opposing "illiberal" democracy, this opposition has been grounded more in what he regards as its narrow, impoverished vision of democratic practice than for any betrayal of individual liberties. Instead, he has sought to shelve this tradition (along with Marxism and his early passion, *autogestion*) as inadequate to the truly difficult and pressing questions about how to structure and conduct democratic politics.[14]

This low estimate of what we have called "Constantian liberalism" is manifest not only in his choice of which historical perspectives on the press are worthy of examination; it comes out as well in his recounting of the clash between Bonapartists and their "liberal" critics in the 1850s-60s. As Rosanvallon presents it, the champions of the free press under the Second Empire did not so much answer the logic behind the Imperial restrictions as merely repeat classical-liberal shibboleths. While he does not criticize the liberals with much explicit harshness, what little he mentions of them indicates a feeling that their reassertion of "the habitual liberal argumentation" was inadequate to a Bonapartist perspective possessed of a "real coherence" (Rosanvallon 2000: 230). This coherence was, as we have seen, anchored in a vision of *democracy*. But rather than combating Bonapartism with an alternate, more attractive conception of democracy, anti-Imperial liberals such as Jules Favre and Jules Simon appear in Rosanvallon's history to have been content simply to reiterate in a question-begging manner the unity and inviolability of the "classical individual liberties" no matter what form their public-political manifestations might take (Rosanvallon 2000: 229). The liberty of expression, they charged, could not be bifurcated into a legitimate half (the printing of books, personal conversations, etc.) and a half that was illegitimate because usurpatory and unaccountable (the collective encroachment on the political sphere that was a newspaper enterprise). But why not, if this was what a healthy, uncorrupt democracy required? The liberal opposition did not have an answer to such a question: they talked past the concerns of Bonapartists by simply reaffirming that the "liberal imperative" had to come before the "democratic imperative" (Rosanvallon 2000: 229-30). Non-doctrinaire French liberals were, then, feeble contenders against the perennial if pathological option of the Jacobin model, for they did not grasp the necessity of crafting a rationale for their preferred policies from *within the ideal of democracy itself* and not only by appeal to natural rights.[15]

---

14 Against *autogestion*, Marxism, and classical liberalism, respectively (cp. Rosanvallon 2015: 200-1; Rosanvallon 2006b; Rosanvallon 1998).

15 Their reluctance to attack the Empire's press regime on democratic grounds fits their own wariness about democracy even during the founding days of the Third Republic

The unwillingness of mid-century liberals to fight on the terrain of democracy brings us to a second commonality between Guizot and the Bonapartists, which is that neither connected the free press to *political* democracy. For the latter, the two were inextricably at odds, since upholding the freedom of the press was tantamount to a declaration from the democratic state that it would not protect itself against usurpations by unaccountable, capital-driven organizations. For the former, there did exist a link between a free press and democracy, but it was democracy understood *socially*, that is, as a post-Revolutionary society in which equality under the law, rights to property, fundamental civil protections, and meritocracy had replaced the *ancien régime*'s system of orders and privileges (Rosanvallon 1985a: 47, 67; Craiutu 2003: ch. 4). In other words, liberty of the press was a constituent part of a specific *condition of society*, but it did not dictate any particular extent of the suffrage and could actually, as we learned earlier, lend itself to the justification of limitations on the franchise.

However, and very importantly, the disconnect between democracy and the free press that occurred on these views was, according to Rosanvallon, not symmetrical. From the Bonapartist standpoint, the conflict was intrinsic and unavoidable. But for the doctrinaires, it appears, this was not so; nothing in Rosanvallon's reconstruction suggested that they could not have added democracy to their compelling account of a free press as an instrument of representation and governmentality. Guizot and his comrades, conservative as they were, drew antidemocratic conclusions out of their theory, but their groundbreaking reorientation of representative government around publicity and communication hardly demanded sky-high censitary requirements for the vote. This is why Rosanvallon treats the Bonapartist as a worse kind of error than the doctrinaire – while Bonapartism figures only as a powerful cautionary tale of the democratic imagination turned "Jacobin" and "monistic," (Rosanvallon 2008: 110) doctrinairism contained positive lessons that could be updated for an era no longer torn about the question of the suffrage. Although Rosanvallon is too sophisticated to pen paeans, it is hard to avoid the

---

(cp. Rosanvallon 2000: 252-65). Nevertheless, these liberal revendications of free discussion were not as flat as and one-dimensional as Rosanvallon's recap makes them out to be. For example, these writers invoked, often with great imagination and nuance, the kinds of consequentialist considerations which, at the same epoch, were being elevated into the "gospel of the nineteenth century" by John Stuart Mill (for this phrase) (cp. Stephen 1872; Dupont-White, 1866: 24-30; Simon 1859). Notably, Rosanvallon has never shown any interest in these Millian lines of argument about the long-run moral and epistemic benefits of expressive liberty.

impression that the doctrinaires represent for him a model for doing political theory, a way out of France's late-twentieth-century political-philosophical morasses.[16] Guizot's teaching on the press was one such area eligible for revival.

Rosanvallon's reconstructions of these positions are exemplary of the genre: economical in their depictions, and distilling an immense mass of material on which little conceptual light had previously been shed into clear and relevant conceptual packages. But for all their virtues, they deserve some scrutiny. Did Guizot really come so near to a plausible, attractive account of the press in modern politics? Can Bonapartism's suspicion about an unshackled newspaper industry really be so neatly cordoned off as an archetypal instantiation of the Jacobin and illiberal tendency in French democracy? On both these counts, qualification of Rosanvallon's account is necessary.

To begin with the doctrinaires: to my mind, Rosanvallon's interpretation of them suffers from two problems, one regarding its *undemocratic* character and the other concerning the degree of *liberty* granted to the press.

First, perhaps due to his admiration for the spirit of the doctrinaires in trying to conceptualize the political meaning of the press beyond the formulas of liberal individualism, Rosanvallon's depiction implies that the undemocratic side of doctrinaire thought is something of a contingent matter in relation to their theorization of the press. This, I think, misconceives the way in which the wider notion of representativeness with which the doctrinaires were working affects the significance which elections can have in a political theory. While I do not have space here to elaborate a full democratic-theoretical argument, the crux of the difficulty can be sketched as follows. Whether or not one assents to the overt elitism of the doctrinaires, as soon as one accords legitimacy to avenues of representation beyond the electoral, one has implicitly abandoned a commitment to strict *political equality*. This is not often recognized explicitly, but the source of this disjunction is not hard to pinpoint. To take the case of the doctrinaires: the periodical press has representative standing, but not all citizens have equal opportunity to express themselves through it. To take another example: the British pluralists, among other schools of political thought, wanted civil-society associations and not just parliament to be considered representatives of the nation or of particular segments of it.

---

16 Guizot's continued relevance lies in his ambition of "making [liberalism] a culture of g*overnment*" more than a "doctrine that would protect the rights of the individual" (Rosanvallon 2006c). In this ambition the crabbed horizons of what Rosanvallon variously decries as *utopian, technical, procedural,* or *rights-based* liberalisms are meant to be surpassed.

This proposal might very well have furthered the cause of inclusivity or accountability or other such norms, but it did not equalize voice in the political process, since of course between citizens there was a vast discrepancy in the number of unions, churches, and other organizations slated for representative empowerment to which they belonged, and in the degree of say which they had in these associations.[17] The source of the attractiveness of these other avenues of representation is that they are supposed to bring the political system into closer accord with some standard than the mere aggregation of equal votes would do; this standard may, to simplify a bit, be either epistemic (conducive to truer outcomes) or descriptive (productive of a more accurate reflection of the nation). Now, if elections are valued only because of their contribution to this broader standard, it is not clear why these have to be conducted on a democratic basis. Why not simply write the electoral rules in such a way as to ensure conformity with the standard adopted? And this is precisely what Guizot sought to do: to ensure the "sovereignty of reason" and not simply rule by "the mere force of numbers," Guizot proposed regulations meant to make certain of the triumph of "reason, truth, and justice" as he conceived them (Guizot 2002: 60, 295, 334). Guizot's anti-democratic side was, correspondingly, not independent of his view of the press as a function of representative government. Indeed, any view that theorizes modes of representation beyond the electoral-parliamentary can, in the last accounting, endorse equal suffrage only on *instrumental* grounds, that is, only because it furthers (or at least is not inconsistent with) the broader epistemic or descriptive standard to which the political system as a whole is held.

Because its attempt to diffuse and extend the notion of representation set it at odds with the egalitarianism that undergirds the commitment to elections under equal universal suffrage, the doctrinaire understanding of the press was *intrinsically* hostile to anything beyond a contingent, instrumental endorsement of democracy. Given the attraction it holds for Rosanvallon, though, it would seem that the doctrinaire theory of the press ought to have provided quite powerful normative considerations of its own to compensate for this loss from the strict egalitarian-democratic standpoint; we might have expected, at the least, that a very robust conception of liberty would underlie all the "political communications" and "reciprocal revelations" which evoked such enthusiasm in the doctrinaires. And yet they had no such conception to offer.

This brings us to a second deficiency of Rosanvallon's reconstruction, which is that it does not convey just how highly constrained the doctrinaire conception

---

17 The indifference to political equality was candidly confessed by one of the great pluralists (cp. Cole 1989: 90).

of *la liberté de la presse* was. It is beyond the scope of this chapter to enter in detail into the very complex legal situation of the period,[18] but the basic outline runs thus. During their time as the liberal opposition Guizot and company were influential in measures to liberalize the press regime under the Restoration, and they ushered out (official) prior censorship with the settlement of Louis-Philippe's reign in 1830. But, on the other hand, both during the Restoration and when they came to power as the leading party during the July Monarchy they did not blanche at cracking down on the press, upholding (and even instituting *de novo*) restrictions and penalties of various sorts; the era of doctrinaire hegemony in the 1830s-40s slotted in perfectly, as one scholar puts it, with the pattern of "each succeeding regime preserv[ing] and expand[ing] [the first Napoleon] Bonaparte's ban on any works injurious to government, church, and public morality" (Cragin 2001).[19] Beyond these specific acts, the doctrinaires unswervingly supported the *cautionnement*, a "caution-money system whereby the publishers of newspapers were required to deposit a significant sum of money with the state in order to secure permission for publication," which openly restricted control of the press to a small stratum of society (Jennings 2012; Rosanvallon 1985: 72). As Jaume has pointed out, a "theory of privilege" undergirded the central constraint that was the *cautionnement*: if the newspaper was not just "the expression of the opinions of individuals" but a "power," then "legislators" had to devise "some guarantees" for their suitable conduct (Jaume 1993: 114; Guizot 1818: 239).

What's crucial to understand is that these policies were not just versions of the familiar failure of those in power to live up to the lofty ideals which they had espoused when out of power. With regard to the press, Guizot the statesman did not break with so much as remain faithful to his principles. For Guizot's support for the *liberty* of the press had always been accompanied by condemnations of – and a willingness to act against – its *license* (Guizot 1814: 26-7). With this distinction available, it was easy to impose an array of restraints without having to confess any infringement of "perhaps the most important" of all liberties, that of the press (ibid: 16, 22).[20]

What Rosanvallon finds so compelling about the Guizotians was that they had a very exalted view of the *function* of the press in modern representative politics,

---

18 Until the definitive settlement of the press question in 1881, France experienced a "profound instability of legislative regimes" (Le Béguec 2002: 22).

19 An astonishing 736 prosecutions against the press were brought between 1831 and 1835 alone (cp. Goldstein 1998; Fozzard 1951).

20 The liberty-license distinction resembles the argument, frequently heard at present, that "hate speech" is not protected by a commitment to "free speech."

an insight which Rosanvallon believes remains true in the present (Rosanvallon 2011: 216-7; Rosanvallon 2014). But because he finds this part of doctrinairism so absorbing, he hardly notices what a mean and stinting view of the *freedom* of the press they offered. Furthermore, as with the undemocratic ramifications discussed above, the meagre notion of freedom in their theory of the press is hard to brush off – it was neither an accidental accrual to their platform nor a logical mistake. The doctrinaire reasoning was that, since the press had a properly political-representative function – since it was a means for achieving public purposes – it was appropriate to regulate and limit it for the sake of ensuring that these purposes were fulfilled. This is a familiar and coherent line of thought (we impose all kinds of special restrictions on public actors of many sorts), and it resembles calls today for governmental and/or corporate entities to control the flow of information to stymy the spread of "fake news" or to impede access to irresponsible outlets. What's more, the Guizotians' eagerness to tie the exercise of the rights of public discussion to the provision of financial securities was a close replay of their capacitarian justification for tying the vote to the amount of tax paid – in each case, money served as security for the responsible performance of a public role. And in each case what one might have expected, in a France that had abolished its "estates," to be a right granted universally wound up instead looking more like a class privilege.

Thus, although they came from opposite directions, in the end there was not much daylight between the doctrinaires and the Bonapartists on the *liberty* of the press (Jaume 1993). In the eyes of the former, because the press had, rightly understood, a public/representative function, it demanded regulation – assurances had to be gotten for its responsible use in the common interest. In the eyes of the latter, it was precisely because the press lacked any such public standing (recall that it was "unaccountable" and "capitalistic") *and yet* touched upon political matters that the state could not afford not to oversee and restrain it. And so, despite having widely discrepant visions of what kind of thing the press was, they both arrived at positions quite unfriendly to its freedom.

Indeed, the argument could be made that Bonapartism was friendlier to the press's freedom than doctrinairism. This counterintuitive result – of which Rosanvallon's writing gives no inkling – derives from the fact that Bonapartism was, at root, *Erastianism* updated for conditions of mass media and plebiscitary democracy. Erastianism was the early-modern position that the state was supreme over the church and therefore could control religious worship and belief; its most famous exponent was Hobbes. Against the prevalent caricature of Hobbesianism, however, it has increasingly been recognized that Hobbes was supportive of toleration (Tuck 1990; Ryan 1998); while he thought it intrinsic to sovereignty that the civil ruler be able to settle the terms of religion within the commonwealth, Hobbes could nevertheless wish for wide latitude to be accorded to religious opinion and practice, at least in certain apt conditions (Hobbes 1991: 479-480). In a precisely parallel manner, what Granier de Cassagnac insisted on as "essential" was the need "to distinguish," on the one hand, between "the appropriateness of leaving to journals" some particular amount of practical "liberty," and, on the other, the "doctrine which consists in imputing to newspapers a natural and absolute right to intervene in public affairs" (Granier de Cassagnac 1860: 23). "We deny," he continued, "the existence of this right attributed to the press, but as clearly and as frankly as we do so we uphold the appropriateness of leaving newspapers free, provided that they do not abuse the liberty" (ibid). On the ground, so to speak, Bonapartism's press regime was characterized by a capacity to expand and contract that offered no guarantee that the more ardent champions of repression and control of speech would be satisfied.[21]

Doctrinairism, on the contrary, had no such wiggle room. While perhaps the sum required might rise or fall, Guizot and company had erected the *cautionnement* – the provision of a (sizable) financial guarantee as a condition for receiving the "privilege" of publishing – into a *principle*. In other words, it was a core theoretical commitment of the doctrinaires to make the newspaper press the "exclusive share" of an "aristocracy" (Jaume 1993: 120). In short, because the fundamental conviction behind the Bonapartists was just that the democratic state must not cede its power to decide on the extent of the press's liberty, the scope allowed could be quite large. But because the doctrinaires understood the financial surety as following intrinsically from the duty of ensuring the responsible use of public power, they offered themselves no such practical latitude.

In sum, Guizot was a theorist of neither a democratic nor a free press, and the degree to which these features were not incidental bugs but essential qualities of the theory is downplayed by Rosanvallon. The latter deficiency, especially, seems not to trouble him. Unlike Rosanvallon, one thinker who was very troubled by the doctrinaires' constriction of the scope of freedom was the author we quoted just above – Constant, who figures in Rosanvallon's discussion of the press only as a foil for Guizot; his appears as, so to speak, a mode of thought to be dialectically surpassed. Constant's notion of a free press was more capacious and less qualified than the doctrinaires, and his personal record regarding policy on the press was

---

21 As Granier de Cassagnac asked, with evident exasperation, "what actually are the matters which the French press has not examined and treated at length in recent times? Which questions of foreign policy or domestic policy has it not freely tackled?"

not blighted by restrictions as was the doctrinaires'.[22] What enabled Constant to be a more stalwart and egalitarian defender of the liberty of the press was not just that he had a powerful idea of individual rights – after all, it is a common occurrence to see a grand principle proclaimed while its instantiation is crippled by qualifications and limitations. The ingredient present in Constant's liberalism that was lacking in Guizot's was the sense that the press was ultimately separated from the state, the recognition that while of course much of what citizens would communicate via the press would bear on politics, it did not follow from this fact that the state was authorized to set the terms of the press's use. (Much of what citizens communicate in the press concerns religion, and yet from this fact we do not derive a justification for churches to control publications.) The promise of Constant's political theory – this is, most notably, the aim of his most famous essay (Constant 1988) – was not just to decree *ex nihilo* a set of inviolable rights, but to show why without these rights the "individual liberty" of the modern person was unimaginable. What the free press serves, from this perspective, is *the free life*, which sets it above or at least outside the determination of the political authorities. Rosanvallon's historiography never, in my estimation, reckons with the *impoverishment* to Guizot's theory of the press that results from its lack of this Constantian attempt to understood the "free" press not only as a function in the sociopolitical system, but also as a condition of self-determining personhood. It should be noted, before leaving Constant, that this was a liberal but not a democratic argument. Constant was an opponent of universal suffrage (Constant 1993: 420-1)[23]; the essential conditions for a free life in modern times did not in his eyes extend to possession of the vote.

Constant's marshaling of individual-rights liberalism against the Guizotian program for the press is remindful of the point covered above, that it was Constantian liberals who mounted the chief opposition against Bonapartism's press regime. This historical datum directs us toward a broader conceptual truth. Rosanvallon treats it as a cause of some dissatisfaction that these conventional and rather stodgy liberals – rather than a movement that championed the unshackling of the press in the name of a fuller, more dynamic *democracy* – were at the head of the charge for a free press under the Empire. But the truth is that appeal to the ideal of democracy itself hardly vanquishes Caesarism. Caesarism is – as Rosanvallon's

---

22 Constant's clash with the doctrinaires is examined well in the texts from Jaume and Craiutu cited above.

23 Despite their common defense of a circumscribed suffrage, Constant was critical of the doctrinaire's version of electoral capacitarianism. Rosanvallon's discussion of Constant in the Restoration debates on the vote is outstanding (cp. Rosanvallon 1992: 275-325).

own captivating scholarship attests, against his political sympathies – a plausible, if to many palates unsavory, interpretation of what democracy in modern states entails. It invokes values such as equality, popular sovereignty, and the accountability of power that have been watchwords for democracy's heralds across time and place.[24] From the purely democratic perspective, popular ratification through a free and fair vote of a government that restricts the press (or associations, or property, or any of the other innumerable objects which it has been desired to elevate into the status of basic rights) poses no particular difficulties[25]; were it

---

24 For a riveting but sadly overlooked acknowledgement of just how potent the Empire's appeal to democratic values could appear *even from the perspective of a liberal anti-democrat*, see the essays collected in (cp. Bagehot, 1965-86: vol. 4, 29-178).

25 One way to escape from the argumentative cul-de-sacs that arise with attempts to link free speech absolutism to democracy – to answer the questions: why should "speech" be special? why shouldn't the state regulate speech for the public interest like it does so many other aspects of our lives, especially when we are aware that the media landscape and the public discourse are shaped by inequalities of resources and power? – is via the democratic theory of Rosanvallon's mentor, Claude Lefort. For Lefort, what characterized democracy was less a specific institutional setup than the acknowledgment of social division and plurality and the acceptance of contestation. If this is the right way to understand democracy, then, Lefort argued, the standard liberal intellectual-expressive-associative rights are constitutive of democracy, since these freedoms make it possible for conflict and pluralism to manifest themselves on the political stage rather than a single ideology being imposed upon the polity (cp. Lefort 1988). Strikingly, though, despite his many evident debts to Lefort, Rosanvallon does not articulate this view, nor does he assent to Lefort's forthright assertion that these freedoms are the most important and "indissociable" elements of democracy (ibid; Lefort 1986: 250-1). What exactly we are to make of this absence in Rosanvallon's oeuvre, it is difficult to say. But considered in its own terms, it is worth noting that Lefort's theory, despite its *democratic* self-presentation, runs the risk of just talking past Caesarist viewpoints in a way similar to how Rosanvallon believes the Constanian liberal opposition did. That is, when the kind of liberal pluralism that Lefort prizes comes up against the popular will as expressed in electoral majorities, why would the *democratic* option be to choose against the latter? Faced with Caesarist democracy, Constanian assertion about the indivisibility of rights or Lefortian identifications of democracy with pluralism both read as simple stipulations of what is true and right before the democratic process has even had a chance to play out – a mode of reasoning and conducting politics which Caesarists judge to lack democratic legitimacy. In the terms of Carl Schmitt, the opposite of Caesarism is not democracy, but liberalism (cp. Schmitt 1988: 34).

otherwise, given the historical record we could not claim that a democratic state had ever existed.

To formulate the point slightly differently: the reason to oppose Caesarism is not because one is more of or more truly a democrat than someone else, but because one wants political power to respect certain limits. No matter what verbal tricks one plays, the freedom of the press can only be guaranteed by denying that the state's self-proclaimed goals and needs trump the claims of individuals to write, speak, read, and listen to what they deem fit. Political philosophy has yet to invent a superior device for resisting the infinity of possible reasons which the state – be it democratic or not – might furnish for interfering with the expression and dissemination of ideas than that of liberal individual rights. As both political theorist and historian, however, Rosanvallon has failed to recognize how deeply intertwined his commitments are with this liberal tradition.

Related to this misidentification of what might constitute a sufficient theoretical rejoinder to the Caesarist crackdown on the press is a second problem with Rosanvallon's analysis of Bonapartism. We might call this problem the magnification of ideological distance. Rosanvallon presents the Second Empire as an extreme instance, a paradigm of a pathology. It serves as at once the epitome and the reductio of the "illiberal" strain in postrevolutionary French politics (Rosanvallon 2000: 201). But this way of framing the nature of Bonapartism obscures as much as it reveals. In particular, it conceals just how much continuity exists between Bonapartism and programs of reform whose "liberal-democratic" credentials go more or less unquestioned today.

For example, there is an evident affinity between Bonapartism and the current trend to call for the government to act against the spread of "fake news." On both views, it is a dereliction of duty on the part of a democratic government – the legitimate, publicly-constituted authorities – to sit idly by while the flow of information is polluted by private interests. Both rest their plausibility quite heavily on the suspicion of the deep impressionability of the citizenry, on the intuition that the average voter is possessed of sound instincts but can be easily led astray by oligarchs feeding them the wrong messages.[26] Likewise, many European countries to which the label "liberal" is applied with little hesitation have instituted large restrictions on expression, often explicitly in the name of "democracy." Strands of the longstanding postwar German commitment to "militant democracy" bear a resemblance to the Bonapartist attitude toward the liberty of speech and the press,

---

26 E.g. the characteristic passage at *L'aristocratie des journaux et le suffrage universel*, 6 about the power of the unbridled newspaper industry to "faire croire à tous, et surtout aux simples" precisely those ideas that we know it "should repudiate and detest."

as well. Indeed, any political system that grants the state, as a concomitant of its democratic nature, a paternalist, interventionist role vis-à-vis the circulation of information and opinion is to that extent allied with Bonapartism.

One surprising sphere in which this alignment appears is on an issue dear to the hearts of many self-conceived liberals: campaign finance restrictions. Angst over the influence of money on the electoral discussion; fear of the ability of corporations, super-PACs, "soft" and "dark" money to impose a particular message on the citizenry – this is hardly distinguishable in its basic shape from the Bonapartist argument that the democratic authorities ought to secure the public deliberation from contamination by private interests. Both today's reformers who seek to monitor private spending on issues of common concern, and the Bonapartists who felt that the democratic powers had to resist the swaying of elections and setting of the agenda by the agglomerations of "capitalists" who steered "writers" in the direction of the "self-interest rightly understood of its shareholders" and "dominated the public powers," (Granier de Cassagnac 1860: 22)[27] share the conviction that it is the state's responsibility to keep the democracy uncorrupted by an unfettered media.

The Bonapartist press regime was opposed by an individual-rights-based "liberal" argument. Naturally enough, so are programs to restrict spending on campaigns – the back-and-forth between these two camps is one of the leitmotifs of American First Amendment jurisprudence. Perhaps, though, it leaps out less to the eye that campaign finance reform and Bonapartist management of the press are liable to a common objection internal to the "democratic" domain. In brief and with admitted simplifications, the objection runs as follows: there are two possible results of publishing a newspaper (or releasing a series of campaign ads) – either citizens will be persuaded by the material it presents, or they will not. If the negative, then the state should refrain from needlessly punishing activities that have no impact. If the affirmative, then in impeding its diffusion the democratic state itself is acting as an impediment to the rule of the general will from which its legitimacy is supposed to derive. After all, it was only the state's accordance with the latter that marked it as democratic in the first place. How is democracy contravened by the fact that some people believe and then vote in accord with what a specific newspaper or series of advertisement has to say? If they do so, is it not after all because they were *persuaded* by what these materials had to say? How exactly is the reduction of newspapers or of campaign messages tantamount to an increase in democracy? These same questions confront both Louis-Napoleon and

---

27 Note how the author turns the Tocquevilian phrase "l'intérêt bien entendu" against the Tocquevillian belief in the free press.

the modern campaign-finance reformer, as different political animals as they are in so many ways. To maintain the state's role as regulator of the press and steward of what we might call the "political economy of information" is to be in sympathy with an important element of the Bonapartist outlook.

Recognizing this affinity, of course, does not settle what is the right or wrong democratic theory of the press. It merely suggests that the liberal-democracies of the early twenty-first century are, on questions of expression and the press, not as far from the Second Empire as might have been imagined. And this is a truth – like our discovery above of how the doctrinaires fell afoul of *both* democratic and liberal imperatives when it came to the press – that Rosanvallon's historiography leaves unspoken.

BIBLIOGRAPHY

Anon. (1864): L'aristocratie des journaux et le suffrage universel, Paris.

Bagehot, Walter (1965-86): The Collected Works of Walter Bagehot, 15 vols., Norman St. John-Stevas (ed.), Cambridge.

Bonaparte, Louis-Napoleon (1840): Des idées napoléoniennes: On the Opinions and Policy of Napoleon, London: Henry Colburn.

Bryce, James (1995): The American Commonwealth, 2 vols., Gary McDowell (ed.), Indianapolis: Liberty Fund.

Cole, G.D.H. (1989): "The Social Theory." In: Paul Hirst (ed.), The Pluralist Theory of the State: Selected Writings of G.D.H. Cole, J.N. Figgis, and H.J. Laski, New York: Routledge.

Constant, Benjamin (1988): "The Liberty of the Ancients Compared with That of the Moderns." In: Biancamaria Fontana (ed.), Benjamin Constant, Political Writings, Cambridge: Cambridge University Press.

Constant, Benjamin (1993): "Pensées diverses sur les élections." In: Benjamin Constant, Oeuvres completes, vol. 11, Berlin.

Conti, Greg/Selinger, Will (2016): "The Other Side of Representation: The History and Theory of Representative Government in Pierre Rosanvallon." In: Constellations 23/4, pp. 548-62.

Cragin, Thomas (2001): "The Failings of Popular News Censorship in Nineteenth-Century France." In: Book History 4, pp. 49-80.

Craiutu, Aurelian (2003a): "Guizot's Elitist Theory of Representative Government." In: Critical Review 15/3-4, pp. 261-284.

Craiutu, Aurelian (2003b): Liberalism under Siege: The Political Thought of the French Doctrinaires, Lanham: Lexington Books.

Dupont-White, Charles (1866a): La liberté de la presse et le suffrage universel, Paris: Hachette.
Dupont-White, Charles (1866b): Le rôle et la liberté de la presse, Paris: Hachette.
Fozzard, Irene (1951): "The Government and the Press in France, 1822 to 1827." In: The English Historical Review 66/258, pp. 51-66.
Furet, François (1992): Revolutionary France, 1770-1880, Antonia Nevill (trans.), Oxford: Blackwell.
Goldstein, Robert (1998): "Fighting French Censorship, 1815-1881." In: The French Review 71/15, pp. 785-96.
Granier de Cassagnac, Adolphe (1860): L'empereur et la démocratie moderne, Paris.
Granier de Cassagnac, Adolphe (1864): L'aristocratie des journaux et le suffrage universel, Paris.
Guizot, François (1814): Quelques idées sur la liberté de la presse, Paris.
Guizot, François (1818): "Des garanties légales de la liberté de la presse." In: Archives philosophiques, politiques, et litteraires 5, pp. 184-243.
Guizot, François (2002): The History of the Origins of Representative Government in Europe, Andrew R. Scoble (trans.), Indianapolis: Liberty Fund.
Hazareesingh, Sudhir (2004): "Bonapartism as the Progenitor of Democracy: The Paradoxical Case of the Second Empire." In: Peter Baehr/Melvin Richter, (eds.), Dictatorship in History and Theory, Cambridge: Cambridge University Press, pp. 129-52.
Hobbes, Thomas (1991): Leviathan, Richard Tuck (ed.), Cambridge: Cambridge University Press.
Jaume, Lucien (1993): "La conception doctrinaire de la liberté de la presse: 1814-1819." In: Guizot, les Doctrinaires et la presse, Val Richer, pp. 111-23.
Jaume, Lucien (1997): L'Individu effacé ou le paradoxe du libéralisme français, Paris: Fayard.
Jennings, Jeremy (2012): "A note on freedom of the press in Restoration France." In: Journal of Modern Italian Studies 17/5, pp. 568-73.
Le Béguec, Diane (2002): "De la rhétorique parlementaire à la rhétorique judiciaire: la défense de la liberté de la presse sous la Restauration." In: Droits 36/2, pp. 21-38.
Lefort, Claude (1986): "Politics and Human Rights." In: John B. Thompson (ed.), The Political Forms of Modern Society, Cambridge: MIT Press, pp. 239-72.
Lefort, Claude (1988): "'The Question of Democracy' and 'Human Rights and the Welfare State.'" In: Democracy and Political Theory, David Macey (trans.), Cambridge: Polity Press.
Price, Roger (1997): Napoleon III and the Second Empire, London: Routledge.

Rémusat (1863): "Liberté et démocratie." In: Revue des deux Mondes 44, pp. 634-57.

Rosanvallon, Pierre (1985a): Le Moment Guizot, Paris: Gallimard.

Rosanvallon, Pierre (1985b): "Préface: Le Gramsci de la bourgeoisie." In: François Guizot, Histoire de la civilisation en Europe, suivie de Philosophie politique. De la souvereaineté, Paris: Hachette, pp. 9-18.

Rosanvallon, Pierre (1988): La question syndicale. Histoire et avénir d'une forme sociale, Paris: Calmann-Lévy.

Rosanvallon, Pierre (1992): Le sacre du citoyen. Histoire du suffrage universel en France, Paris: Gallimard.

Rosanvallon, Pierre (1993): "Les Doctrinaires sonts-ils des liberaux?" In: Darío Roldán (ed.), Guizot, les Doctrinaires et la presse, 1820-30, Val-Richer.

Rosanvallon, Pierre (1994a): La monarchie impossible. Les Chartes de 1814 et de 1830, Paris: Fayard.

Rosanvallon, Pierre (1994b): "The Republic of Universal Suffrage." In: Biancamaria Fontana (ed.), The Invention of the Modern Republic, Laura Mason (trans.), Cambridge: Cambridge University Press, pp. 192-205.

Rosanvallon, Pierre (1998): Le peuple introuvable. histoire de la representation démocratique en France, Paris: Gallimard.

Rosanvallon, Pierre (2000): La démocratie inachevée. histoire de la souveraineté du peuple en France, Paris: Gallimard.

Rosanvallon, Pierre (2002): "Fondements et problèmes de l'"illiberalisme' francais." In: Thierry de Montbrial (ed.), La France du nouveau siècle, Paris, pp. 85-93.

Rosanvallon, Pierre (2006a): "Political Rationalism and Democracy in France." In: Samuel Moyn (ed.), Pierre Rosanvallon, Democracy Past and Future, New York: Columbia University Press.

Rosanvallon, Pierre (2006b): "Marx and Civil Society." In: Samuel Moyn (ed.), Pierre Rosanvallon, Democracy Past and Future, New York: Columbia University Press, pp. 160-186.

Rosanvallon, Pierre (2008): Counter-Democracy: Politics in an Age of Distrust, Arthur Goldhammer (trans.), Cambridge: Cambridge University Press.

Rosanvallon, Pierre (2011): Democratic Legitimacy: Impartiality, Reflexivity, Proximity, Arthur Goldhammer (trans.), Princeton: Princeton University Press.

Rosanvallon, Pierre (2014): Le parlement des invisibles, Paris: Seuil.

Rosanvallon, Pierre (2015): Le bon gouvernement, Paris: Seuil.

Ryan, Alan (1998): "A More Tolerant Hobbes." In: Susan Mendes (ed.), Justifying Toleration, Cambridge: Cambridge University Press, pp. 37-60.

Schmitt, Carl (1988): The Crisis of Parliamentary Democracy, Ellen Kennedy (trans.), Cambridge: The MIT Press.

Siedentop, Larry (2012): "Two Liberal Traditions." In: Raf Geenens and Helena Rosenblatt (eds.), French Liberalism from Montesquieu to the Present Day, Cambridge: Cambridge University Press, pp. 15-35.

Simon, Jules (1859): La Liberté, Paris: Hachette.

Soltau, Roger (1931): French Political Thought in the Nineteenth Century, New Haven: Yale University Press.

Stephen, Leslie (1872): "Social Macadamisation." In: Fraser's Magazine 16/32, pp.150-68.

Thompson, James (2013): British Political Culture and the Idea of Public Opinion, 1867-1914, Cambridge: Cambridge University Press.

Tuck, Richard (1990): "Hobbes and Locke on Toleration." In: Mary Dietz (ed.) Thomas Hobbes and Political Theory, Lawrence: University of Kansas Press, pp. 153-71.

Zeldin, Theodore (1958): The Political System of Napoleon III, London: Macmillan.

Zeldin, Theodore (1963): Émile Ollivier and the Liberal Empire of Napoleon III, Oxford: Oxford Clarendon Press.

9 Pierre Rosanvallon in Context
The Crisis of Republicanism
and the Democratic Experience

Daniel Schulz

As is so often the case in the French tradition, Pierre Rosanvallon is an academic and a public intellectual at the same time. Not only is he distinguished by his scholarly works, but he is present as well in central political debates. This crossing of borders between the academic and the political public sphere is reflected also in his biography, which does not match a classical academic career path in France: Rosanvallon's early writings are not being produced within the context of academia, but stem from the world of the French trade union *Confédération française démocratique du travail* (CFDT). The CFDT was a reformist competitor of the communist Confédéreation générale du travail (CGT) and was close to Mitterand's *Parti socialiste* (PS) – under the influence of the idea of autonomous self-administration ("*autogestion*"), the union was more and more turning its back on the still dominant orthodox Marxist discourse and moving towards social democracy, a current that was in the minority in the PS for a long time and could not really become an important force on the French left until the nineteen nineties (Judt 1990). Other than many known intellectual figures in France – Jean-Paul Sartre, Raymond Aron, Jacques Derrida, Michel Foucault, Pierre Bourdieu etc. – Rosanvallon is not an alumni of the famous Parisian *École normale supérieure*. The young Rosanvallon studied at the *École des hautes etudes commerciales de Paris* (HEC), a renowned business school. After graduation, he worked for the CFDT as a counselor from 1969 to 1972 and as editor in chief for the journal *CDFT Aujourd'hui* from 1973 until 1977. Back at that time, he was already part of the reformist current in the PS under the lead of Michel Rocard, who, taking into account the anti-authoritarian impulse from May 1968, pleaded for taking a distance from a hierarchical and centralistic understanding of politics – an understanding that was common sense on the left as well as on the right of the French party-spectrum at that time.

Rosanvallon quickly became one of the most important thinkers of the so called *Deuxième gauche*, the "second left", a movement within the socialist party in the nineteen seventies that considered a liberalization of the leftist tradition as an urgent task, criticizing the new government under president Mitterand for his statist policies of nationalizations and taking the coalition with the communist party up a blind alley (Hamin/Rotman 1984). His works *L'âge de l'autogestion* (1976) and *Pour une nouvelle culture politique* (1977) have been part of this development, even though they had little success within the PS, dominated by Mitterand's presidency and his hegemonic fixation on the state and its authority.[1]

Instead of pursuing a political career, Rosanvallon at the end of the seventies entered academia and started writing a thesis under the direction of Claude Lefort. The work was published in 1979 under the title *Le capitalism utopique* and analyzes the political ideas and the political theory of early liberalism. This book, reflecting the strong influence of Albert O. Hirschman and his seminal work *The Passions and the Interests,* published two years earlier in 1977, sees Rosanvallon describe the idea of the market as the political and the social utopia of the liberal tradition. The special punch-line of his consideration is that the liberal utopianism of the 18th century and the socialist utopianism of the 19th century are much closer to each other in their normative structure and their idea of autonomy than the polemic discourse of socialist anti-capitalism would suggest. The question then is how to overcome this deep division, and how to build a political theory based on autonomy. While Smith and Marx are substituting the political with the economic from opposite sides, Rosanvallon, in following Lefort, points back to Machiavelli as a possible reference in the history of ideas (Lefort 1972):

"With Machiavelli rather than Rousseau as a starting point, one could develop a notion of the political which is neither conceived as a harmony of interests (Smith) nor as overcoming all oppositions (Marx) or as unity of the common will (Rousseau)." (Rosanvallon 1979: 61)

Shortly after, Rosanvallon presents a second doctoral thesis, published in 1985 under the title *Le moment Guizot* and revealing the connections between liberalism and democracy in the post-revolutionary France, which had until then been mostly concealed in their somewhat paradoxical and intricate nature (see below). In 1983

---

1   Cp. Rosanvallon (1983) and (1988).

he becomes *Maître de conférences* at the *École des hautes études en sciences sociales* (EHESS), six years later he is *Directeur d'études*. From 1992 until 2005 he is head of the influential *Centre de recherches politiques Raymond Aron*, the role of which for the discussions in political and democratic theory can hardly be overestimated. François Furet, Claude Lefort, Bernard Manin, Marcel Gauchet, Dominique Schnapper, Vincent Descombes and Mona Ozouf are only some of the names of those who are engaged in a regular intellectual exchange beyond the narrow limits of academic fields and the various disciplines of the social sciences and the humanities. It is in this context that a whole series of important studies in the history of political ideas see the light: Next to Rosanvallon's own work on François Guizot, there are works on Alexis de Tocqueville, on Benjamin Constant, on Condorcet and others, all being connected by the same interest in the liberal, antitotalitarian and representative tradition of the political which should gradually enlarge the narrow frame of republican political ideas still dominating in France.[2] In this context Rosanvallon conceives his fundamental works on the genesis of democracy in France: *Le sacre du citoyen. Histoire du suffrage universel en France* (1992), *Le peuple introuvable. Histoire de la représentation démocratique en France* (1998) and *La démocratie inachevée. Histoire de la souveraineté du peuple en France* (2000) are forming a first trilogy addressing central problems of democracy along a historical perspective from the French Revolution until the early 20th century.

Up to this point, Rosanvallon's works are closely related to the French development and its reconstruction, but they nevertheless possess a conceptual potential that leads beyond this reference, opening insights into the fundamental theoretical problems and paradoxes of contemporary democracy. Rosanvallon pursues this comparative enlargement of perspectives and a more systematic approach when in 2001 he becomes elected as indirect successor of Michel Foucault and Pierre Bourdieu to the *Collège de France*. In this institution occupying the peak of academic reputation in France, he occupies a chair named *Histoire moderne et contemporaine du politique*. In a subsequent series of four monographs, Rosanvallon is questioning modern democracy on its historical genesis and its normative potentials at once: *La contre-démocratie. La politique à l'âge de la défiance* (2006), *La légitimité démocratique. Impartialité, réflexivité, proximité* (2008), *La société des égaux* (2011) and *Le bon gouvernement* (2015).

---

2   On Tocqueville cp. Aron (1967, 1997), Manent (1982), Mélonio (1993), Gauchet (2005), Lefort (1992), and Audier (2004); on Constant cp. Gauchet (1997), on Condorcet cp. Jaume (1989), and Rosanvallon (2000).

At the same time, he takes the role of one of the most important French public intellectuals. Already from 1982 until 1999, he directed the *Fondation Saint-Simon,* a center-left, reform-oriented think tank. Together with François Furet and Jacques Juillard, in 1988 he writes the programmatic essay *La république du centre,* stating the long goodbye from the French history of radical upheavals towards a balanced political order. Since 2002 he has directed the project *La vie des idées*, a journal and a book series directed to a larger educated public and that has established itself as an intellectual forum for public discussions.³ His latest project *Raconter la vie* is trying to provide a public platform through widely available biographical essays in order to bring together different ways of life and different biographical experiences, thus engaging in a conversation bridging the deepening social, political and cultural splits that threaten to destroy the public space and thus the foundations of society. It is the declared aim of this enterprise to overcome the silence between different social milieus in France and to allow for a face and a voice of those excluded from the public.

1. THE REDISCOVERY OF FRENCH LIBERALISM

Before presenting his works on democratic theory, it is necessary to account for Rosanvallon's achievements in the field of the history of political ideas. More precisely it was his rediscovery of the French liberal tradition that provides the background for his notion of democracy. In the 1970s, the French intellectual discourse was largely dominated by the attempt to leave the authoritarian and paternalistic elements of Marxism behind. Paradoxically enough, it was exactly this tradition which had claimed to represent progress and the emancipation of mankind from the chains of heteronomy. The post-structuralist critique of enlightenment was itself a result of bringing together elements from Marxism, psychoanalysis and heterodox philosophical traditions such as Nietzsche and Heidegger. What was commonly overlooked, especially in the strong reception of post-structuralism in western Europe and in the USA, was that the critical deconstruction was not dealing primarily with liberalism and its theory of the market and of law. Rather, its initial object of critique was the French republican tradition with its dominant political imagination of unity, as represented in the nation, the people, and the state (Schulz 2015). The critical reconstruction of French liberalism however stood much less under the sign of radical deconstruction, but instead attempted to break up the sclerotic understanding of political order in republicanism by recurring to the

---

3   Cp. www.laviedesidees.fr, and its english version www.booksandideas.net

largely forgotten alternatives in political thinking. It was the dialogue with the post-revolutionary development that could bring to the fore the blind spot of the Jacobin paradigm and thus resolve the confusion over the question of what a democracy would look like. The work of Pierre Rosanvallon not only focused on well-known figures such as Tocqueville, Constant or Condorcet, but also rediscovered the historian and politician François Guizot. Beyond the clichés about the July monarchy and its slogan *enrichissez-vous*, little more was known in France about this eminent figure in the history of post-revolutionary democracy. However, Rosanvallon shows the degree to which Guizot ties many of the central discourses of his time to being desperately in search of a political constitution for a post-revolutionary society (Rosanvallon 1985a). The *Guizot moment* refers to the liberal political culture in the years between 1814 and 1848, being exposed to multiple front lines and finally failing in a double sense: Against the restauration of absolutist monarchy, liberalism fights for parliamentarism and fundamental rights, both finding only weak and transitory expression in the imposed constitution from 1814 (Rosanvallon 1994). In the July revolution of 1830 the constitutional order could be renewed but kept claims for democratic participation at bay. The search for a liberal balance failed again in 1848 and it preliminarily ended in the plebiscitarian rule of Bonapartism under Napoleon III. With his focus on Guizot, Rosanvallon brings back a political liberalism that has been largely overshadowed by the economic strand of liberal thinking. Guizot, an author commonly overlooked by the history of ideas, merits attention because he is one of the first thinkers to ask the question of a constitutional *government* – and thus shifting the attention from the big philosophical issues of justification and political legitimacy towards the problems of how to realize those rights and constitutional ideas which were articulated for the first time during the French Revolution. Even though Rosanvallon does not share Guizot's reflections and solutions, he nonetheless deserves attention as a historical figure because he has to fulfill the post-revolutionary task of forming a permanent political constitution on the basis of the philosophical principles of the Revolution. Guizot deals with this task with some liberal-conservative retention. After the experience of the *terreur*, one caveat of constitutionalism at that time is that this event of democratic self-destruction must never repeat itself under any circumstances. Rosanvallon shows how the political semantics of that time go through different options in order to realize the idea of a free commonwealth with a universal and equal legislation. The liberal discourse tries on the one hand to deal with the experience of the revolutionary reign of terror in the name of popular sovereignty, and on the other hand to satisfy the idea of a universal legal order implied by reason. The core problem is, however, that the liberalism of this epoch cannot fall back on a single idea of political order but rather produces multiple blind spots due to the conflicting nature of his motifs: As political liberalism, it is not democratic; as economic liberalism, it reveals a strong utopian moment and, by the effects of industrialization and the growing social differences, involuntarily undermines its own egalitarian principles of justice. This development culminates in the marginalization of liberal thought in France, continuing well into the twentieth century. Even though, according to Rosanvallon, there are no direct solutions which could be drawn from this for modern democracies, the reconstruction of those intellectual circumstances is nonetheless important because, notwithstanding their failure, it points to an alternative perspective, thus relativizing the absolute claims of monarchism, Bonapartism, socialism and republicanism to represent the whole set of ideas at the origins of modern French societies. Regarding the history of ideas, this view also shows the connections between German idealism and the French discourse, which have long been hidden. Rosanvallon draws a connecting line from Hegel to the group of the doctrinaires, of which Guizot was a member, and which then had a strong influence on Tocqueville and his search for the stabilizing contexts of a modern liberal constitutional setting (Rosanvallon 1985: 50). When Guizot's liberalism wants to limit the democratic participation with reference to the reasonable liberal elites, then this is an echo of the Hegelian theory of the state, having itself translated the spirit of liberal reforms in Prussia into the system of the philosophy of right. Guizot changes this into a quite paternalistic liberalism of the state, which has to create conditions of its own validity by enlightening and reforming the society on which it is based – and thus avoiding being at the mercy of irrational passions in a society not sufficiently cultivated in a liberal sense. Tocqueville, however, facing the American experience with democracy, should draw completely different conclusions. Instead of looking for the rule of reason embodied in the institutions of the state, he searched for conditions that could render the democratic autonomy of free citizens permanent.

2. THE CONCEPT OF DEMOCRACY: THE FRENCH DEVELOPMENT

Rosanvallon's main works have been dedicated to the question of democracy. Even though throughout his entire works he connects the history of democracy with the theory of democracy, one can still distinguish some shifts in focus. His first trilogy dealing with democracy is dominated by the history of ideas and the history of democratic practices, taking France as its central reference. Even though he already develops theoretic categories and concepts with relevance beyond the narrow question of democracy in France, it is mostly the following series of four consecutive monographs that puts to the fore the approach to the theory of democracy.

The history of the state in France he developed in *L'Etat en France de 1789 à nos jours* is connected to his work on Guizot and the state-centered liberalism and, taking the perspectives of Tocqueville and Marx on the continuity of a centralized state between the *Ancien régime* and the revolution, represents the role of the administration as a political instrument to produce the French society – thus showing how it is only this process of political intervention in the social structures which slowly creates the social reality declared by the revolutionary principles in 1789. As with Guizot, there is a strong paternalistic dimension in the liberal reprogramming of the state power in the nineteenth century, linking it to the principles of 1789 and thus giving a rationalized, elitist answer from above towards the challenge posed by the Jacobin politics of a permanent mass-mobilization.

This aspect of a dynamic change in the political self-description and its interplay with the institutional structures was also at the center of the three volumes Rosanvallon published on the history of democracy from 1993 until 2000. This trilogy is at the same time conceived as a history of discourses and practices and uses an impressive amount of historical material to develop its conceptual and systematic consequences. The first part, *Le sacre du citoyen* (1992) reconstructs the history of universal suffrage. With its revolutionary proclamation, this right begins to exist as a principle, but it was far more than just a legal form of a revolutionary claim. Quite the contrary: As a symbolic leverage the suffrage caused a long process of transformation, thus creating the social prerequisites of the "one man one vote"-principle even though the right was perceived as being the expression of those conditions. As an imaginary figure of the new, democratic dispositive of legitimacy, the male citizen eligible to vote existed long before its political and legal realization. The history of political suffrage shows how a universal claim is not reducible to a legal right. The legal discourse is creating a social and a politico-cultural dynamic leading to a mutual transformation of the political, the social, and the legal structures. The citizen appears as a specific form of subjectivation in modern democracy, the form of which cannot be determined a priori. Rather, the figure of the citizen receives its form in the course of a changeful, nonlinear history.

The second volume undertakes a similar reconstruction, this time taking the case of democratic representation. While before it was the question of individual subjectivation of the citizen, now Rosanvallon in *Le peuple introuvable* (1998) reconstructs the genealogy of the people as collective subject of democracy. Rosanvallon shows how the complex relation between the political subject "the people" as a symbolic unity and as a social presence triggers a political quest for its appropriate institutional translation. Thus, the meaning of democratic representation was and still is the subject of ongoing political conflicts. Therefore, at the core of the democratic project there is an aporia which cannot be solved. While the people as a symbolic subject is supposed to guarantee the imagined unity of political self-legislation, it always loses this quality when the social subject tries to transform itself into this imaginary role. Instead of universal unity with itself, the people reveals itself as a fragmented, amorphous entity with blurred edges, unclear belonging and polyphonic voice. The symbolic and the social body of the people cannot be formed into a unity. Rather, instead of this unity, they permanently reveal their inner differences. It is for this reason that the process of democratic representation is permanently bound to fail, unless it takes notice of its inner tension and draws institutional consequences from the impossibility of creating a real identity of the people with itself.[4]

La démocratie inachevée (2000) demonstrates how the triumph of the sovereignty of the people actually poses more questions than the legal formalization of this sovereignty in the democratic constitutions can answer. Here too, the French Revolution was not the end and the result of a successful democratization, but rather the beginning of a long history of experiments with democracy. There is no direct path leading from the philosophical principle of autonomy towards an institutional form which transforms this principle into a political and social practice. Rosanvallon shows the different, mutually exclusive and concurring conceptions which existed during the course of the nineteenth century in France. A Jacobin-republican idea of a central embodiment in form of a legislative assembly is opposed to a Napoleonic logic of popular sovereignty, reclaiming the democratic principle in the plebiscitary form of Bonapartist leadership. In between those opposites, there are numerous attempts at mediation and compromise, but it is not until the second half of the twentieth century that the form of democracy ceases to be a matter of intense political conflict. It is exactly here that we can find the punch line of democracy: A successful democracy has to find a form to integrate the possibility of a permanent quest for itself, if it does not want to perish. In France and in Western Europe, this long and sometimes violent search has created a preliminary balance in the guise of the democratic welfare state, before this institutional construct began to be slowly dissolved in the process of liberalization, globalization, and deregulation.

---

4   For a theory of democracy that continues to think along these lines cp. Colliot-Thélène 2018.

3. THE CONCEPT OF DEMOCRACY: A THEORETICAL SYSTEMATIZATION

The resulting theoretical, conceptual and systematic challenges for democracy have been treated in a following series of monographs. The first volume *La contre-démocratie* develops an analysis that is directed against the traditional image of voluntaristic theories of democracy and that could be described as negative theory of democracy: Democratic legitimacy for Rosanvallon is not only based on positive acclaim and the trust in institutions and representatives, but rather to the same degree by dissent and mistrust. Not only does the power survey the people in the sense of Foucault, but the people also survey the power by the permanent presence of public opinion (Rosanvallon 2006: 38). The public scandal, muckraker journalism, the always-precarious reputation of public actors similar to the notion of honor in pre-modern societies, the evaluation of public action by citizens – all these are elements of democracy that have, according to Rosanvallon, not received enough attention in the fiction of unity defended by traditional republicanism. Instead he points to a multitude of new, heterogeneous actors ranging from social movements to advocacy groups, think-tanks and the much-discussed rating agencies, having gained a power of interpretation over the credit-worthiness of states that may deeply affect their capacity for political action and even threaten their very existence. Adding to that are the new digital media companies that have broken up the monopoly of information held by public, often state-owned media (ibid: 71). The theory of democracy should, according to Rosanvallon, take into consideration the potential legitimacy of other, indirect and intermediary powers. It is those powers which could not be justified within the Jacobin framework of a unitary national sovereignty – a framework that has also been associated with an understanding of democratic legitimacy, which is dear to Carl Schmitt, and his followers on the left and on the right. It is also put into question in the context of a mixed constitution, giving expression to an extensive understanding of a separation of powers. Not only the political integration by trust, but also the productive force of mistrust must become part of a theory of democratic legitimacy – even though the populist wave of mistrust in Europe and the United States illustrates the fact that this mistrust may itself become a problem for political legitimacy.

This tentative trial to describe the changing face of democracy under the transformed conditions of statehood and political action has been undertaken by Rosanvallon in his book on democratic legitimacy: The legitimacy of democracy is based on traditional forms of direct or representative participation in the legislative process, but also goes beyond this by including the criteria of non-partisanship, reflexivity and proximity. Compared to a purely voluntaristic paradigm of the democratic will, the focus is thus enlarged: Rosanvallon aims at taking into account those instances, that would have the common reputation of lacking legitimacy and therefore be perceived as alien to the democratic process. Given the French background of those ideas, it seems remarkable the way in which institutions like constitutional courts or an independent central bank are now declared as being part of the democratic dispositive, since they represent the capacity of non-partisan judgment dear to many citizens. Due to these qualities, they embody a corrective in relation to traditional forms of democratic decision-making. It is not Rosanvallon's intention to justify a new elitist rule but rather to describe the new institutional forms which are proper to democratic representation today. This does not lead him to follow the pessimistic diagnosis of post-democracy. His aim is to develop a realistic model mirroring the plurality of influences and factors that play their part in contemporary democratic decision-making processes without at the same time inflating the status quo as a normative ideal. Quite the contrary: This approach shows the large range of democratic possibilities beyond the limitation on votes and elections. At the same time however, there is a certain realistic estimation concerning the possible range of democratic actions. If the democratically-elected governments become part of an overarching constellation of veto-players and non-elected powers, then the expectations towards the capabilities of governments have to be adapted to these conditions instead of raising those expectations with every new electoral campaign, systematically producing disappointments which undermine the democratic legitimacy in the long run. Rosanvallon uses the term of complex sovereignty in order to describe this constellation, allowing modern democracies to include the possibilities of self-criticism and self-limitation in the political constitution itself. The numerous veto-powers within democracy do not serve the destruction of political rationality and autonomy, but rather enlarge the perspectives of decision-making. It is for this reason that also the criteria to judge a good citizen are transformed: Next to the integration into the political will, dear to voluntaristic approaches, it is the development of political judgment that becomes crucial for democratic legitimacy.

The transformation of democracy is menaced however by the growing erosion of its fundamental assumptions: *La société des égaux* describes how the growing inequality in western industrial societies is eroding democracy as a social form. As a result, the political form of democracy is losing more and more of its credibility. Both sides of the concept of democracy – the social and the political aspect – have belonged inseparably together since Tocqueville's analysis. Rosanvallon is basing his diagnosis on the works of Thomas Piketty and poses the urgent question of in which respect the citizens of a democracy have to regard themselves as equals if a pure legal quality seems insufficient to guarantee the bonds of society.

Tocqueville's famous discussion of democratic equality serves as a guideline to analyze the historical change of the notion of equality in its different forms, and also in its multiple pathologies. Democracy as a society of similarities (Rosanvallon 2011: 27) can take quite different shapes and leads to quite different political consequences depending on the concept of equality that it relies on. The historical recourse on the development of the idea of democratic equality shows once more the central role of the citizens: As legal subjects they are created by the constitutional guarantee of a general and equal right to vote. Beyond this legal dimension, the citizens are at the same time part of a culture of solidarity and mutual recognition, providing the political and the social foundation of the democratic project. The problem however is that it is not clear how such a form of civic sense can be generated under conditions of a generalized market society and its transformation of social solidarity. Rosanvallon's answers to this remain much more vague than his lucid descriptions of the problems – at least if one is not entirely convinced by the renationalization of democracies recommended in the final chapter (ibid: 411).

With his last volume on *Le bon gouvernement* (2015) Rosanvallon in a certain sense makes a link to his work on Guizot and is searching for a political culture of government in contemporary democracy.[5] Behind this link is the insight that the question of good government has become more and more important, but at the same time it has become also more and more neglected in the theory of democracy. The concept of democracy developed by Rosanvallon aims to differentiate between democracy as active participation, democracy as an institutional structure, democracy as a society of equals, and finally democracy as a form and a practice of government (ibid: 31). In the light of the growing predominance of the executive and the personalization of the political in parliamentary regimes – described by Rosanvallon as the "presidentialization of democracies" – the absence of the executive in the theory of democracy must become highly problematic.

In using material from the history of ideas, Rosanvallon shows how the executive dimension of democracy has been rendered invisible by the cult of the law and is counterpart, the cult of the impersonal during the course of the French Revolution. With Napoleon, the idea of the *homme-peuple*, the personal embodiment of popular sovereignty appears on the scene of political representation. After this early experience with democratic Caesarism the function of government will only be slowly rehabilitated, and experiences a recovery with the change from the legal state to the executive state in mass democracy during the first half of the twentieth

---

5   Back then he had already declared that „La nécessité d'en faire une culture de gouvernement est partout ressentie" (Rosanvallon 1985: 25).

century. In the light of enlarging state activity, the liberal-technocratic neutralization of the political and the executive political order of the state of exception – theorized by Carl Schmitt – are facing a confrontation without a possibility of reconciliation. Rosanvallon reconstructs the effect of presidentialization in different contexts, ranging from Max Weber and Charles de Gaulle to the USA and the New Deal. They finally converge in a *démocratie de l'exercice*, having as a common denominator a basic illiberal tendency. Even though a new aspect of impersonal power, for instance the emergence of constitutional courts, is rising in the same period, the decisive question for the theory of democracy remains, how a government can be possible in the form of non-domination – a government, not founded in its efficient functionality, but in its quality as a specifically democratic government. Rosanvallon is thus interested in nothing less than a democratic refoundation of a politico-cultural theory of government. To this end, he discusses different problems: The necessary readability of government actions cannot be guaranteed by increased visibility. On the contrary, the decision-networks of globalized orders create new forms of opacity and of the secret, which animate conspiracy theories rather than democratic legitimacy. In a similar way, the question of government-responsibility loses its focus because it becomes more and more difficult to link actions to actors. Adding to that is the tendency to replace political responsibility with the legal concept of guilt. It is an open question whether a republican language of frankness, which would weaken the hiatus between the language of electoral campaigns and the language of government, could really counterbalance this tendency. Even more problematic is the question of whether the political integrity of the governing should really be linked to the citizen's claim of transparency in order to trump the protection of personality rights. All of these proposals however are able to stir up a vivid discussion and to challenge the theory of democracy with its alleged certainties. Also, the separation of labor between political theory and the studies of comparative government has come too close to a pact of mutual non-recognition in the last decades – a fact that should be reconsidered on this occasion.

If then the final volume of the series of work on democracy gives opportunity to critical discussion, the immanent connection between historical and the normative dimension of democracy is a highly innovative methodological way to think about the contemporary political order and its problems. Even if not all institutional propositions are entirely convincing, the intellectual stimulation of his work prevails, offering a whole range of ideas not only for political theory but also for comparative government-studies. Norms are put into contexts and contexts are analyzed referring to norms without falling into the trap of normative particularism. Rosanvallon draws his picture of democracy as a space of possibilities, being reconstructed from social practices and historical discourses, without compressing it into a closed philosophical system of justification. The central concern of his theory of democracy is the question of appropriate representation. With this concern, he marks an accent that is more political than the equally reconstructive, but much more normative, position represented by Axel Honneth (2011; Arentshorst 2016). In a similar way to Rosanvallon, the philosophical question of the foundation of norms has been recently transformed into a question of thinking in possibilities open to experiences (Möllers 2015). This kind of democratic reflection has to be understood as an opening, facing what is democratically possible with regard to its history of experiences. Even as a regime of institutionalized self-critique and self-reflection, democracy cannot fully overcome its constitutive indetermination.

BIBLIOGRAPHY

Arentshorst, Hans (2016): "Towards a reconstructive approach in political philosophy. Rosanvallon and Honneth on the pathologies of today's democracy." In: Thesis Eleven 134 (1), pp. 42-55.
Aron, Raymond (1967): Les étappes de la pensée sociologique, Paris: Gallimard.
Aron, Raymond (1997): Introduction à la philosophie politique. Démocratie et revolution, Paris: Le Livre de poche.
Audier, Serge (2004): Tocqueville retrouvé. Genèse et enjeux du renouveau tocquevillien français, Paris: VRIN.
Colliot-Thélène, Catherine (2018): Democracy and Subjective Rights: Democracy without Demos, London: ECPR Press.
Furet, François/Julliard, Jacques/Rosanvallon, Pierre (1988): La République du centre. La fin de l'exception française, Paris: Calmann-Lévy.
Gauchet, Marcel (1997): "Benjamin Constant: L'illusion lucide du libéralisme." In: Marcel Gauchet (ed.), Benjamin Constant: Écrits politiques, Paris: Gallimard, pp. 12-110.
Gauchet, Marcel (2005): "Tocqueville, l'Amérique et nous. Sur la genèse des sociétés démocratiques." In: Marcel Gauchet (ed.), La condition politique, Paris: Gallimard, pp. 305-404.
Hamon, Hervé/Rotman, Patrick (1984): La deuxième gauche. Histoire intellectuelle et politique de la CFDT, Paris: Gallimard.
Hirschman, Albert O. (1977): The Passions and the Interests. Arguments for Capitalism before its Triumph, Princeton: Princeton UP.
Honneth, Axel (2011): Das Recht der Freiheit. Grundriß einer demokratischen Sittlichkeit, Berlin: Suhrkamp.

Jaume, Lucien (1989): Le discours jacobin et la démocratie, Paris: Fayard.

Judt, Tony (1990): Marxism and the French Left: Studies on Labour and Politics in France 1830-1982, Oxford: Clarendon.

Lefort, Claude (1972): Le travail de l'oeuvre Machiavel, Paris: Gallimard.

Lefort, Claude (1992): "Tocqueville: démocratie et art d'écrire." In: Claude Lefort, Écrire. À l'épreuve du politique, Paris: Calmann-Lévy, pp. 55–90.

Mélonio, Françoise (1993): Tocqueville et les Français, Paris: Fayard.

Möllers, Christoph (2015): Die Möglichkeit der Norm. Über eine Praxis jenseits von Moralität und Kausalität, Berlin: Suhrkamp.

Müller, Jan-Werner (2016): Was ist Populismus?, Berlin: Suhrkamp.

Raphael, Lutz (2013): "Demokratiegeschichte als Problemgeschichte und Gegenwartsanalyse. Das Werk Pierre Rosanvallons." In: Neue Politische Literatur 58, pp. 7-20.

Rosanvallon, Pierre (1976): L'Âge de l'autogestion, Paris: Seuil.

Rosanvallon, Pierre (1977): Pour une nouvelle culture politique, Paris: Seuil.

Rosanvallon, Pierre (1979): Le capitalisme utopique, Paris: Seuil.

Rosanvallon, Pierre (1983): Misère de l'économie, Paris: Seuil.

Rosanvallon, Pierre (1985): Le moment Guizot, Paris: Gallimard.

Rosanvallon, Pierre (1985a): "Préface: Le Gramsci de la bourgeoisie." In: Pierre Rosanvallon. (ed.), François Guizot: Histoire de la civilisation en Europe, Paris: Hachette, pp. 9-18.

Rosanvallon, Pierre (1988): La question syndicale. Histoire et avenir d'une forme sociale, Paris: Calmann-Lévy.

Rosanvallon, Pierre (1990): L'État en France de 1789 à nos jours, Paris: Seuil.

Rosanvallon, Pierre (1992): Le sacre du citoyen. Histoire du suffrage universel en France, Paris: Gallimard.

Rosanvallon, Pierre (1994): La monarchie impossible. Les Chartes de 1814 et de 1830, Paris: Fayard.

Rosanvallon, Pierre (1998): Le peuple introuvable. Histoire de la représentation démocratique en France, Paris: Gallimard.

Rosanvallon, Pierre (2000): La démocratie inachevée. Histoire de la souveraineté du peuple en France, Paris: Gallimard.

Rosanvallon, Pierre (2003): Pour une histoire conceptuelle du politique, Paris: Seuil.

Rosanvallon, Pierre (2004): Le modèle politique français. La société civile contre le jacobinisme de 1789 à nos jours, Paris: Seuil.

Rosanvallon, Pierre (2006): La contre-démocratie. La politique à l'âge de la défiance, Paris: Seuil.

Rosanvallon, Pierre (2008): La legitimité démocratique. Impartialité, reflexivité, proximité, Paris: Seuil.
Rosanvallon, Pierre (2011): La société des égaux, Paris: Seuil.
Rosanvallon, Pierre (2014): Le parlement des invisibles, Paris: Seuil.
Rosanvallon, Pierre (2015): Le bon gouvernement, Paris: Seuil.
Schulz, Daniel (2009): "Minderheit, Mehrheit, Allgemeinheit: Die Krise der Repräsentation im Spannungsfeld des französischen Republikanismus bei Pierre Rosanvallon." In: Soraya Nour (ed.), The Minorities Issue: Law and the Crisis of Representation, Berlin: Duncker & Humblot, pp. 103-116.
Schulz, Daniel (2015): Die Krise des Republikanismus, Baden-Baden: Nomos.
Weymans, Wim (2004): "Pierre Rosanvallon und das Problem der politischen Repräsentation." In: Oliver Flügel/Reinhard Heil/Andreas Hetzel (eds.), Die Rückkehr des Politischen: Demokratietheorien heute, Darmstadt: Wissenschaftliche Buchgesellschaft, pp. 87-112.
Weymans, Wim (2006): "Freiheit durch politische Repräsentation – Lefort, Gauchet und Rosanvallon über die Beziehung zwischen Staat und Gesellschaft." In: Reinhard Heil/Andreas Hetzel (eds.), Die unendliche Aufgabe. Kritik und Perspektiven der Demokratietheorie, Bielefeld: transcript, pp. 185-207.
Weymans, Wim (2007): "Understanding the present through the past? Quentin Skinner and Pierre Rosanvallon on the crisis of political representation." In: Redescriptions. Yearbook of Political Thought, Conceptual History and Feminist Theory, pp. 45–60.
Weymans, Wim (2015): "Demokratie als Gesellschaftsform. Pierre Rosanvallon und die vielfältigen Stimmen des Volkes." In: Oliver Flügel-Martinsen/Franziska Martinsen (eds.), Demokratietheorie und Staatskritik aus Frankreich. Neuere Diskurse und Perspektiven, Stuttgart: Steiner, pp. 167–185.

10 Organizing the Political

Understanding the Crisis of Democracy with Rosanvallon

Felix Heidenreich

INTRODUCTION

Although the debate on the crisis of democracy seems to date back to the earliest days of democracy, a fundamental shift seems to be taking place in western established democracies (Della Porta 2013). The diagnosis that liberal representative democracy is in acute danger is not an overstatement: Donald Trump, the situation in countries such as Hungary or Poland, even the latest developments in Austria make it obvious that "democracy" is not just an institutional framework which, once it is established, will prevail. On the contrary, the developments in many countries show that a democratic framework relies on democratic virtues that need to be reproduced in a vivid civic society. In fact, it may be true that the American democracy has seen severe crisis before. However, the continental European experience tells us that democrats should not rely on democracy to save itself.

It is important to see that the term "crisis" is, in itself, a conceptual framework which implies specific assumptions. Wolfgang Merkel has argued that the "crisis" refers to an imaginary in which a point of decision is reached. Just as in a medical crisis the patient will either survive and get better soon, or die: A crisis always has a tipping-point (Merkel 2015). Merkel therefore proposes to conceptualise the current situation rather as a process of *erosion*, a term that describes a slow and mostly unnoticed process in which the social pre-conditions in which democracy is "embedded" (Merkel 2004) are slowly questioned. Rising social inequality, the erosion of democratic discourse and the loss of democratic control caused by globalisation then destroy democracy without making an autocratic takeover necessary

(Merkel 2015b: 490).[1] David Runciman's description of "how democracy ends" takes a similar stance, since he also emphasises that we should not mislead ourselves over a stretched comparison with the classic forms of totalitarianism such as fascism or Stalinism. The end of democracy may come slowly and calmly, without people in uniforms parading the streets (Runciman 2018).

A third concept (or guiding metaphor) that might be used in this context is "decline". The "decline of democracy" describes a rather different aspect of the changes in the system of international relations; it points to the relative loss of influence and importance of democracies in comparison to autocratic regimes such as Russia or China. The *Journal of Democracy* has recently outlined this perspective at great length. What appears to be a "crisis" of democracy could also be viewed as a process in which democracies simply are pushed into the defensive against autocratic foes. It is well known that the Russian government has a systematic policy which aims at destabilizing established democracies. To what degree turmoil, populist movements and polarization are the result of external interference is, however, hard to say.

Pierre Rosanvallon has on several occasions outlined a fourth perspective that can be summarized in the term of *malaise*, or, to use the Freudian term, discontent (*Unbehagen*). He points out that democracy inevitably produces dissatisfaction by making promises it cannot keep: "the people" is an entity that cannot be identified once and for all (*le people introuvable*); it can therefore only be imperfectly represented by elections, parliaments or government. Democracy therefore always produces discontent and an important task of political theory is to explain why these frustrations are partly essential to democracy.[2]

However, Rosanvallon provides a conceptual framework which allows us to gain a new perspective on one of the most important battlegrounds in the crisis of democracy: the broken relationship between citizens and politicians, between "the people" and the elites. In his book on counter-democracy Rosanvallon gives an inspiring description of how this relation was organized in different democratic frameworks. John Keanes' term of "monitory democracy" allows a comparison to

---

[1] In 2015 Merkel explicitly stated that right-wing parties in Switzerland, Austria, Scandinavia or France were problematic but neither capable nor willing to destroy democracy (cp. Merkel 2015b: 492). It can be doubted if this optimistic view is still realistic as the situation in countries such as Austria, Poland or Hungary has changed dramatically.

[2] I have compared the four guiding concepts – crisis, erosions, decline and discontent at great length: cp. Heidenreich 2017.

another attempt to understand the constant tension between political actors and their citizens.

The debate on Rosanvallon as a political theorist is just about to start; his books have often been viewed as contributions to the history of ideas – which, of course, they are. However, recent attempts to view his work also as a contribution to the debate on the theory of democracy have triggered a new debate.[3] In particular his book on counter-democracy has been discussed (cf. Schmitter/Porter/Warren 2010, Dahlgren 2012; Della Porta 2012), although it may look as if Rosanvallon's defence of the decisive role of civil society may be, in the Anglo-Saxon world, not sufficiently innovative to provoke a major debate (whereas it is of great interest in France where the Republican idea has since 1789 questioned self-organizing civil society) (Moyn 2015).[4]

A second reason for the rather cautious reception of Rosanvallon on the international level may be found in his extraordinary method. As Paula Diehl and Daniel Schulz have pointed out, Rosanvallon practices an approach of historical reconstruction which is directly opposed to all attempts to "ground" political ideas in deductive operations (Diehl/Schulz 2012: 287). This reconstructive approach becomes a true challenge for the reader, since all the decisive arguments are developed by going through a vast amount of historical material.

It is in particular in the first and the last chapter that Rosanvallon gives a conceptional account of his view: The term 'counter-democracy' serves to give a more in-depth comprehension of the crisis of democracy without pretending to allow a simple way out of this crisis. His approach therefore allows us to question some illusions about democracy and to adapt our expectations to a more realistic level, in particular in regard to the idea of a political representation without distortion: Not feeling "properly" represented is a default-setting in democracy.[5] Therefore, in Rosanvallon's view the options for organizing counter-democracy are always a choice between options that provide specific solutions–and with them, specific problems. His book would be misunderstood if it was taken for a plea for more counter-democratic mechanism. The task is rather to give a precise description of the different ways in which democracies organize counter-democratic institutions.

---

3 For Germany cp.: Weymans 2004, 2006, Diehl/Schulz 2012, Schulz 2015: 178-197.
4 Samuel Moyn recalls the attempts by Mark Lilla to get Rosanvallon's books translated into English. In the USA, Rosanvallon is basically viewed as a researcher in the field of the History of Ideas (cp. Moyn 2015: 65f.).
5 Also cp.: Rosanvallon 1998.

The fact that Rosanvallon's systematic contributions to political theory sometimes risk being concealed under the mass of historical references may have contributed to the hesitant reception. In contrast to Michel Foucault, Hans Blumenberg, Niklas Luhmann or Charles Taylor, Rosanvallon has chosen to only rarely publish programmatic texts to complement his work. Only in interviews or in his inaugural talk at the *Collège de France* does he gives a hint that allows us to decipher his method (Rosanvallon 1995; 2012; also see: Guénard 2015). The reader is therefore confronted with a way of writing the history of ideas (and practices!) which connects historical examples with contemporary empirical research and thereby allows analogies that bridge time and place –one of the major allurements of his writing.

This paper aims at giving a comprehensive account of the term counter-democracy and tries to sketch its potentials and limits. In what way does the idea of counter-democracy help to understand the relation between citizens and elites, voters and their representatives? In order to answer this question, I first will take a closer look at Rosanvallon's view of the crisis of democracy (2.). I then will try to define what he calls counter-democracy (3.) and compare it to Keanes' concept of "monitory democracy" (4.). I will then sketch consequences concerning our concept of populism (5.) and try to re-frame the tension between "politics" and "the political" by referring to Rosanvallon (6.). My final remark will raise the question of whether, and to what degree, Rosanvallon's political theory is based on assumptions linked to the French tradition of Republicanism. Maybe counter-democracy is not an answer to the crisis of democracy, but also partly one of the causes. Mechanisms and institutions of counter-democracy could then be viewed as attempts to *organize the political*, i.e. to give the tension between politics and the political a *form*, that allows civil society and the "corps intermédiaires" to operate properly. Political parties, I argue, would have to play a much larger role in Rosanvallon's analysis (7.).

1. THE QUESTION TO WHICH THE CONCEPT OF COUNTER-DEMOCRACY IS THE ANSWER

Rosanvallon starts his book on counter-democracy by sketching a panoramic picture of the contemporary crisis of democracy, pointing in particular to the importance of trust and mistrust in democracy. His first major point is that democracies all over the world are in a state of "malaise", of discontent, referring to Freud's idea of an inevitable mismatch between the biological and psychological condition of Man on the one hand and modern culture on the other, which forces him to control and tame his nature constantly.

Rosanvallon refuses to contrast the contemporary state of democracy with its often purely imagined golden ages or sheer ideals. In the view of many citizens, he argues, democracy does not keep its promises. This is why many voters, in Eastern Europe in particular, leave politics behind altogether. The declines in participation both in elections and with political parties are the key-indicators for this growing discontent. Before taking a closer look at these new modes of participation, Rosanvallon zealously points out that a certain mismatch between expectations towards democracy and the real outcome can be expected: Democracy always produces "promises" and "deceptions" at the same time. It is both a privilege and a rather unpleasant imposition. All forms of democracy are necessarily imperfect. However, this doesn't mean that back then, in an imagined golden age of democracy, everything was better or "more democratic".

In spite of joining the choir of pessimists (in France the "déclinisme" has become a whole literary sub-genre) Rosanvallon proposes to change the viewpoint. The first step to do so is to deconstruct the myth of the passive citizen. Citizens are neither passive nor are they disinterested in politics, Rosanvallon claims. However, the *demos* seeks other channels in order to express its voice.

The history of democracy would be insufficiently reconstructed if we were to exclude all the informal ways and strategies "that serve to compensate the erosion of trust in organisations by organizing mistrust" (Rosanvallon 2006: 12). The idea of a crisis therefore looks less dramatic if the history of democracy is seen as a series of techniques of channelling counter-power. James Madison and Benjamin Constant are classic examples of such a strategy invoked by Rosanvallon since they explicitly stated that democracy needs to be viewed as a form of governance that institutionalizes mistrust of citizens against representatives. In particular the liberal tradition has produced arguments, mechanisms and workflows that seek to contain the expression of an unlimited sovereignty of the people.

Rosanvallon proposes to summarize all these practices and institutions in the term "counter-democracy". Although he does not give a definition in the strict sense (*genus proximum, differentia specifica*), he continues by characterizing counter-democracy:

"Counter-Democracy is by no means the opposite of democracy. It is rather a form of democracy working against the other democracy. It is a democracy of disseminated and indirect forces, a democracry of mistrust opposed to the democracy which is legitimized by elections. This counter-democracy forms a system of legal democratic institutions. It aims at enlarging and expanding its impact; at the same time it is a counter-power. In order to be understood and anlayzised as such, it needs to be considered as a true political form. The work at hand tries to characterise and evaluate it." (Rosanvallon 20016: 16, transl. F.H.)

It is of great importance that Rosanvallon in an almost logical sense takes the difference between democracy and counter-democracy for a *categorical* difference. Producing a democratic decision can be obtained by formulating preferences – or by negating options. In the same sense Rosanvallon distinguishes between two kinds of sovereignty. "In the shadow of a 'positive' sovereignty [...]" there is a "negative social sovereignty" (ibid: 21). Rosanvallon seems to refer to Hegel's term of "abstract negation". The contestation of political mass can take the form of an undefined "not that!".[6] It does not necessarily have to imply a positive vision of what is to be done. "Negative sovereignty" does not need to elaborate consistent policy-packages. This is why "negative majorities" (ibid: 21) are more easily established.[7]

The mode of expressing political preferences however does have ramifications for the subject of this expression. The subject of counter-democracy is more heterogeneous, ephemeral, a fluid *demos*, agreeing only on what needs to be stopped. The limitational concept (*Grenzbegriff*) of this tendency would be a "veto-*demos*" (ibid: 22). The driving engine of the political process would then not be a positive vote, but just a chain of objections by citizens to which the representatives have to react. As this veto-*demos* forms and reforms more or less spontaneously, it becomes more and more difficult for elites to anticipate the objections and their impact. The reactive mode of contemporary politics, the lack of vision and plan, the complete absence of utopic ideas, can then be read as a result of these heterogeneous claims of different veto-*demos*.

In the citation one concept however peeks out: *form*. Rosanvallon here seems to formulate an implicit distance to Foucault. While Foucault had on several occasions underscored the undefined, "formless" character of contestations against governmentalities[8], Rosanvallon points to the potential of taking a form already present in the abstract negation. The counter-democracy Rosanvallon has in mind

---

6   The best example for this "abstract negation" seems to be the formula "dégage!" that the Tunisian opposition used in order to chase Ben Ali out of the country. "Dégage!" is best translated as "buzz off!".

7   Amartya Sen made a similar point in "The Idea of Freedom" by taking a closer look at the coalition which made the end of slavery possible.

8   Cp. e.g. the famous text "What is critique?" (Foucault 1996).

is a form-seeking kind of objection, a protest condensing in constitutions, organisations, courts, becoming, in Hegel's terms, *substance*. It might be helpful to illustrate this point briefly.

2. COUNTER-DEMOCRACY: SURVEILLANCE, HINDERING, SUING

a) Surveillance or oversight

The way in which Rosanvallon re-interprets Foucauldian terminology is most obvious in the case of his analysis of surveillance. He claims that Foucault's work was "ground-breaking" (Rosanvallon 2006: 37), but at the same time he aims to show that Foucault missed the decisive point of modern surveillance technology. While Foucault used the paradigm of Bentham's *panopticon* in which a centre observes the periphery, Rosanvallon argues that the direction of the observational power has shifted 180 degrees: It's the periphery which observes the centre, and it's the citizens that have a constant grip on politicians and exercise power by observation. The representatives today are subjects of a constant control, followed by smartphone-cameras and hackers, moving through a *panopticon* that is ready to use anything against them, be it private or public.

Rosanvallon claims that this mechanism starts to be established in the late 18th century: Democracy also implies accountability in the sense of a quasi-religious need to justify one's actions. Although the control of the representatives by the citizens has a long history, it's the technological innovations of our time that let mechanism escalate. The critical public can target absolutely everyone. In many cases – and here Rosanvallon seems to join Foucault again – it is not the actual interference, but the anticipated control, the internalisation of imperatives and expectations which guides the behaviour. The unnatural way of speaking that some politicians practice (called "langue de bois" in French), the professional preparation of well-calibrated "wordings", the politically correct empty talk, could therefore also be interpreted as a defensive strategy that helps to cope with the constant control: It shows captives trying to gain the benevolence and favor of their observers.

Rosanvallon's main interest however does not focus on these "pathological" forms of citizens' involvement. His core point is that mistrust is needed to keep representatives doing what they are supposed to do. The trust expressed in elections needs counter-democratic correlates to counter-balance the relation.

The centrepiece of "surveillance" is of course a critical public sphere – and in this regard there seems to be an important convergence with the theory of Jürgen Habermas. In the view of Habermas, a democratic public sphere needs to be well-structured; there need to be clear lines drawn between the informal communication in families and among friends (the so-called "Life-World") on the one hand and then the broader public sphere of journals and television on the other hand. The "political system" in the narrow sense forms a third sub-genre of public sphere, the sphere of parliamentary debate, of constitutional courts or government press-conference. Habermas had always argued that democracy gets into trouble when the differences between these sub-spheres dissolve, when politicians talk as if they were in the bar with friends, when journalists pretend to be normal citizens or when rhetorical standards in parliaments perish.[9] I will get back to this important point later on.

(b) *Prevention – the right to object*: The second dimension of counter-democratic practices is called prevention (*empêcher*). The right to organize a strike plays a key-role for Rosanvallon; this tool of counter-democracy has for many years been an important element to prevent reform in France.

In the case of prevention, the advantages of abstract negation mentioned above kick in: 'X' can be prevented without proposing a 'Y'. Rosanvallon claims that prevention has become a dominant tool in modern democracies.[10]

It must however be noted that successful practices of prevention in general are put in place not by spontaneous groups, but by institutions that can operate in a well-established pattern. Constitutional courts, labour unions and other "veto-players" (Tsebelis 2002) have the best chances of successful prevention.

b) Taking to court/suing/condemning – the people that accuses

When Rosanvallon talks about the "people that judges" or the "people as a judge" ("le peuple-juge") he tries to coin a term which is able to catch all the practices of citizens attacking representatives via the judicial system. *Impeachment* and *recall* are the most obvious examples, but we could also think of the possibilities to coun-

---

9   Cp. in particular „Between Facts and Norms" (Habermas 1998).
10 The generalisations he produces in this context are not always convincing: "Nous sommes entrés dans un âge indissociablement faible et négatif du politique." (Rosanvallon 2006: 191) Who exactly is the "we"? Since when exactly have we entered this stage of negativity?

ter specific political decisions with the tools of administrative law. German administrative law defines that a priori every decision made by an administration can be taken to court by citizens. Rosanvallon emphasizes that in Athens political citizens were always voters and judges, as Aristotle underscored (Rosanvallon 2006: 199ff.). Citizens *literally* becoming judges therefore is the most extreme form of this kind of counter-democracy. In Rosanvallon's view these mechanisms have a compensational function; they repair what has been broken elsewhere.[11]

When taking the common law as the norm, the picture would look rather different. Law and the rule of law here have always been the decisive tool of the civil society to oppose aristocratic tyranny. Law here is not about compensating a democratic sovereignty going wild, but about defending individual sovereignty in the first place. From an Anglo-Saxon point of view, the 'rule of law' precedes the sovereignty of the people and does not just compensate its flaws.

However, Rosanvallon goes even farther: He claims that a second source of law has been created in counsels, juries and commissions. He calls those circles the "shadow-law-makers" ("législateur de l'ombre") which side-line the law-making in parliaments. An important example he gives is the ACLU, the most important American Association of human-rights interested lawyers that keeps pressure on the legal system in order to prevent violations of human rights. (ibid: 227ff.). Rosanvallon does not in detail discuss the fact that other lobbying organizations with rather different agendas take influence also. Couldn't we imagine a history of "counter-democracy" which sketches these practices as attempts of elites to counter the will of the people? Rosanvallon seems to insinuate that in counter-democratic practices the subaltern get a voice. This view can be contested. In many cases counter-democratic mechanisms can be used to silence the voice of the excluded.

The ability to "take to court" is oftentimes an option linked to a specific knowledge that can be found among the elite rather than among the oppressed. Gandhi and Martin Luther King may be counter-examples (in particular Gandhi who was a lawyer), but they are not the norm.

However there is a flip-side to the counter-democratic practices of taking political issues to court. Dealing with politics in terms of law has a ramification on the way we view the law: Not only is politics perceived in juridical terms, but the law is also politicised. Courts run the risk of turning into the stage of a political

---

11 The exact quote is: „[...] contre-pouvoirs [...] *destinés à compenser l'érosion de la confiance par une organisation de la défiance*" (ibid: 12, original emphasis). From a liberal point of view, counter-democracy is a lot more than just compensation.

mise en scène (ibid: 240). Moreover, the difference between the result of an election and the result of a judicial process may dissolve. This is true in particular when we think of a commission of inquiry. These commissions emulate the form of judicial process, although they have mainly a political function. They can force politicians to resign, but they cannot put citizens into jail. The act of judging or "bringing to court" therefore has its clear limits.

The third dimension of counter-democracy also shows that in many cases counter-democratic practices look bottom-up driven, but are mainly dependent on elites, on lawyers and on specialists of administrative law.

3. TRUST AND MISTRUST IN COUNTER-DEMOCRACY AND "MONITORY DEMOCRACY" (JOHN KEANE)

Linking Rosanvallon's analysis to long debate on trust and mistrust in democracy might help to shed some more light on this concept. Piotr Sztompka has pointed out an important tension that dominates the relation of democracy and its institutions to its citizens. On the one hand democratic institutions need to allow citizens to express their mistrust and to take seriously their suspicion: "people are more prepared to trust institutions and other people if the social organization in which they operate insures them against potential breaches of trust" (Sztompka 1999: 143). Some forms of counter-democratic control might therefore increase the trust of citizens in elites. Sztompka however draws a clear distinction between the possibility of control and actual control: Counter-democratic mechanisms of control only increase trust if they are not used too often and if their possibility has a disciplining effect.[12] In order to show in which way Rosanvallon deals with this ambivalence, I will briefly draw a comparison to John Keanes' concept of "monitory democracy".

Keane for the first time used the term "monitory democracy" in his book *The Life and Death of Democracy* (2009) and then gave a more detailed outline in an article in 2011. Keane makes a rather brief reference to Rosanvallon (Keane 2011:

---

12 "Democratic principles institutionalize distrust because they assume that trust can potentially be breached and provide correctives for such a contingency. The fact that the principles are put to use, that the corrective mechanisms are activated, controls actually applied, indicates that trust had in fact been breached. As long as this happens sporadically, exceptionally, as a last resort, the culture of trust is not undermined, but rather enhanced by the confirmation of effective accountability. But there is some threshold where this may backfire and the trend reverses itself." (Sztompka 1999: 145-6)

216), and it might almost look like there was no huge difference between the two concepts. Keane too does not give a strict definition, but rather a characterization: "Monitory democracy is the age of surveys, focus groups, deliberative polling, online petitions and audience and customer voting." (Ibid: 214; also see Keane 2009: xxvii f.)

Rosanvallon and Keane both agree on the rise of mechanisms of control and objection in modern democracies. However, a first important difference concerns the details of this historical thesis. While Rosanvallon claims that "counter-democracy" has from the beginning of democracy been an important dimension of democratic rule, since it is in a sense the logical correlate of input-legitimacy, Keane states that the rise of "monitory democracy" only begins after 1945 (Keane 2009: xxvii; Keane 2011: 213). Since Keane does not only use the term for contestation in the strict sense, but rather for all kinds of input from civil society (Keane 2011: 215), everything which isn't part of the electoral political system somehow is part of "monitory democracy".

Linked to this widening of the concept, a second element is to be noted: Whereas the classical representative democracy has some clearly defined borders (ibid: 217), *monitory democracy* forms a network of transnational actors that operate across borders. *Monitory democracy* can be practised by foundations and NGOs, but also by more dubious actors and agents, prepared to instrumentalize the mechanisms of monitory democracy for specific purposes (Keane 2009: 695f.). Rosanvallon however seems not to take the de-territorializing effect of counter-democracy for an important side-effect. His examples mainly refer to structures and procedures in nation-states or clearly defined political entities such as the EU.

A *third* central difference can be found in the way the two authors conceptualise the relation between counter-democracy and monitory democracy and the media. The difference in the historical thesis already makes it clear that from Rosanvallon's point of view counter-democracy may use different media, but is not essentially linked to them. Keane in contrast views the rise of modern media after 1945 as the decisive trigger for the rise of monitory democracy. The media bring *monitory democracy* in "communicative abundance" (ibid: 736) into life in the same way a new offer creates new demand. (Keane 2011: 229). Keane also argues that inequalities in the use and competence of modern media therefore pose a major threat to democratic equalities. Most of the time, it's the elites in media that use the tools of monitory democracy in order to make things go their way, thereby side-lining the equalizing effect of elections.

The fact that Rosanvallon and Keane take these different perspectives makes them also deal differently with the paradox that Sztompka outlined so well. Both agree that there can be a certain effect of over-using a tool, which then backfires and acts counter to the original intention: Control is hoped to make trust possible; however, if control is over-used only mistrust will be created. Keane argues in this way when he talks about political media in general. Too much political information, he claims, might trigger what is called "wilful ignorance" (Keane 2009: 747).[13] In Rosanvallon's analysis, it's the overdoses of counter-democratic practices that produce a populist attitude which intends to establish identity of represented citizens and representatives in order to re-establish credibility in politics. Let's take a brief look at this theory of populism.[14]

4. POPULISM AS A PATHOLOGICAL FORM OF COUNTER-DEMOCRACY

Rosanvallon does not only expound with great zeal the ambivalences of counter-democratic practices. He also tries to join his arguments together in order to propose a genuine theory of populism which he views as a "pathology of counter-democracy" (Rosanvallon 2006: 257ff). The starting point of this pathology is an imbalance in the relation of democracy and counter-democracy. Forms of "negative sovereignty" can – by blocking all possible options – literally replace the positive sovereignty that is expressed in elections or referendums (ibid: 257). Rosanvallon also calls this phenomenon a form of political consumerism: Citizens start to behave like spoiled kids, refusing all kinds of positive propositions without formulating propositions themselves: *Not in my backyard*. In reaction to this attitude, representatives try to find the path of least resistance, aiming to avoid all decisions that might wake up the Behemoth of contestation. The observation of the elites provokes a kind of non-politics, sometimes hiding behind the formula *there is no alternative*.

It is this mechanism that explains in Rosanvallon's view the rise of governance-technologies and governance–research. Administration and politics are being intertwined in order to form a network that manages to avoid or buffer counter-democracy. Rosanvallon claims that "hierarchic systems" (ibid: 265) allowed more accountability – a thesis that can be questioned. It could be argued – and

---

13 Concerning the "diverse faces" of "standby citizens" also cp.: Amna/Ekman 2013.
14 Both approaches at the same time invite us to re-consider the upsides of classical elections. The convergence of both approaches is evident: Keane fears political apathy; Rosanvallon is afraid of counter-democratic hyper-activity. It could be argued that in many cases both attitudes replace each other in a constant back and forth.

Foucault would be a classic source of this idea – that the self-representation of power as pyramidal powers with well-defined centres and sovereign power have always been fictional self-descriptions that served to legitimize power. Anyway, at least the regulatory idea of accountable top-down responsibility seems to be questioned in modern societies (also see Rosanvallon 2015).

In the case of counter-democratic mechanisms losing their moderation, the centre of power is imagined as a strong network of elitist circles that can only be taken over with extreme counter-democratic measures. In the case of populism surveillance, contestation and hindering can take the extreme form of a complete deconstruction of democratic power. Political representatives are then taken for criminals, and the distinction of friend and foe is becoming the dominant mind-set in an aggressive political rhetoric. This mind-set can use different ideological patterns such as nationalism, socialism or extreme liberalism.

Not the ideological core is decisive, Rosanvallon claims, but the counter-democratic form of populism. Rosanvallon's formal definition of populism – populism as an extreme form of counter-democracy – puts the emphasis on the co-evolution of counter-democracy and populism.

Populism in this framework can be interpreted as a reaction to the crisis of political representation and de-politicisation combined with the refusal to take part in "positive" productive input-aggregation. This would also allow for drawing a sharp line between populism and nationalism: Populism is about being "against" the elites in an abstract sense. Once in power, the populist and nationalist movements have to end their populist protest against elites and have to start formulating "positive" decisions.

This distinction seems to make sense, since populists indeed often express an abstract feeling of dissatisfaction. However, in many cases populist movements and parties do a lot more than this. The *Front National* in France actually does formulate rather concrete political propositions. Can there be another *differentia specifica* of populist movements? It could be argued that the core element of populist thought consists in an idea of political representation that imagines the identity of the representatives and the represented. The leader is thought to represent a homogenous people without any distortion. In this case populist communication could have both a "democratic" (by input) and "counter-democratic" (surveillance, contestation or hindering) spin.

Rosanvallon's concept of populism only allows practical conclusions in a limited way. The thin red line between "sane" and "pathological" counter-democracy is hard to draw. When exactly does mistrust towards representatives become "pathological"? When is the idea of "the people as the judge" populist? In Rosanvallon's definition populism seems to become a problem of dosage. Maybe the more decisive point is to be found in the way the "people" is imagined and represented.

Rosanvallon seems to have seen himself that it is hard to define populism by reference to the concept of counter-democracy. In a more extensive paper on populism he proposes three elements of populist thought: an "identitarian" concept of the *demos*, an over-simplified view of political procedures and the central role of the distinction between friend and foe (Rosanvallon 2011: 6ff).

5. COUNTER-DEMOCRACY AS AN ALTERNATIVE TO A ROMANTIC VISION OF PROTEST

Rosanvallon has a tendency to mark differences to other theories of democracy only by elegant allusions. His approach of reconstruction evidently underscores the elements that let his vision look stronger while excluding opposing views.[15] However, it is not hard to see against what kind of theories and philosophers his work is also pointed. His work does not only oppose a simplistic vision of political representation, but also contradicts a romantic vision of protest. The legitimation of political power by elections and representation, in contrast needs to be reconciled with the counter-democratic mechanisms, he claims. The contradiction between these two sources of legitimacy needs to turn out as false contradiction. This vision is aimed against all those who – claiming to be 'radical'– hope that counter-democratic grassroots participation may one day not only complement but *replace* the classical form of election. The German sociologist Niklas Luhmann has described a certain tendency to oppose "the system" whilst being part of it in the German left-wing movements of the 1970s (Luhmann 1996: 156). It is the same paradoxical gesture of being radical inside a system that Rosanvallon seems to have in mind when he shows that "counter-democracy" has been, for hundreds of years, part of the democracy. There is no such thing as a "radical", "authentic", "original" or "real" democracy outside democracy. Rosanvallon's political thinking therefore strongly opposes any kind of political romanticism that operates with an unmediated distinction of "politics" and "the political".

A brief comparison with Alain Badiou may help to draw this line more sharply. Badiou's distinction between "sheer politics" on the one hand and the political "happening" (*événemment*) seems to reproduce in an ideal-type clarity the distinction Rosanvallon opposes. Badiou distinguishes between changes that keep the

---

15 Here some methodological questions arise in a similar way as for Honneth's "normative reconstruction".

rules of the game intact, and incidences that change the rules. In one case we are witnessing pseudo-reforms, in the other we see a true revolution going on. In this framework "politics" turns into a bad version of "the political"; all the classical procedures of democracy (elections, parliaments etc.) that look like obstacles to a "true" revolution. Even the mechanisms of counter-democracy are viewed to be part of the "system" since they only accompany the democratic mechanisms without ever really questioning them. In contrast Rosanvallon's phenomenology of democratic procedures tries to show that *the political* and *politics* are always intertwined, that extraordinary moves can slowly change the rules of the game without looking like an incidence of revolutionary scope.[16]

6. ORGANIZING THE POLITICAL

The idea that Rosanvallon's concept of counter-democracy could also be read as an attempt to answer some radical-democratic ideas very present in the French public sphere implies a possible critique. Since it could be argued that Rosanvallon's vision of counter-democracy is intensely linked to the specific situation in France, I therefore want to discuss possible objections against Rosanvallon.

(a) A French answer to a French problem? Rosanvallon himself states that many of the counter-democratic practices he analyses are part of the classical toolbox of democracy, in particular of the liberal tradition. Could the term 'counter-democracy' probably give an answer to a question that only arises in France, under the specific condition of French republicanism? Pointing to the elements of counter-democracy as necessary counter-elements against a sovereignty of the people that risks to trump individual rights – this could be viewed as a Rousseauist scenario. Defending constitutional courts, legal limits, rights to object to political decisions, defending also the "corps intermédiaires" seems to be necessary only where republicanism has systematically questioned these elements. In Great Britain, where civil society always continued to play an important role (e.g. in education) none of these elements seem to be very of interest since they are completely normal and trivial. Counter-democracy would then be just another term for "liberal democracy".

---

16 In his inaugural speech for the *Collège de France* Rosanvallon states this aim quite clearly. "In fact it is never easy to distinguish the sublime from the ordinary, the small egoistic calculations from the great ambitions, the impressing language of truth from the scams of manipulation, the consideration of long-term effects from practical constraint." (Rosanvallon 2012: 63, transl. F.H.)

The fact that individual defensive rights should allow every citizen to oppose political decisions by referring to the idea of a *rule of law* just seems to be a classical liberal idea. Jürgen Habermas has outlined this idea in an important paper on the co-originality of the liberal idea of the rule of law on the one hand and the republican idea of the people's sovereignty on the other (Habermas 1994). In Rosanvallon's terminology operating under French presuppositions, "democracy" and "counter-democracy" seem to take the place of "sovereignty of the people" and "rule of law". Sovereignty of the people without the rule of law is despotism; the rule of law without the sovereignty of the people is expertocracy. The "counter-democracy" then might be misleading, because it suggests that the rule of law is in some way an opposite to democracy. Rosanvallon's view makes sense when outlined in the context of a post-revolutionary France with a civil society (*les corps intermédiaires*) almost destroyed by a centralised Republic. In his book *Le modèle politique français* (2004) he takes a closer look at the specificities of the French experience and reconstructs the Jacobin attack against the *corps intermédiare* in France (ibid: 432).

However, the fact that Rosanvallon gives a French answer to a French problem does not need to be problematic. It could also mean that something more general can be learned from the specific French perspective. The question then would be not if there are counter-democratic mechanisms, but rather how they work and how they are institutionalized. The heuristic framework of democracy/counter-democracy then could be used in order to compare different ways of organizing *surveillance*, *prevention* or *taking to court*. The different variations of counter-democracy then become of great interest. The term 'counter-democracy' would then name a neo-institutionalist question pointing at the legal frameworks that allow a productive collision of democracy and counter-democracy. I would like to elaborate on this point by taking a closer look at political parties.

(b) *Organizing the political – in political parties.* It is surprising to see that in Rosanvallon's book on counter-democracy, political parties are almost completely absent.[17] This is surprising since the role of political parties is discussed at great length in the debate on the crisis of democracy. In *Le peuple introuvable* Rosanvallon had outlined a genealogy of party-democracy (Rosanvallon 1998: 173-217), trying to show where the systematic problems come from that parties face trying to represent the "unfindable people". The more recent writings of Rosanvallon seem to categorize political parties as part of the "representative-legal" mechanism. However, it is obvious that political parties are extraordinary examples of the intertwining of "democratic" and "counter-democratic" mechanisms,

---

17 Exceptions cp. e.g.: Rosanvallon 2006: 177ff.

since they clearly have defined procedures of surveillance, of objection and contestation. The most striking example is, it can be guessed, the process of excluding a member from a political party in the German party-law. Excluding a member for misbehaviour is a rather complex process that includes formalized stages and decision-making.

Political parties therefore are important examples that help to illustrate that "democracy" and "counter-democracy" do not collide as institutions (elections vs. contestation), but within institutions. Political parties produce "positive" programs, ideas of what should be done. However, at the same party meetings a whole range of counter-democratic mechanisms are practiced, e.g. surveillance of delegates. In the same way, the leaders of parties are constantly confronted with the mistrust of the members, and have to face contestation and objections.

New forms of integrating party members into the inner-party decision-making process (referendums on the candidates in which every member has a voice) in most of the cases strengthen this tendency.

Comparing political parties across countries and their roles in different political systems shows the huge differences that can be found between different ways of giving political parties a legal framework. Whereas in the USA political parties have a rather loose structure and are of great importance mainly in elections, Germany's parties are huge organizations with a great influence on the public sphere, owning newspapers or exacting influence on the public radio and public TV stations.

The decline of the Republican party in the US could then be viewed as the result of an escalation of the conflict between democratic and counter-democratic dynamics. The Republican party apparently failed to give counter-democratic protest an adequate form – and then ended up with the tea party movement taking over important positions and finally making Donald Trump possible. Rosanvallon's concept of populism here would apply to an inner-party movement, including the possibility of a complete take-over by populists.

Giving counter-democracy a well-defined form then seems to be a promising measure against populism even within parties. The case of Germany is of great interest here since Germany has one the most elaborate laws regulating in detail how political parties are to function, to be financed and to be structured. The German party law has, without any doubt, played an important role in stabilising German democracy. Parties that are organized more like tribes or clans never managed to establish themselves in the German party system; the requirements for inner-party democracy are too high and would make a leader-centric political party impossible. In the Netherlands, the "Party for Freedom" has only one member, the leader Geert Wilders. All the other MPs are not officially members of the party.

In France the *Front National* has for many years given the impression of a clan-based family business in which father, daughter and cousin Le Pen held all the important positions.

In all these cases of *organizing the political*, organizing the intersection of democracy and counter-democracy is the decisive challenge. Counter-democratic impulses need to have their well-defined place in political parties in order to make sure they do not completely take them over. Giving counter-democracy a well-defined place seems to be the best way of keeping democracy alive and successful.

Taking a closer look at Rosanvallon's book on the 'good government' (*Le bon gouvernement*) can be helpful. In the introduction, Rosanvallon explains at great length why he does not believe that political parties will play an important role in the re-definition of democracy in the 21st century (Rosanvallon 2015: 23-28). On the one hand there is the constant rise of individualism which lets the percentage of party-members shrink constantly. On the other hand, Rosanvallon claims that political parties have been degraded to organizations only serving executive power. The process of "presidentialization" is turning political parties from bottom-up organizations to top-down hierarchical "movements". The example of Emmanuel Macron's *La République En Marche* would be striking.

However, Rosanvallon does not take into account that in France the law only gives very general prescriptions on how to organize a political party. In Germany an organization such as LREM would probably not be allowed to operate as a political party in the first place. *Organizing the political* therefore is essential, in particular in political parties. In Germany too, political parties are subject to political lobbying or attempts to take financial influence. The law regulating inner-party democracy and financing however, prevents a situation such as in the Netherlands or France, where the Front National never even tried to hide the fact that it is financed partly from Russia. In other words: the range of different types of legal frameworks for political parties is huge. Maybe it is not by accident that democracy is in a deep crisis in those countries which under-regulate political parties, namely the USA, where the crisis of the Republican party has made Trump possible.

When Rosanvallon talks about new approaches to counter the crisis of democracy he seems to take the other way: instead of taking political parties seriously (and regulating them seriously) he proposes new institutions. A "council on the well-functioning of democracy" (*conseil du fonctionnement démocratique*) might judge political actors for their misbehaviour, he claims. And how should it be organized? On a "collegial basis", just as the *Académie française* („organisé sur une base collégiale") (Rosanvallon 2015: 386). But can we really expect "councils" to have an impact when they oppose representatives? Or will this only look like one part of the elites fighting another part? Organizing counter-democracy in this way looks dangerous.

This problem shows, it seems, the problems due to the approach of historical reconstruction. Comparing different historical phenomena is helpful – but maybe it needs to be put in a more systematic dialogue with the comparison of different political systems. Rosanvallon's focus on the organization of the tension between democracy and counter-democracy gives an important impulse that needs to be answered with more detailed comparative work.

BIBLIOGRAPHY

Alonso, Sonia/Keane, John/Merkel, Wolfgang (eds.) (2011): Representative Democracy, Cambridge: Cambridge University Press.

Amna, Erlin/Ekman, Joakim (2013): Standby citizens: diverse faces of political passivity. In: European Political Science Review 1, pp. 1-21.

Badiou, Alain (2008): "Ereignis und Gesetz: Die drei Negationen." In: Henning Teschke/Gernot Kamecke (eds.), Ereignis und Institution, Tübingen: Gunter Narr, pp. 17-27.

Baecker, Dirk (2007): Studien zur nächsten Gesellschaft, Frankfurt (Main): Suhrkamp.

Bedorf, Thomas (2010): "Das Politische und die Politik – Konturen einer Differenz." In: Thomas Bedorf/Kurt Röttgers (eds.), Das Politische und die Politik, Berlin: Suhrkamp, pp. 13-37.

Brodocz, André/Llanque, Marcus/Schaal, Gary S. (2007): Bedrohungen der Demokratie, Wiesbaden: Springer VS.

Chatriot, Alain (2015): "La représentativité des syndicats dans l'oeuvre de P-. Rosanvallon." In: Al-Matary, Sarah/Guénard, Florent (eds.), La démocratie à l'oeuvre: Autour de Pierre Rosanvallon, Paris: Seuil, pp. 127-141.

Dahlgren, Peter (2012): "Social Media and Counter-Democracy: The Contingences of Participation." In: Proceedings of the 4th IFIP WG 8.5 International Conference, September 3-5, 2012, Kristiansand, pp. 1-12.

Della Porta, Donatella (2012): "Critical Trust: Social Movements and Democracy in Times of Crisis." In: Cambio 2(4), pp. 33-43.

Della Porta, Donatella (2013): Can Democracy Be Saved?, Oxford: Polity Press.

Diehl, Paula/Schulz, Daniel (2012): "Was ist demokratische Legitimität? Eine Auseinandersetzung mit der Demokratietheorie Pierre Rosanvallons." In: Zeitschrift für Politische Theorie 2, pp. 287-297.

Foucault, Michel (1996): "What is Critique?" In: James Schmidt (ed.), What is Enlightenment?: Eighteenth century answers to twentieth century questions. Berkeley: University of California Press.

Gaboriaux, Cloé (2015): "Faire l'histoire des corps intermédiaires en France. Quelques remarques sur le modèle politique français." In: Sarah Al-Matary/Florent Guénard (eds.), La démocratie à l'oeuvre: Autour de Pierre Rosanvallon, Paris: Seuil, pp. 113-126.

Giebler, Heiko/Lacewell, Promise Onawa/Regel, Sven/Werner, Annika (2015): "Niedergang oder Wandel? Parteitypen und die Krise der repräsentativen Demokratie", In: Wolfgang Merkel (ed.), Demokratie und Krise: Zum schwierigen Verhältnis von Theorie und Empirie. Wiesbaden: Springer VS, pp. 181-220.

Guénard, Florent (2015): "Le système conceptuel de Pierre Rosanvallon." In: Sarah Al-Matary/Florent Guénard (eds.), La démocratie à l'oeuvre: Autour de Pierre Rosanvallon, Paris: Seuil, pp. 9-27.

Habermas, Jürgen (1992): Faktizität und Geltung, Frankfurt (Main): Suhrkamp.

Habermas, Jürgen (1994): "Über den internen Zusammenhang zwischen Rechtsstaat und Demokratie." In: Ulrich K. Preuß (ed.), Zum Begriff der Verfassung. Die Ordnung des Politischen, Frankfurt (Main): Fischer, pp. 83-94.

Habermas, Jürgen (1998): Between Facts and Norms (Studies in Contemporary German Social Thought): Contributions to a Discourse Theory of Law and Democracy, Cambridge: MIT Press.

Habermas, Jürgen (2012): Nachmetaphysisches Denken II: Aufsätze und Repliken, Berlin: Suhrkamp.

Heidenreich, Felix (2014a): "Was politische Parteien sein könnten – Versuch einer normativen Rekonstruktion aus gegebenem Anlass." In: Felix Heidenreich/Daniel Schulz/Didier Mineur (eds.), Die Bürger und ihr Staat in Deutschland und Frankreich. Les citoyens et leur État en France et en Allemagne, Berlin: LIT, pp. 55-63.

Heidenreich, Felix (2014b): "Welche Idee der Republik für Frankreich und Europa? Neo-republikanische Theorien und ihre Implikationen." In: Stefan Seidendorf (ed.), Frankreich in der Krise: die Suche nach dem verlorenen Selbstverständnis, Wiesbaden: Springer VS, pp. 43-58.

Heidenreich, Felix (2015): "Unvermittelte Gegensätze: Blumenbergs Analyse des gnostischen Denkens." In: Melanie Möller (ed.), Prometheus gibt nicht auf: Antike Welt und modernes Leben in Hans Blumenbergs Philosophie, Paderborn: Wilhelm Fink, pp. 141-153.

Höffe, Otfried (2009): Ist die Demokratie zukunftsfähig? Über moderne Politik, München: C.H. Beck.

Honneth, Axel (2011): Das Recht der Freiheit, Berlin: Suhrkamp.
Ipsen, Jörn (ed.). (2009): 40 Jahre Parteiengesetz: Symposium im Deutschen Bundestag, Osnabrück: Vandenhoeck & Ruprecht.
Keane, John (2009): The life and death of democracy, London: W. W. Norton & Company.
Keane, John (2011): "Monitory Democracy?" In: Sonia Alonso/John Keane/Wolfgang Merkel (eds.), Representative Democracy, Cambridge: Cambridge University Press, pp. 212-235.
Klein, Markus/von Alemann, Ulrich/Spier, Tim (2011): "Warum brauchen Parteien Mitglieder?" In: Tim Spier/Markus Klein/Ulrich von Alemann/Hanna Hoffmann/Annika Laux/Alexandra Nonnenmacher/Katharina Rohrbach (eds.), Parteimitglieder in Deutschland, Wiesbaden: Springer VS, pp. 19-30.
Luhmann, Niklas (1996): Protest: Systemtheorie und soziale Bewegungen, Kai-Uwe Hellmann (ed.), Frankfurt (Main): Suhrkamp.
Al-Matary, Sarah/Guénard, Florent (eds.) (2015): La démocratie à l'oeuvre: Autour de Pierre Rosanvallon, Paris: Seuil.
Merkel, Wolfgang (2004): "Embedded and Defective Democracies." In: Aurel Croissant/Wolfgang Merkel (eds.), Special Issue of Democratization Vol. 11: Consolidated or Defective Democracy? Problems of Regime Change 5, pp. 33-58.
Merkel, Wolfgang (ed.). (2015a): Demokratie und Krise: Zum schwierigen Verhältnis von Theorie und Empirie, Wiesbaden: Springer VS.
Merkel, Wolfgang (2015b): "Schluss: Ist die Krise der Demokratie eine Erfindung?" In: Wolfgang Merkel (ed.), Demokratie und Krise: Zum schwierigen Verhältnis von Theorie und Empirie, Wiesbaden: Springer VS, pp. 471-498.
Möllers, Christoph (2008): Demokratie: Versprechen und Zumutungen, Berlin: Wagenbach.
Monod, Jean-Claude (2011): "Die Krisen der Gouvernementalität." In: Felix Heidenreich (ed.), Technologien der Macht: Zu Michel Foucaults Staatsverständnis, Baden-Baden: Nomos, pp. 97-109.
Moyn, Samuel (2015): "'De l'eau à la rivière?' La réception anglo-américaine de P- Rosanvallon." In: Sarah Al-Matary/Florent Guénard (eds.), La démocratie à l'oeuvre: Autour de Pierre Rosanvallon, Paris: Seuil, pp. 65-77.
Müller, Jan-Werner (2016): Was ist Populismus? Berlin: Suhrkamp.
Petring, Alexander (2015): "Parteien, hört Ihr die Signale? Bevölkerungseinstellungen zur Ungleichheit und der Responsivität der Parteien." In: Wolfgang Merkel (ed.), Demokratie und Krise: Zum schwierigen Verhältnis von Theorie und Empirie, Wiesbaden: Springer VS, pp. 221-243.

Rancière, Jacques (2002): Das Unvernehmen: Politik und Philosophie, Frankfurt (Main): Suhrkamp.

Rosanvallon, Pierre (1995): "Faire l'Histoire du politique – Entretien avec Pierre Rosnvallon." In: Esprit 209/2, pp. 25-42.

Rosanvallon, Pierre (1998): Le Peuple introuvable: Histoire de la représentation démocratique en France, Paris: Gallimard.

Rosanvallon, Pierre (2001): Fondements et problèmes de l''illibéralisme' français (http://www.asmp.fr/travaux/communications/2001/rosanvallon.htm).

Rosanvallon, Pierre (2004): Le modèle politique français: La société civile contre le jacobinisme de 1789 à nos jours, Paris: Seuil.

Rosanvallon, Pierre (2006): La contre-démocratie: La politique à l'âge de la défiance, Paris: Seuil.

Rosanvallon, Pierre (2011): "Penser le populisme." In: Pierre Rosanvallon, La vie des idées, September, 9 2011 (http://www.laviedesidees.fr/IMG/pdf/2011092 7_populisme.pdf).

Rosanvallon, Pierre (2012): "Für eine Begriffs- und Problemgeschichte des Politischen: Antrittsvorlesung am Collège de France vom 28. März 2002." In: Mittelweg 36/6, pp. 43-66.

Rosanvallon, Pierre (2013): Demokratische Legitimität: Unparteilichkeit – Reflexivität – Nähe, Bonn: Bundeszentrale für Politische Bildung.

Rosanvallon, Pierre (2015): Le bon gouvernement, Paris: Seuil.

Runciman, David (2018): How Democracy Ends, London: Basic Books.

Schaal, Gary S. (2004): Vertrauen, Verfassung und Demokratie: Über den Einfluss konstitutioneller Prozesse und Prozeduren auf die Genese von Vertrauensbeziehungen in modernen Demokratien, Wiesbaden: Springer VS.

Schmitter, Phillipe C./Della Porta, Donatella/Warren, Mark E. (2010): "Democracy and Distrust. A Discussion of Counter-Democracy: Politics in an Age of Distrust." In: Perspectives on Politics 8/3, pp. 887-895.

Schulz, Daniel (2015): Die Krise des Republikanismus, Baden-Baden: Nomos.

Sen, Amartya (2008): Die Idee der Gerechtigkeit, München: C.H. Beck.

Siri, Jasmin (2012): Parteien. Zur Soziologie einer politischen Form, Wiesbaden: Springer VS.

Sztompka, Piotr (1999): Trust – A Sociological Theory, Cambridge: Cambridge University Press.

Tsebelis, George (2002): Veto Players – How Political Institutions Work, Princeton: Princeton University Press.

Weymans, Wim (2004): "Pierre Rosanvallon und das Problem der Politischen Repräsentation." In: Oliver Flügel/Reinhard Heil/Andreas Hetzel (eds.), Die

Rückkehr des Politischen – Demokratietheorie heute, Darmstadt: Wissenschaftliche Buchgesellschaft, pp. 87-112.

Weymans, Wim (2006): "Freiheit durch politische Repräsentation – Lefort, Gauchet und Rosanvallon über die Beziehung zwischen Staat und Gesellschaft." In: Reinard Heil/Andreas Hetzel (eds.), Die unendliche Aufgabe: Kritik und Perspektiven der Demokratietheorie, Bielefeld: transcript, pp. 185-207.

11 Governing Democratically

A Reconceptualization of the Executive
based on Pierre Rosanvallon

Anna Hollendung

In terms of rulership, how can the relationship of a government to its subject be understood in a way that does not contradict the democratic ideal? How can the extent to which the executive is democratic be determined? The fact that something like a government that rules against its subjects exists, is obviously in tension with the democratic demand that is expressed in the key concept of 'popular sovereignty'. While this is discussed broadly in terms of the legislative processes, such considerations are relatively absent concerning the institutions of the executive.

In *Le bon gouvernement* Pierre Rosanvallon (2016) points to this theoretical void (Part I) on the basis of his own thoughts on democracy (Part II & III). As he makes clear, this theoretical shortcoming resonates in recent developments that he summarizes under the heading of the "presidentialization of democracies" (Rosanvallon 2016: 99-164), which remain under-theorized (Part IV). This transformation contributes to the vulnerability of democracy to collapse into authoritarian or totalitarian systems – a threat that, as we know from Lefort, is inherent to democracy but that is sharpened under the condition of a growing personalization of politics and a prevalent strengthening of the executive sphere.

Rosanvallon supplies the discussion with an acceptable heuristic, that allows evaluating the status quo (Part V), as well as some suggestions for a more democratic institutional setting (Part VI). However, his main achievements (Part VII) are not the examination of the executive institutions and their valuation of them in the spirit of democracy: he shows profound transformative processes, and radical social and political changes that happen without broad public reflection. Considering the inherent danger of recent developments (presidentialization) the book's most important contribution lies not in the field of ready-made concepts and clear instructions in how to implement more democracy into the executive, but in its power to give an insight into the institutional setting and its conceptual fluidity, which allows for public deliberation and democratic opinion forming.

I. THE UNDER-THEORIZATION OF THE EXECUTIVE

Jean-Jacques Rousseau (2002), who is frequently called the father of modern democratic theory, introduced the differentiation of executive and legislative power into theoretical reflections. Meanwhile he emphasized that "[d]emocracy is [...] founded upon the twin principles of self-government and direct legislation by the people" (Rosanvallon 1995: 141). The undervaluation of the executive form of government for democracy also emanates from his thoughts. The lack of theorizing in regard to the executive power, that motivates Rosanvallon's engagement in *Le bon gouvernement*, already existed in Rousseau's debate on that problem. Rousseau divorced the legislative from the executive power and sidelined the latter instead of including it in his democratic ideal. His often cited doxa "[t]he people, being subjected to the laws, should be the authors of them; it concerns only the associates to determine the conditions of association" (Rousseau 2002: 179), which is often seen as the essence of his democratic theory[1], displays this imbalance. The subordination of the executive power allowed him to assign the executive responsibility to a single person or a distinct group (Rosanvallon 2016: 177f.). His concept therefore reflects a non-identity of the citizens and the (executive form of) government.

Rousseau aims at the realization of democracy in a paradoxical form, namely as a rulership of those who are ruled, whereas Rosanvallon argues that the claim to govern oneself must fail because of the non-identity of the citizen (representing the generality) and the particular individual. While the idea of the legislating people remains a regulatory ideal, Rosanvallon dismisses the utopia of self-governing as an impossibility, arguing that the functional differentiation between those who are governing and those who are governed is already implicated in the concept of "government" (ibid: 19, 165-191). The individual must be governed in order to become a citizen: Government produces and organizes a compatibility of these two separated instances (ibid: 178).

---

1   This view is fundamentally questioned by Catherine Colliot-Thélène who rejects the idea of self-legislation as an illusion (cp. Colliot-Thélène 2011: 95).

The idea of self-government[2] was further modified throughout the 18th century: The question of "who governs?" was reconsidered in democratic theories that demanded institutions which guarantee a continuous rule of law, discussing the making of law, its implementation and execution. Nevertheless, compared to the broad discursive efforts to define democratic modes of legislation, the theoretical reflection of the executive mode of governing remained relatively silent (Richardson 2008: 207).

The theoretical reflections concerning government had a tendency to argue for its conceptualization as a counterpart to popular sovereignty: conservatives balanced it against the dangers inherent to democracy, and leftists saw the executive as a hindrance to the realization of people's sovereignty, that therefore needs to be minimized (Dormal 2016a).

II. THE IDEA OF DEMOCRATIC REPRESENTATION

The idea of representation, paradigmatically informed by Thomas Hobbes, who argued that representation is the mechanism that not only allows for the organization of a society but is its constitutive condition, has been broadly discussed and reconsidered since the second half of the 18th century. Revolutionaries like Thomas Jefferson aspired to translate the Athenian democratic organization into mechanisms that enable democracy for much greater communities. He and many of his political contemporaries claimed that the democratic principle therefore needs to be amended by the concept of representation (Lembcke 2016: 25).

As Dolf Sternberger (1970) retrospectively makes clear, this description plays down the real continuities that mark the political structures before and after the revolutions: "It was not representation that was grafted onto democracy, but conversely democracy was grafted onto representation." (Sternberger 1970: 14, transl. A.H.) Parliamentary representation was not an invention of the revolutionary era. Rather it is the appearance of the people (the *demos*) as central political actors and the implementation of their demand to be represented in governmental politics that formed the fundamental break with the old order (ibid).

Despite this, the above cited 'democrats' did not speak about 'democracy': the term 'democracy' was in their time almost exclusively used with great skepticism and in reference to the Aristotelian schema of forms of government, to ancient

---

2   Abraham Lincoln (2001 [1863]: 734) famously sketched the idea of self-government in his "Gettysburg Address" one hundred years after the publication of Rousseau's Contrat Social as "government of the people, by the people, for the people".

republics or rather odd structures of some Swiss cantons or German cities (Colliot-Thélène 2011: 70-75). Evoking connotations of archaism and instability, the concept of democracy didn't play a role in the debates about the constitution or on universal suffrage that were discussed in the 18th century (ibid: 70f.).

In the French Revolution the revolutionaries described their ideals in terms of 'representative government' (the moderates) or 'popular sovereignty' (the radicals). Criticism on the failures of representation did not refer to the notion of self-government but deployed procedures of surveillance and the popular ratification of law (Rosanvallon 1995: 144; Rosanvallon 2008c: 22-25).

Beginning with d'Argenson, Robespierre, Kant and Christian democrats, the concept of democracy became detached from the notion of popular sovereignty and continues to cling to equality and full civil rights. As opposed to the contemporary interrelatedness of the concepts of popular sovereignty and democracy, there was a striking asynchronicity in their development. "[I]t was not until 1848 that the word 'democracy' really became current in political discourse in France – long after the principle of popular sovereignty was formulated and recognized" (Rosanvallon 1995: 140). While in liberal vocabulary the term was associated with archaism and the Terror of 1793-94, it became a broadly accepted description of modern egalitarian society only after the dawn of universal suffrage in France. 'Democracy' came to be a universal point of reference, incorporating manifold different and sometimes even contradictory meanings, characterizing a political regime, social structures or a common acceptance of the worthiness of equality (ibid: 145-149). This development was at last accomplished in 1835 with the publication of Alexis de Tocqueville's *Democracy in America* (Tocqueville 2000).[3]

Philosophers like John Stuart Mill (1971) who interpreted representative regimes as democratic systems, pushing forward the concept of 'representative democracy'[4], partook in the process that characterized the democratic universe in the 19th century through the notion of representation (Richardson 2008: 206-211). In terms of progress, this development in political theory can be described as a shift from direct democratic ideas,[5] which evoke a premodern essentialism that ensued

---

3 Cp. John Keane (2009), for a historical perspective on the variety of democratic regimes.

4 The earlier foray of the Marquis d'Argenson passed nearly unnoticed. He differentiates "false" and "legitimate" forms of democracy, anticipating the intervention of representative democracy: "In true democracy, one acts through deputies, who are authorized by election" (d'Argenson cited in: Rosanvallon 1995: 140f.).

5 In the Contrat Social Rousseau unambiguously comments on the question of representation: "For the same reason that sovereignty is inalienable it is indivisible; for the will

from an identity of the political sovereign (the people) and the physical reality (multitude), to constitutional procedures, intermediary and representing institutions.

Representability is a regulative principle, not a reality. This implies that contemporary democracies suffer a lack of democratic representability. Nonetheless, this is a fact that requires consideration. Representation is considered to mediate between the empirical plurivocality and the ideal political entity of the people. The shape of society is therefore determined by various instances of intermediation, as post-fundamentalist approaches emphasize.[6] The two most prominent intermediating institutions are universal suffrage and an administration that is expected to serve public values. In *La légitimité démocratique* Rosanvallon describes their impact as institutional affirmation of universality, a notion that is highly contested in political theory. Both institutions achieve legitimacy by social acknowledgement and by compliance with accepted norms. As Rosanvallon (2011a: 5-9) argues, this scheme needs further supplements since the administrative power has suffered a loss of legitimacy, while elections only express the will of the majority vs. minorities, but are unable to represent a generality.

III. ROSANVALLON'S UNDERSTANDING OF DEMOCRACY

Rosanvallon formulates a strong dissent to the idea that democracy is fully defined by the procedure of election on the one hand and the rule of law on the other. In his eyes it is not enough to ideally ground state institutions in citizen vote and to insist on participation in decision-making within administrative bodies – this needs to be complemented. In *Le bon gouvernement* he therefore pleads to fundamentally reconfigure the relationship between the government and the people.

---

is either general, or it is not; it is either that of the body of the people, or that of only a part of it" (Rousseau 2002: 171). This reasoning allowed Carl Schmitt (cp. 1989) to refer to Rousseau conceptualizing a homogenous entity of the people in terms of identity, not representation. They come without differentiation between those who rule and those who obey. The concept of a coherent general will persists in contemporary republican discourse in France (cp. Weymans 2004: 100-105). In contrast to this idealistic interpretation of Rousseau's thoughts, a pragmatic one is essentially compatible with the modern system of parliamentary representation, as Catherine Colliot-Thélène (cp. 2011: 87-91) shows.

6   The relevant theories are broadly discussed by Oliver Marchart (cp. 2013).

This ought to prevent social dislocations and dictatorial elements (Rosanvallon 2016).

He refers to three additional modes that in his eyes aim for universality and therefore express distinct dimensions of democratic legitimacy. This legitimacy always remains unstable and precarious. He points to impartiality as it can be observed in supervisory and regulatory authorities, reflexivity as it is incorporated through constitutional courts, and proximity, meaning that political actors and institutions live up to the expectation that everybody's singularity be respected (Rosanvallon 2011a: 75-218).[7]

Previously, in *Le peuple introuvable*, he already addressed the inner aporetic tension between the mainly abstract constitutional concept of the people as a political entity and the demand to reflect the empirical heterogeneity and plurivocality of the citizens (Dormal 2016b: 23; Rosanvallon 1998: 31). As a scholar of Lefort he does not see this as a problem which requires resolution, but as an example of the 'emptiness of the place of power' that Lefort (1990) famously described. In contrast to monarchy, democracy has no instance that embodies power and the whole of society like the monarch does, connecting the whole of his regime with the divine infinity. Rather, this place is left empty. Democracy in Lefortian analysis centers on an ongoing contestation of power and is therefore a dynamic and precarious configuration. Its inherent endangerment is conveyed in comparison to totalitarianism, which is characterized formally as a regime that fills this void and suspends the social contest (ibid).[8]

Rosanvallon therefore identifies this tension within the democratic subject as part of the structural groundwork whose contestation allows for the democratic shaping of society. In democracy "the people is no longer a natural fact, but only exists through intermediation" (Weymans 2004: 89). A people exists only in dependence on those intermediating institutions that shape its form and constitute it.

Rosanvallon names such instances, pointing to political parties, directorates, institutions of the social welfare state, trade unions and alike on the one hand, and the cognitive and poetic dimension of representation through poets, authors and

---

7   For a broad discussion of La légitimité démocratique cp. Paula Diehl and Daniel Schulz (2012) and Dirk Jörke (2012).
8   The obscurity of Lefort's conception is illuminated with a view to the range of interpretations and advancements by his scholars, that range from the approach of Gauchet, who understands democracy as "a permanent threat to itself" (Ingram 2007: 40) and who therefore argued in a liberal vein for the subordination of popular sovereignty under constitutionality, to Abensour, who conceptualizes Democracy as the capacity of the demos to question, challenge and transform the institutional setting (ibid).

social researchers on the other (Rosanvallon 1998: 279-301, 354-361; 2000: 96-102; 2014: 23-31, 35-47, 56f.; Weymans 2004: 104f.; 2007: 54f.; 2015: 180-182). Weymans consequently adds contemporary media (from pop songs to cartoons) to the latter category (Weymans 2004: 112). [9]

This broad range of intermediaries is not necessarily reflected within the concept of representative democracy that pinpoints first and foremost the state and its institutions. The executive part "of government was understood as lacking coherence [and] [...] practically disappeared behind the exercise of its own power" (Rosanvallon 2011c: 122). Consequently the changes of the executive power remain under-theorized as well.

Rosanvallon's description of democratic institutions and their mode of action is led by basic assumptions. In reference to Lefort, he understands democracy as a system that institutionalizes conflict, and recognizes the fundamental division of the social body and the existence of opposing worldviews, interests and opinions. Democracy not only allows for the articulation of dissenting opinions, but is centered on the institutionalized competition between them. It is a relentless process of shaping the form (*mise en forme*) of society, which for Rosanvallon is not reducible to election campaigning.

In following with his thoughts, political theory should *not* diminish the opacity which adheres to the concept of democracy. On the contrary, Rosanvallon insists that the meaning of democracy is *essentially* floating. While there are certainly democratic institutions, democracy cannot be reduced to them. Democracy in this sense is not a form of sovereignty but a relentless search, experimenting and exploration of a substantiation of equality that, as he points out, manifests in various and changing institutional settings (Rosanvallon 2008a: 2, 2008b: 546f.). It does not allow for its hypostatization. In this sense Rosanvallon states "that democracy *is* a history" (Rosanvallon 2011b: 59). As Emanuel Richter paraphrases:

"[...] democracy is not to be understood as a certain 'system' of governing in touch with the people, but as a pursuit of ways to its obtainment. Hence, the history of democracy is rattled throughout by a tension between a promise and its noncompliance. Historically [...] [t]he promise was composed of the democratic reaction concerning the social desire for equality and autonomy, and the problem consisted of the clusiveness of this noble objective." (Richter 2016: 55, transl. A.H.)

---

9   For a deeper investigation into the problem of political representation in Rosanvallon's work cp. (Conti and Selinger 2016; Disch 2008; Weymans 2006).

Democracy in this sense is a public manifestation of critique on domination, withholding surveillance, vetoing and juridical modes of intervention by the citizens, without the ability to define its *demos* conclusively (Rosanvallon 2011b: 49). The people (in its vague, precarious, contested and changing form) not only installs the government but fulfills more functions in its capacity to perform surveillance, to veto and to judge. In this way the people forms the active basis for the good working order of the government (Rosanvallon 2008c, 2013).

Rosanvallon's inquiry into the nature of democracy goes further: In *La contre-démocratie* he outlines that institutionalized democracy (legitimated by vote) has a continuous existing counterpart. This "counter-democracy" (Rosanvallon 2008a) is motivated by mistrust against the political elites. It is also, as he shows, institutionally admitted by those possibilities that allow citizens to influence representative politics through oversight (ibid: 29-120), prevention (ibid: 121-190) and judgement (ibid: 191-248). *La contre-démocratie* points to political activities of non-state actors and institutions that are nourished by distrust and scrutiny. Ranging from social movements to rating-agencies and think tanks, indirect intermediating actors play a role in contemporary democracies that characterizes them as a potentially legitimating force, and one that needs consideration in democratic theories (Bizeul and Rohgalf 2016; Heidenreich 2016; Rosanvallon 2008a).[10]

In order to shed light on the question as to how a democratic executive ought to be, he focuses on the relationship of the government to those being governed and points out the normative expectations, which go far beyond the fact that the latter authorize the former. Especially when the executive is dominating, there is a need to establish forms of control through society. His description of a theoretical void concerning the valuation of executive institutions by their democratic accuracy resonates with a theoretical inability to reflect adequately on recent developments – namely of how the growing domination of the executive characterizes the current situation. Rosanvallon (2016: 99-164) identifies a "presidentialization of democracy" as a contemporary development that is not fully intelligible within the existing theoretical framework.

---

10 For a more differentiated discussion of the Anglo-Saxon reception cp. Samuel Moyn (2016).

IV. THE HEGEMONY OF THE EXECUTIVE OR THE "PRESIDENTIALIZATION OF DEMOCRACY"

The "presidentialization of democracy" (Rosanvallon 2016: 99-164, transl. A.H.) is a relatively new phenomenon that shapes many contemporary democracies. Succeeding an era where the executive power was revaluated, as a counterpoint to social destabilization and as reconfiguration that promises more efficiency and strength of purpose than parliamentary decision-making. In reaction to the expansion of governmental duties, presidential systems evolved in the United States, Ireland, Finland, Portugal, France and non-European countries. This refers to questions of social and economic policy (ibid: 63-80).

The "trend to personalize the executive power" (ibid: 136, transl. A.H.) is to be understood as a break from the succeeding "cult of impersonality" (ibid: 137, transl. A.H.), which was formerly associated with democracy and epitomized in administrative anonymity. The benefits of the presidential systems are the greater overall transparency and the clear-cut assignment of responsibility to the president, in contrast to an assembly that structurally diffuses responsibility. The direct ballot of the president, as in France, provides "superlegitimacy" to his acts (ibid: 146). On the other hand, the great power of the president makes the system vulnerable to autocracy.

The recent authoritarian developments in Hungary and Turkey, for example, are therefore not random changes, but have to be interpreted as parts of the general process of presidentialization. With an eye on the danger of authoritarianism, it is of great importance to point out mechanisms that curb the danger of illiberalism and strengthen the compatibility of presidential systems with democracy.

V. READABILITY, RESPONSIBILITY, REACTIVITY, TRUTH-SPEAKING AND INTEGRITY

Rosanvallon strives to "define the conditions of the representatives' non-sovereignty against those who are governed, while acknowledging the unavoidable asymmetry of their relationship" (ibid: 187, transl. A.H.). This aim structures the second part of *Le bon gouvernement* (ibid: 165-340). In these chapters he refers to five motives that are used to describe the ideal relationship between those who govern and those who are governed (these are: readability, responsibility and reactivity), or else characterize good governing representatives (which are: truth-speaking and integrity). This way he depicts an ideal state of government and society at large.

The readability of governmental activities is certainly a precondition for democratic control. Therefore there is a need for mediating instances like school and media that structure the information and balance the growing visibility of the governmental actions with concepts and tools to understand them (ibid: 193-225). Accordingly, their functionality can be measured against the empowerment of citizens to participate in democratic processes.

With the concept of responsibility, Rosanvallon points to the parliament's loss of control in the course of presidentialization, and a diffusion of authorship that frustrates attempts to assign responsibility to individual actors. Rosanvallon addresses the accountability of political leaders. Their responsibility can relieve the damage to their offices in political scandals, but more than that it comprises the fact that the conflicts dividing society are brought to light, which ought to allow for reform (ibid: 227-249).

Reactivity refers to the ideal that the citizens are included in all knowledge formatting structures in order to compensate for the decline of parties and unions (which prevents them from fulfilling this function anymore) and the change of social configurations (that diffuses old patterns of representation). This actual state is far from Émile Durkheim's ideal of a permanent interaction between society and their representatives. Durkheim described democracy as a site where both sides interact together in broad reflections, deliberations and criticism of public concerns. He thought of this collective effort in social self-reflection as premise for the irreducible unity of government and society (Durkheim et al. 1988; Rosanvallon 2016: 251-270). This demands bringing the institutional setting more in line with the Habermasian ideal of deliberative democracy.

In democracy, there is not just an obligation to speak the truth, but democracy's foundational indeterminacy, which was mentioned above, forces a permanent dispute over its partial and incomplete realization (ibid: 293-316). "[D]emocracy can be defined only when it originates from permanent research into the conceptual premises of its own indeterminacy." (Ibid: 309, transl. A.H.) With reference to this requisition, not only the talk-practices of individual representatives are challenged but also the systematic structures that prevent actors from complying with the norm.

The value of integrity refers to the problem of corruption and designates transparency as the most important mechanism to overcome it. The imperative of instrumental transparency is a prerequisite for a well-adjusted relationship between the citizens and their representatives. Transparency in this sense enables the citizens to control their representatives and places them in a powerful position. This presupposes not only the protection of whistleblowers, but Rosanvallon emphasizes the French efforts concerning the pecuniary circumstances of administrative and political leaders through the *Haute Autorité pour la transparence de la vie publique* (HATVP). The HATVP implements a form of preventive control of the fortune and tax behavior of office-holders. Transparency has not only the potential to increase the accountability of political leaders, but it may legitimize and therefore support the institutions in question and stress their orientation towards the common good (ibid: 317-341).

Due to their long history in western democracies and their inclusion into a broad consensus concerning the ideal government, the remaining potential of readability, responsibility, reactivity, truth-speaking and integrity for innovation is rather low. Hence, they belie exaggerated expectations that Rosanvallon's description implies. Only with a distance from his explicitly stated aims can these five elements be taken to form an acceptable heuristic for a survey of the contemporary state of western democracies.

While these elements can only be seen as regulative ideals that allow for judging the common state of democracy, Rosanvallon reflects on some additional possibilities for an optimized institutionalization of democracy.

VI. A SUPPLEMENT OR SUBSTITUTE FOR DEMOCRACY?

There is high potential for the further development of democracy, and democratic theory is in three fields of attention; (1.) in countering powers that balance out the weaknesses of elections,[11] (2.) in mechanisms that strengthen the parliamentary authority concerning the executive power, (3.) in the substitution of powers that are legitimized by elections by impersonal ones (ibid: 151-164).

Rosanvallon refers to the fact that such mechanisms are already at work in the temporal restrictions of offices (especially the presidential office), suspension proceedings (like impeachment, connected with the idea of imperative mandates or recall), and in parliamentary authority to control, judge and interpellate executive

---

11 Structurally, ballots have four immanent tensions: (1) The arithmetic discrepancy distance between the society and those who actually gave their vote, (2) the difference between the characteristics one must have to run a successful election campaign and those needed for good governing, (3) the conflicting expectations concerning the nature of the president to be near to the ordinary people in order to represent them and to be an exceptionally gifted person who is able to make a difference and (4) the discrepancy between the election campaign language that raised hopes and made promises in contrast to the real politics after inauguration (cp. Rosanvallon 2016: 141-146).

actions. The parliament rationalizes itself through procedural regulations and unambiguous majorities. The establishment of supervisory and regulatory authorities and autonomous constitutional courts that articulate the public good complements that system (ibid: 151-164).

The latter institutions are not legitimated by majority vote. Rosanvallon's endorsement of such institutions may come as a surprise. It nurtured Dirk Jörke's (2012) skepticism of this approach. Jörke warns that it is a traditional antidemocratic attitude to replace the constitutive political conflict with institutions that promise to be more rational and/or neutral. He argues that independent agencies need democratic control[12] (ibid: 151-153). Analogously Michel Dormal (2016a) criticizes Rosanvallon and urges him to set up a "republic of notables 2.0".

Jörke's and Dormal's disapproval is based on the assumption that Rosanvallon's suggestions are supplements and not substitutes to the traditional ones. In that sense Jörke rejects Rosanvallon's thoughts in *La légitimité démocratique*, arguing that it forms an enucleation of democracy. He points out the inherent elitism of Rosanvallon's model of democratic legitimacy. Therefore he warns not to dismiss the existing democratic institutions too hastily (Jörke 2012).

Unlike Jörke, I assume a different reading of Rosanvallon that resonates with Felix Heidenreich:

"Thus, Rosanvallon does not make a naïve plea for an extension of counter-democratic proceedings, as it is sometimes asserted. It is rather a question of making counter-democratic institutions and practices as such nameable and analyzable." (2016: 55, transl. A.H.)

In following with this, the objections of Jörke and Dormal are based on a confusion of the character of Rosanvallon's suggestions. These suggestions are supplements and not substitutes to the democratic institutional setting and they are efforts to take account of the empirical reality that already shapes the faces of western democracies: The European Central Bank, constitutional courts, regulatory and supervisory authorities actually form part of liberal-democratic orders. They are counterparts of those institutions open to citizen participation or based on their vote, as Jörke (2012: 153) himself confirms, thereby affirming Rosanvallon's perspective.

Even Rosanvallon's criticism on electoral procedures does not imply that he proposes an end to the whole institution of suffrage, as his discussion in *Le sacre*

---

12 Mainstream political theory sees democratic control established by the mechanism of ballots that are interpreted as allowing for sanction of the misbehavior of representatives and via the system of checks and balances that provides intra-institutional control.

de citoyen makes clear, but to critically examine systems that allow for balancing its weaknesses and to include those mechanisms in the universe of democratic theory. These remarks do not refute the objections mentioned by Jörke and Dormal, but reorient them towards the current situation we live in: If the traditional institutions are losing influence, while the rising complementary institutions are missing certain elements that belong to the democratic core (like legitimation by vote), we are confronted with a transformation that indeed causes concerns. Reformulated in this way, Jörke and Dormal's objections display empirical evidence in the contemporary political state, which is made visible through the analysis of Rosanvallon. The integration of new elements into the institutional setting invites criticism on the democratic shortcomings of those alterations. This calls for a discussion of their possible democratization and to deliberate on their potential for further improvement via complementary procedures or mechanisms.

At the end of *Le bon gouvernement,* Rosanvallon sheds light on some further ideas that may advance democracy: (1) He suggests organizing a Council that is concerned with democratic progress. On the basis of a 'Charter of Democratic Action' it would observe the transparency and integrity of representatives, political measures, and institutions. This Council would report the state of democracy on an annual basis, and hold the representatives accountable for justifying their actions. Furthermore, it would protect whistleblowers. (2) Public Commissions would evaluate administrative practices and the procedures that realize initiatives, and they would initiate public debates about it. They would evaluate whether the political procedures of preparation and of decision-making are democratic. (3) Organizations of civil surveillance would control governmental activities and engage in information, participation and education of citizens. (4) An annual 'Day of Democracy' should be considered to induce the self-assurance of the actors and to involve citizens extensively (Rosanvallon 2016: 341-348).

VII. (ONLY) TRANSIENT CONCLUSIONS

Rosanvallon's concept of democracy, that defines it as a relentless search, experimenting and exploration of its own substantialization, contradicts the old idea of 'popular sovereignty', which is a direct translation of democracy from its Greek origin. While the Greek term highlights the power of the people not just to control the public realm but further their "*strength* and *ability* to act within that realm and [...] to reconstitute the public realm through action" (Ober 2008: 7) – a concept of power that resonates in Arendt's discussion of the political and her concept of freedom – Rosanvallon is oriented toward forms of critique, control and reform.

Emphasizing the dynamic processes and contestation at the very center of democracy, Rosanvallon defines democratic institutions in terms of public criticism on domination, surveillance of the political leaders, the citizen's power to veto (counter-democracy) and to intervene via juridical modes.

Rosanvallon's concrete proposals for institutional improvements request mechanisms that allow for surveillance and resistance against political actions that create public disfavor. The task of surveillance can be assigned to the broad public, to specialized committees or the parliament. Its implementation improves the government in a way that opens sluices for its further progression and reconfiguration from below.

Rosanvallon's conceptualization comes without an embodied popular sovereign, but democracy gets located in the tradition of counter-sovereign power. This places him in proximity to another scholar of Lefort, namely Abensour. Contrasting the two highlights the reformism of Rosanvallon's account: Abensour (2012) rejects every intention to reconcile democracy with the state and restricts the concept of democracy to activities that are beyond the state, at a distance from the state or in opposition to it. For him the rebelling democracy marks a fundamental break between two regimes.

Conversely, Rosanvallon exhibits the large number of correctives and adjustments, trials and explorations that go along with the process of democracy. This concerns, *inter alia*, the election procedures, the question of representability and parity, mechanisms that allow for citizen participation in nomination procedures, other mechanisms that foreclose the abuse of administrative authority or the accumulation of offices, impersonal administrative work, systems of checks and balances, the use of supervisory and regulatory authorities, and the role of the constitutional courts. In comparison to Abensour, Rosanvallon integrates the democratic forces countering the state institutions into the institutional setting. Therefore, his account can be described as deradicalized interpretation of the counter-hegemonic struggles.

Furthermore, his perspective might conceal the caesuras within that history, the fundamental reconfigurations and new beginnings. He is unable to conceptualize and explain radical change.

Rosanvallon's primary achievement is to reveal the incompleteness of the quest for legitimate institutions and actors that materialize the democratic project, and the need for its continuous consultation. He pleads for an understanding of "democracy ensuing from the problems of its implementation and the permanent danger of its lapse into an oligarchic regimen […]. In other words to understand it as a work in itself […]" (Rosanvallon 2016: 349, transl. A.H.). In this sense, the improvement of the institutional setting has a history that is not yet finished. By designating the actual state of democracy in a broad manner and naming the problems that accompany the tendency to presidentialization, he fuels this ongoing quest. Therefore, his analysis should be valued against the deliberative efforts it permits and less by its concrete institutional proposals (that indeed do not fulfill his pledges), as his work is primarily an invitation to participate in the debates and actions that will further shape the history of democracy.[13]

BIBLIOGRAPHY

Bizeul, Yves/Rohgalf, Jan (2016): "Singularität und Verschmelzung. Rosanvallons contre-démocratie und der Wandel des demokratischen Imaginären." In: Zeitschrift für Politische Theorie 7(1), pp. 33-51.

Colliot-Thélène, Catherine (2011): Demokratie ohne Volk, Hamburg: Hamburger Edition.

Conti, Gregory/Selinger, William (2016): "The Other Side of Representation: The History and Theory of Representative Government in Pierre Rosanvallon." In: Constellations 23 (4), pp. 548-562.

Diehl, Paula/Schulz, Daniel (2012): "Was ist demokratische Legitimität? Eine Auseinandersetzung mit der Demokratietheorie Pierre Rosanvallons." In: Zeitschrift für Politische Theorie, 3(2), pp. 287-297.

Disch, Lisa (2008): "The People as 'Presupposition' of Representative Democracy: An Essay on the Political Theory of Pierre Rosanvallon." In: Redescriptions 12, pp. 47-71.

Dormal, Michel (2016a): Ein demokratischer Fürstenspiegel.

Dormal, Michel (2016b): "Eine Phänomenologie der Ränder und Antinomien. Pierre Rosanvallons Beitrag zur Methodenfrage in der Ideengeschichte." In: Zeitschrift für Politische Theorie 1, pp. 17-31.

Durkheim, Émile/Müller, Hans-Peter/Schmid, Michael/Luhmann, Niklas (1988): Über soziale Arbeitsteilung. Studie über die Organisation höherer Gesellschaften, Frankfurt am Main: Suhrkamp.

Heidenreich, Felix (2016): "Die Organisation des Politischen. Pierre Rosanvallons Begriff der 'Gegen-Demokratie' und die Krise der Demokratie." In: Zeitschrift für Politische Theorie 7(1), pp. 53-72.

Ingram, James (2007): "The Politics of Claude Lefort's Political: Between Liberalism and Radical Democracy." In: Thesis Eleven 87, pp. 33-50.

---

13 I owe gratitude to Kate Stollmann for her patient and pleasant correction of this paper.

Jörke, Dirk (2012): "Demokratietheorie ohne demos." In: Jürgen Nordmann/Katrin Hirte/Walter Ötsch (eds.): Demokratie! Welche Demokratie? Postdemokratie kritisch hinterfragt, Marburg: Metropolis, pp. 139-158.
Keane, John (2009): The Life and Death of Democracy, London/Sydney et al.: Simon & Schuster.
Lefort, Claude (1990): "Die Frage der Demokratie." In: Ulrich Rödel/Katharina Menke (eds.): Autonome Gesellschaft und libertäre Demokratie, Frankfurt am Main: Suhrkamp.
Lembcke, Oliver W. (2016): "Theorie demokratischer Repräsentation." In: Oliver W. Lembcke/Claudia Ritzi/Gary S. Schaal (eds.): Zeitgenössische Demokratietheorie, Wiesbaden: Springer VS, pp. 23-58.
Lincoln, Abraham (2001 [1863]): "Address Delivered at the Dedication of the Cementary at Gettysburg (Nov. 19, 1863)." In: Roy P. Basler (ed.): Abraham Lincoln: His Speeches and Writings, New York: Da Capo Press.
Marchart, Oliver (2013): Das unmögliche Objekt: eine postfundamentalistische Theorie der Gesellschaft, Berlin: Suhrkamp.
Mill, John Stuart (1971): Betrachtungen über die repräsentative Demokratie, Paderborn: Schöningh.
Moyn, Samuel (2016): "Coals to Newcastle? On the Anglo-American Reception of Pierre Rosanvallon." In: Zeitschrift für Politische Theorie 7(1), pp. 7-16.
Ober, Josia (2008): "The Original Meaning of 'Democracy': Capacity to Do Things, not Majority Rule." In: Constellations 15, pp. 3-9.
Richardson, Henry S. (2008): "Demokratie." In: Stefan Gosepath/Wilfried Hinsch/Beate Rössler (eds.): Handbuch der Politischen Philosophie und Sozialphilosophie, Berlin: De Gruyter, pp. 206-211.
Richter, Emanuel (2016): Demokratischer Symbolismus. Eine Theorie der Demokratie, Berlin: Suhrkamp.
Rosanvallon, Pierre (1995): "The History of the Word 'Democracy' in France." In: Journal of Democracy 6(4), pp. 140-154.
Rosanvallon, Pierre (1998): Le peuple introuvable. Histoire de la représentation démocratique en France, Paris: Gallimard.
Rosanvallon, Pierre (2000): The New Social Question. Rethinking the Welfare State, Princeton: Princeton University Press.
Rosanvallon, Pierre (2008a): Counter-democracy. Politics in an age of distrust, Cambridge et al.: Cambridge Univ. Press.
Rosanvallon, Pierre (2008b): Democratic Universalism as a Historical Problem.
Rosanvallon, Pierre (2008c): Le sacre du citoyen: histoire du suffrage universel en France, Paris: Gallimard.

Rosanvallon, Pierre (2011a): Democratic legitimacy: impartiality, reflexivity, proximity, Princeton: Princeton University Press.

Rosanvallon, Pierre (2011b): "Für eine Begriffs- und Problemgeschichte des Politischen. Antrittsvorlesung am Collège de France." In: Mittelweg 36 20(6), pp. 43-66.

Rosanvallon, Pierre (2011c): "The Metamorphoses of Democratic Legitimacy: Impartiality, Reflexivity, Proximity." In: Constellations 18(2), pp. 114-123.

Rosanvallon, Pierre (2013): Die Gesellschaft der Gleichen, Hamburg: Hamburger Edition.

Rosanvallon, Pierre (2014): Le parlement des invisibles, Paris: Seuil.

Rosanvallon, Pierre (2016): Die gute Regierung, Hamburg: Hamburger Edition.

Rousseau, Jean-Jacques (2002): Social Contract and The First and Second Discourses, The Rethinking of the Western Tradition, New Haven: Yale University Press.

Schmitt, Carl (1989): Verfassungslehre, Berlin: Duncker & Humblot.

Sternberger, Dolf (1970): Ursprung der repräsentativen Demokratie, Erlenbach-Zürich/Stuttgart: Eugen Rentsch.

de Tocqueville, Alexis (2000): Democracy in America, New York: HarperPerennial.

Weymans, Wim (2004): "Pierre Rosanvallon und das Problem der Politischen Repräsentation." In: Oliver Flügel/Reinhard Heil/Andreas Hetzel (eds.): Die Rückkehr des Politischen. Demokratietheorien heute, Darmstadt: Wissenschaftliche Buchgesellschaft, pp. 87-112.

Weymans, Wim (2006): "Freiheit durch politische Repräsentation – Lefort, Gauchet und Rosanvallon über die Beziehung zwischen Staat und Gesellschaft." In: Reinhard Heil/Andreas Hetzel (eds.): Die unendliche Aufgabe. Kritik und Perspektiven der Demokratietheorie, Bielefeld: transcript, pp. 185-207.

Weymans, Wim (2007): "Understanding the present through the past? Quentin Skinner and Pierre Rosanvallon on the Crisis of Political Representation." In: Redescriptions. Yearbook of Political Thought, Conceptual History and Feminist Theory, pp. 45-60.

Weymans, Wim (2015): "Pierre Rosanvallon und die vielfältigen Stimmen des Volkes." In: Oliver Flügel-Martinsen/Franziska Martinsen (eds.): Demokratietheorie und Staatskritik aus Frankreich, Stuttgart: Steiner, pp. 167-184.

12 Coals to Newcastle

Samuel Moyn

I first met Pierre Rosanvallon at a conference at Columbia University in April 2004 entitled "Liberalism's Return." At that moment in the United States, Rosanvallon's importance seemed to be part of so-called "New French Thought," to recall the title of a book series founded by Mark Lilla, the Columbia University political theorist, that allowed several hitherto unknown authors an audience in the English language, including Rosanvallon. The first book in his career that appeared in English was *La nouvelle question sociale*, published in Lilla's series only in 2000.

But by the 2004 conference, Lilla was grim. The series had not succeeded, intellectually or commercially, he reported. And Lilla, who had intended it to offer the message that "new French thought" was liberal and even traditional rather than leftist or postmodernist in nature (contrary to what most people believed French thought is about), knew why. In the end, it was because contemporary French liberals had nothing to teach Anglo-Americans, who hardly needed outside help, especially from French thinkers who had so often proved wayward and unreliable. Hence "Coals to Newcastle," the old saying that Lilla used as the title of his lecture: the attempt to create and import "New French Thought" was akin to trying to sell something to somebody already famous for inventing it. (Newcastle is the city in the northeast of England that once had a royal monopoly on coal. Importing Rosanvallon's version of liberalism into the United States, Lilla was suggesting, was the equivalent of selling coal to a city that already had plenty of it.)

I already knew, having written with my colleague and friend Andrew Jainchill a long study of Rosanvallon's trajectory (published, also in early 2004, in the *Journal of Modern History*), that his thought partook little in the sort of romance of Anglo-American liberalism that was the hallmark of Cold War authors such as Isaiah Berlin, Karl Popper, or Jacob Talmon. In spite of Rosanvallon's early years as the theoretician of *le socialisme autogestionnaire*, however, Jainchill and I emphasized that he incorporated into his own work his mentor and advocate François Furet's Cold War contrast of the Anglo-American defense of the rights and interests of civil society against Jacobin political excess. It was true, of course, that Rosanvallon from the beginning claimed that *economic* liberalism – in Adam Smith and even in Karl Marx – was equally utopian and indeed proto-totalitarian as the sort of political fusion that characterized the politics the revolutionary imaginary. If so, he did not rest content with the invocation of supposedly prepolitical "droits et intétêts" as the hallmark of more anodyne sort of representative democracy than in the Jacobin tradition, as Furet did at the end of *Penser la Révolution française*. But Rosanvallon also distinguished that very economic liberalism from political liberalism and presented the latter as worth exploring after a long era in which it had been forgotten – including, of course, in its native French versions. I would still insist, for this reason, that there is no way to understand Rosanvallon's early career apart without inserting it into the antitotalitarian moment in French thought of the mid-1970s and its long-term legacy, which created a political thought whose first principles were a negative denunciation of political evil and the reinvention of a left only within terms of that denunciation. Emancipation might still beckon, but only chastened by vivid memory of the disasters of the past.

Yet we can now see, ten years later, that the original reception of Rosanvallon in the United States was based on a mistake of its own. In spite of his original inclusion in "New French Thought," the tensions between Rosanvallon's body of work and that ideological project stand out more. Indeed, in his inaugural volume for the series, called eponymously *New French Thought*, Mark Lilla did not even mention Rosanvallon, preferring to lavish most of his attention in his defense of the "legitimacy of the liberal age" (as he entitled his introduction to the volume) on Marcel Gauchet, Pierre Manent, and others. In doing so, Lilla played in tune with a widespread depiction of the recent history of French thought that offered a very simple narrative. From the French Revolution on, French thinkers were beset by the same extremist oscillation as their polity suffered, excluding a liberal moderation and ultimately opening them to the communist temptation in the twentieth century. Belatedly recognized as a hero who guarded the flame of liberal reason in the maelstrom of philo-communist passion, Raymond Aron allowed liberalism to return to France after Alexander Solzhenitsyn finally broke the grip of illusion and irresponsibility over the French mind. This narrative owed much to Furet, though Tony Judt was its great propagator on the Anglo-American scene. It was not altogether false. But this narrative screened out what was more interesting in Rosanvallon's contribution. If it has not yet had the Anglo-American reception that it deserves even today, it was hardly because Rosanvallon's thought merely brought liberalism to a place that invented it.

The stark limits of the attempt to force Rosanvallon into the Procrustean bed of "liberalism" became even clearer to me a year later, when I spent my sabbatical in Paris and began to go backwards, in order to situate his work better in what I came to see as a distinctive tradition of political thinking with no precedent or peer in Anglo-American intellectual history. Originating in Maurice Merleau-Ponty's precocious break with Marxism, it was built above all by Claude Lefort, who emerged over time, I believe, as a much more permanent and durable resource for Rosanvallon than Furet. Lefort's reception in the English language had occurred under completely different auspices, namely the left of the generation of 1968 and its leading figures like Jean Cohen and Dick Howard (both of whom were friendly with Rosanvallon for decades without introducing his work to English-language readers). Lilla simply didn't know how to make sense of the fact that the new French thought he celebrated had leftist roots, not to mention a massive debt, through Lefort, to the very Continental philosophy from which he insisted French liberals were breaking. (Of Lefort, Lilla commented simply: "After leaving 'Socialisme ou barbarie' he then slowly drifted closer to the liberal tradition.") Where in Lilla's hands Gauchet and Manent looked like the natural outcome of Aronian liberalism, on second glance Gauchet seemed the heretical follower of Lefort with Rosanvallon his more faithful heir. In any case, the best scholarship on all these figures now recognizes the different branches of the tree, once falsely reduced to a unitary "new French thought" (that promotional phrase having since dropped completely out of use).

I hardly need enumerate the features of the Lefortian tradition that Rosanvallon took to new levels of depth and sophistication, first from a historical and later from a contemporary perspective. To begin with, it centered on the world-historical significance of democracy (rather than liberalism), which it interpreted as a regime in the classical sense of a social ensemble, rather than a formal mechanism of governance alone. The people who rule do so in the symbolic order, and are never localizable in real terms; modern history can be interpreted as a reckoning with this necessary symbolic division. But it was not really the philosophical intricacy of these notions, fecund as they have been in Rosanvallon's historiography, that have accounted for the limited impact of this tradition in Anglo-American thought. Rosanvallon showed peerlessly in comparatively lucid exposition how much work they can do in a unique synthesis of history and theory that few scholars could match. In many ways, Lefort provided the challenging model and for the past forty years Rosanvallon has explored and deepened it with rigorously historical investigation that also opened it to a much broader audience. If Lefort was discovered only by a discreet circle Anglo-Americans as the crisis of "French theory" had set in, Rosanvallon made some of his central premises independently and easily accessible. And his own Anglo-American connections, which went far beyond the generation of 1968 to range from figures like Albert Hirschman to Michael Sandel and Charles Taylor might presumably have allowed for a greater impact.

It proved most fateful for his Anglo-American reception, I think, that Rosanvallon's chief achievement, certainly until the new millennium, was to vindicate some of these premises on the terrain of specifically French history. Though he began his career highly interested in transnational study, notably in *Le capitalisme utopique*, starting with *Le Moment Guizot* Rosanvallon explored the unfolding of democracy, like Furet and indeed Lefort himself, by showing how much value they offer in understanding the specifically but narrowly French national narrative and theoretical canon. Intellectually, the choice made sense given the French Revolution's importantce. Internationally, however, it was not a propitious moment to do so.

The 1990s and since have been the great age of the crisis of French historiography in the Anglo-American academy. It is worth dwelling on the reasons for this, for it was certainly bad timing to vindicate a general theory of democracy on the grounds of a national history that now interests the world less and less, for better or worse. The historiography of France had been a consensual laboratory of reflection for all fields of under a specific set of assumptions that are now no longer taken for granted. Its story of cascading regimes – liberal and right, with an occasional promise or threat of left-wing breakthrough – remains compelling. But the disappearance of strong working class projects that made French history the glory of Marxist historiography struck a major blow against Franco-centrism. One way to read the classics of the middle of Rosanvallon's career during the 1990s – from *Le sacre du citoyen* to *La démocratie inachevée* – is indeed as an attempt to substitute for such a narrative, retaining the importance of French political history on completely new footing. Yet other forces proved too strong for such a substitution to find the audience that French history once did outside of France, and especially for Anglo-American audiences. With the Cold War over, France's geopolitical importance declined swiftly. Perhaps above all, the loss of any emancipatory leftist project has decentered the French Revolution in world history, and even though its radicalism and the democratic experimentalism it introduced traveled the globe, few think it is crucial to explore it as the foundation of modernity in quite the same way many did for many decades. Simply put, if the French experience was merely local and not also universal, then its status as a global testing ground became increasingly unbelievable.

We can add to this analysis of why a particular geographical forum for global historiographical interests suddenly seemed uninteresting to many who had once studied it that an entire era suffered the same fate: the nineteenth century. Alon Confino has recently argued that the central event of world history was once the French Revolution, but with the crisis of emancipation the Holocaust of European Jewry has taken its place; and it is a shift with wide-ranging ramifications. It altered not solely the place but also the time of historiographical absorption – from the heritage of the French Revolution's emancipation in one century to the making of catastrophic political evil in the next. Further and perhaps above all, it both reflected and abetted a widespread sense of what is ultimately at stake in politics: from hope for liberty, equality, and fraternity to fear of blood, soil, and slaughter. Even the history of human rights, a topic on which I have personally worked recently, looks very different depending on whether one chooses to anchor them in the visionary claim to liberate human beings from oppression for the sake of autonomy, or in the horrified response to barbarity and genocide for the sake of preservation of bare life. Alas, the latter view has generally prevailed both intellectually and mobilizationally – and one can understand why in view of historical experience. One can even argue that by so doggedly reading the French Revolution in the light of twentieth-century totalitarianism, Furet and his epigones – though intending to renovate the study of the meaning of progress – hastened not simply the loss of historiographical interest in France but in the country's revolutionary tradition and its accoutrements. Instead, a historiography about twentieth-century dictatorship and its overcoming became much more exigent. If emancipation mattered primarily for leading to horror, then the climactic twentieth-century with its bloodlands and terror might matter more – especially if its study seemed to bolster the credentials of a "liberalism of fear" primarily valuable because it starts with insight into how easily politics can decline into calamity for all concerned.

All of this had direct implications for Rosanvallon's potential Anglo-American audience. Generations of American and British historians once made an education in the vicissitudes of France's long nineteenth century central to what it meant to be a professional in the discipline, and of course many chose to contribute to the field directly through their own research and writing. Now almost no one is trained in it, or even cares about it. Anyone who, like me, who has tried even to teach Karl Marx's *Eighteenth Brumaire of Louis Napoleon* will find the students lost before the opacity of the events, before even Marx's interpretation of them is debated. Obviously, much more could be said about these developments, which seem to me symptoms of a very great political reorientation, and not simply an intellectual fad. Even a new and much celebrated work that purports to give readers a new reason to care about the nineteenth century, Jürgen Osterhammel's mammoth *Die Verwandlung der Welt* (recently translated into English as *The Transformation of the World*), succeeds only partway in restoring attention to the century, and then only by viewing it as a laboratory not for democracy but for globalization. But focusing overwhelmingly on France's experience between the first revolution and the Great War, Rosanvallon's work was out of step with the Anglo-American trend of global history. In fact, it broadly excluded a now almost obligatory focus on empire that has done most to provide French historians in the Anglo-American world a potential response to decline of broader interest in their materials. I cannot think of any part of Rosanvallon's writings all the way along the course of his career that has made France's imperial incursions even tangentially relevant to "the experience of democracy," whereas for better or worse today students of French history writing in English, like those who write British history, risk the obverse emphasis, making their field nothing but imperial (and in the latter part of the twentieth century post-imperial) history.

Alongside these factors concerning the marginality of France's democratic experiment is the related but distinct and overwhelming shipwreck of its intellectual nobility. Abruptly, Paris lost its centrality to intellectual life in general that it enjoyed from the Enlightenment (if not before) to the era of the *Annales* and the once prestigious series of existentialism, structuralism, and deconstruction. And its leading figures became ciphers rather than saints. Suddenly, it did not go without saying that a professor at the Collège de France had the command of a worldwide attention. The few used bookstores that remain throughout the English-speaking world make the dusty volumes of Roland Barthes, Henri Bergson, Claude Lévi-Strauss, or even Pierre Bourdieu or Maurice Merleau-Ponty widely available, for they were celebrities and *maîtres à penser* for diverse fields on inquiry and even the general public, far beyond their Parisian homes. By contrast, shockingly, no book of Rosanvallon's was even favored to appear in the *New York Review of Books* until last year; as for the *London Review of Books*, with its vestigial nostalgia for academic Marxism, the sole mention of him to date comes in Perry Anderson's notorious diagnosis of French thought, later published in French in *La pensée tiède*, which adopted Lilla's original dichotomy of liberalism versus Marxism, with the sympathies reversed. The results of Rosanvallon's exploration of the vicissitudes of French democracy did not rise to the attention of an Anglo-American public – including when I tried to showcase them in *Democracy Past and Future*, which offered selections of some of the principal themes of Rosanvallon's still untranslated major works of the 1980s and 1990s.

I should add that Rosanvallon has been perfectly lucid and persuasive in rejecting – or is it transforming? – the model of the *intellectuel français* precisely when it was coming to grief worldwide. Some of his loveliest pages concern how scholarship and citizenship most plausibly interact, precisely to avoid the imperious model of the great thinker. While his personal writings are obviously prodigious, and he has made many individual political interventions, he has preferred to operate in the public realm in a new way, by thinking of the scholar as providing long- and medium-term social intelligibility rather than short-term programs. His own institutional ventures, from the Fondation Saint-Simon to the Vie des Idées, have had their participatory *équipes* rather than singular figures and their indeterminate duration rather than episodic sloganeering. Perhaps the best analogy for what he has done in this regard is the American think tank, but saving it from its typically American pathologies of crude ideological conformism and propagandistic mobilization – the terrible form of "counterdemocracy," in his own term, that has sapped so much confidence or interest in electoral affairs in my country.

It is true that Rosanvallon's election to the Collège de France coincided with a series of events that seemed as if they might change the equation to that date and escape the confining dynamics of the factors I have mentioned so far. For one thing, the antitotalitarian moment definitively passed. Even if it remained popular for longer in Anglo-American intellectual life to celebrate the so-called legitimacy of the liberal age, and perhaps always will, more and more began to agree with Rosanvallon's perpetual starting point that liberal democracy is more problem than solution. The events of 1989 did not end history but, in a way, restored the possibility of viewing the drama in the history of democracy from its inception. Arguably, Rosanvallon departed from the limitations of a simply antitotalitarian consensus, after Furet's death. The *affaire* around the publication of Daniel Lindenberg's *Le rappel à l'ordre*, which showed the strains between the left-wing and centrist (or even right) components in the old "consensus," marked an important shift of priorities. There was no way, after this point, to believe that he was one more confused merchant of coal importing it to a land already transformed by its energy and effluents alike.

Just as important, Rosanvallon impressively chose to write a new style of book that would engage frequently with American history, in contraposition to the French experience, a valuable step in the direction of transnational or at least comparative history. And given his new visibility, these works – beginning with *Le modèle politique français* – finally appeared in English. (It is also worth noting that *La contre-démocratie* was also given as the highly prestigious Seeley lectures at the University of Cambridge; and even though Rosanvallon criticized it in his own theoretical writings, the so-called Cambridge school of John Dunn, Quentin

Skinner and others could recognize in Rosanvallon a peer who was testing the border between history and political theory just as they had been doing). And Rosanvallon strayed further into the twentieth century (and even beyond) than he had done in the 1980s and 1990s. A native's interest in revolutionary France and the once obsessive but currently unfashionable interest in the nineteenth century might no longer hinder his reception.

But these reorientations have faced new obstacles. Grievously, not liberalism but a series of academic trends in Anglo-American historiography and political theory have generally excluded the specific model that Rosanvallon's newer investigations allowed – at least so far. As far as I can tell, the inveterate nationalism of American historians of their own country continues to immunize them against work by outsiders or comparativists, of the sort Rosanvallon began offering them in the new millennium. A few great figures since Friedrich von Gentz and Alexis de Tocqueville have organized their thought around a comparison of French and American experiences – but in our time, as I will mention in a moment, it was not Rosanvallon but another figure who has been celebrated for doing so. The most glaring tendency, however, is not one that took place among historians at all, but a dedicated normative approach in political theory and philosophy which, when allied to the formal and empiricist bent of Anglo-American thought, made little space for the conceptual, experiential, and historicist vision of democracy that Rosanvallon has continued to offer in his recent studies of legitimacy and equality. It was not just the Cold War liberals whom Rosanvallon resembled little, but the normative democrats, like John Rawls and his heirs, to say nothing of the reigning sort of political "scientist" in thrall to science-envy and its data and models.

It is in part the very proximity of the historically novel Anglo-American interest in the theme of democratic order that makes our immunity to foreign ways of conceptualizing so disappointing. After all, so-called "democratic theory" has risen far and fast in Anglo-American thought, yet primarily in ways that repeated the country's generally formalistic bent and more recently an ahistorical or antihistorical quest for democracy's true or proper normative principles. This situation made for exceptional hospitality only for external figures like Jürgen Habermas, but not for Rosanvallon, and in part because they were so close to the way people already knew how to think in the English-speaking world. It is almost as if Anglo-America were condemned to receive only those who come close to its own style of liberalism or else those – like the Alain Badious and Slavój Žižeks – who reject it root and branch. More hopefully, however, there are also signs that the sort of political theory that has remained dominant is not likely to last, if recent so-called "realist" assaults on the reigning commitment to neo-Kantian normativity in Anglo-American thought are indicative of future trends. But even this is a hazardous prediction.

Let me close with a different illustration of both the immunity of Anglo-American thought to Rosanvallon's brand of inquiry and the new opening it may now permit. For Rosanvallon's work was never merely in dialogue and competition with other political theories. As his French career shows, it stood out as a prominent attempt to offer academic synthesis and public dialogue on matters of burning civic concern, whether these were the fate of the welfare-state, the transformation of trade-unionism, or the role of government in the face of the explosion of civil society. And even if this role is broadly unavailable in American and English intellectual life, we have been witness to a recent debate in which academic insight was injected into popular consciousness, on the very topic of inequality that Rosanvallon has most recently made his own. I refer, of course, to the spectacular reception of Thomas Piketty's *Capital in the Twentieth Century* – an excellent point of comparison.

The puzzle Piketty's success is interesting on its own, of course, but doubly so when compared to Rosanvallon's very different readership, in general and for *The Society of Equals* in particular. That the two authors share much is self-evident, from their affiliation with a certain sort of socialism, to their favored Franco-American comparison, to their common translator, Arthur Goldhammer.

But if Piketty's breakthrough account of the history of inequality became an unexpected bestseller in my country, the comparison helps to show that it was in part because it shared so much with dominant styles of thought there. Piketty's project is empirical demonstration, at least in the first place, as well as deciphering the laws of capital that explain the data. Rosanvallon, by contrast, cites the data of Piketty and his colleagues, as a point of departure in a very different exploration. Much has been made of Piketty's contempt for disciplinary economics, but his departure from it is hardly very pronounced in the scheme of things. Creditably, Piketty observes that his discipline became a site for mathematical virtuosity, rather than civic commitment, and his book surely demonstrates how to remedy that defect. But his much celebrated turn to historical analysis or even "political economy" seems much less pronounced at second glance than at the start. Its rigor played to the pseudo-scientificity of the social disciplines (not to mention a popular culture enamored of economics), while criticizing it too. Moreover, it lacked many of the historical commitments it claimed. Above all, the account of the now clearly exceptional period when inequality was moderated relies on vague allusions to unspecified events that, as others have observed, enter Piketty's picture nearly as external forces to capitalism – "akin to natural disasters." Redistributive politics are illustrated but not themselves explained. One is forced to conclude that Piketty's success is due not only to an obvious intellectual brilliance and favorable ideological conjuncture but an interesting proximity to analytical frameworks that it purports to challenge.

Rosanvallon's *The Society of Equals* is, on the other hand, a radically different kind of exercise on the same topic – much more of an alternative in intellectual style to what we know in Anglo-America, complementary in spirit to Piketty's venture though it is. Yet it may be no accident that *The Society of Equals* is Rosanvallon's first book to receive broader attention, often in explicit relation to the current political debate on inequality that preceded and hopefully will outlast the Piketty phenomenon. (The *New York Review of Books* ran its long review, as I mentioned earlier the first of any of Rosanvallon's books, accompanied by a photograph of actor Leonardo DiCaprio standing on his yacht from his title role in "The Wolf of Wall Street.") Unlike Piketty, who focuses on a very specific sort of inequality (essentially, in income and wealth), Rosanvallon opens up a broad taxonomy of different modes of similarity and difference as they have been perceived and pursued in sequence across modern history. Recalling the one time radicalism of political equality that made the pursuit of other sorts of equality imaginable, while saving us from Tocqueville's mistaken belief that Christianity paved the way for it, Rosanvallon insists if anything on a story of inequality that has an even longer *durée* than Piketty's (fortunately Rosanvallon is not limited by the availability of state-collected population data).

More important, when it comes to the rise of industrial capitalism that ruined the optimism of the early nineteenth century that political equality might translate naturally into rough social equality, Rosanvallon gives a much more plausible historical account – even a political economy – of the origins of redistributive politics. Unlike others who pine somewhat nostalgically for a return to the social-democratic state, Rosanvallon shows that redistribution from Otto von Bismarck on depended on what he insightfully calls a "reformism of fear." It occurred, that is, only in the presence of an active working class and, ultimately, a frightening communist enemy. From this analysis, there emerges for our times not the prospects of a global wealth tax but the great challenge of discovering a functional replacement for the fear – not to mention mass carnage around the world – that created a moment of comparative strength for the social bond that recent generations no longer know how to experience. In a long-term theme in Rosanvallon's work, owing to his reading of Louis Dumont in the 1970s, a new solidaristic politics would have to work compatibly with, rather than wish away, the contemporary zest for singularity. All this seems far beyond where the reception of Piketty's book has taken Anglo-American discussion, notwithstanding the importance of having the rise of inequality empirically proven and the laws of capital made once again a topic of permissible speculation.

The frontiers of Rosanvallon's work and those of our own political moment thus coincide. One thing seems clear: in the reception of Pierre Rosanvallon's thought, it was most definitely not a matter of bringing coals to Newcastle. Instead, it was to offer fuel for a future and necessary politics, as befits his exemplary demonstration of how to synthesize the roles of scholar and citizen, and – among the many other imperatives he has offered so far – to rethink more deeply present inequalities and their alternatives in light of the longer histories of both.

13 Pierre Rosanvallon's Pragmatic Turn

Stephen W. Sawyer

> "One must not however, use cataclysmic events as a pretext to avoid investigations of longer more ordinary moments."
>
> *(Rosanvallon 2018b: 9)*

Pierre Rosanvallon's oeuvre has opened numerous doors into the history and theory of modern democracy. He has also offered promising methodological statements in the form of lectures, articles, interviews and throughout his many monographs. These proposals provide important insights into key elements of his work and, at the same time, offer scholars interested in similar questions points of departure. What follows, therefore, does not seek to overstate the importance of his methodological propositions[1] – in particular his interview "Faire l'histoire du politique" (Rosanvallon 1995), his article "A Philosophical History of the Political" (Rosanvallon 1986; 2006a) and his inaugural lecture at the Collège de France "A Conceptual History of the Political" (Rosanvallon 2003; 2006a)[2] – but rather to use them as an entry point for analyzing his history and theory of modern democracy. In particular, it highlights a shift that has taken place within Rosanvallon's

---

1 "I am often asked to more thoroughly formalize 'my method.' This would no doubt be an important thing to do if I wanted to serve as the head of a school. It seems to me that the real problem in the social sciences is writing books about social facts. Of course, there are methodological requirements that I try to adhere to. But each book to be written requires a new research investment and not just a recipe that must be applied. It is clear that researchers who are content to 'apply' a given conceptualization are not those who are rebuilding a field of research." (Gaumer/Smadja 2011: 193-194)

2 Hereafter, only the English translation from Rosanvallon 2006a will be cited.

own concept of the political. While it consciously attempts not to push Rosanvallon to the head of a potential school of the history of democracy, the chapter does explore the transformations within his own thought in order to better grasp how future historical and theoretical investigations of democracy may be both informed by and build on his work.

CONCEPTUALIZING THE POLITICAL

Rosanvallon argues that a focus on the political in his work is at once an *aim* and a *method*, or *a field* and *a project*. The "aims and the methods are indissociable," (Rosanvallon 2006a: 74) he argues, because the political is at once a mode of collective existence and an ambition for the common realization of a self-defined group or polity: "In speaking of 'the political' as a noun, I thus mean as much a modality of existence of life in common as a form of collective action." (ibid: 36) The political, then, is the "synthetic order" (ibid: 34) within which the vast range of social activities take place. It is the mark of a "society acknowledged by its members as a whole that affords meaningfulness to its constituent parts" (ibid: 34). Elsewhere, showing his debt to the work of Claude Lefort, Rosanvallon clarifies that the political is the "set of procedures that institute the social." It may therefore be understood as a process within which the full diversity of human actions of a given collectivity progressively shifts from an unconnected set of engagements to constituent (and contested) parts of the life of a community. In this way, the political becomes the mode of operation through which a community works upon itself once the variety of social activities have formed into a "general interpretive framework." Thus Rosanvallon insists that the political must be grasped as a "terrain where society is at work on itself" (ibid: 74).

It is precisely for this reason that the political offers a fecund entry point into an analysis of the democratic. Understanding democracy as a social form and political regime, democracy at once frees the social from all organic or traditional social structures that are imposed from outside of it at the same time that it allows for a tremendous plasticity in the kind of institutional arrangements that serve this social form.

"The question is thrown into the relief it deserves in democratic societies, that is to say, in those societies in which the conditions of life in common are not defined a priori, engraved in a tradition, or imposed by an authority. Democracy, in fact, constitutes the political in a field largely open to the very fact of the tensions and the uncertainties that underlay it." (Ibid: 36)

It is precisely because democracy embraces a constantly changing, profoundly uncertain social imaginary that it is politically saturated. Every aspect of social life, including modes of domination or even the rule of law, therefore remain potentially subject to contest. The political provides the realm within which this democratic debate may take place.

Building on these constituent parts, we see that "the political can therefore be defined," writes Rosanvallon, "as the process that allows the constitution of an order accepted by all by means of deliberation about the norms of participation and distribution" (ibid: 61). This definition is sufficiently rare and concise that it merits the highlighting of three key traits. First, according to this characterization, the political is not a thing, but is rather a *process*. In other words, it develops over time. Here we come to one of Rosanvallon's most commonly stated arguments on the place of democracy in a conceptual history of the political: it is insufficient to understand democracy through history because democracy emphatically *is* a history. In other words, there is no space outside of the democratic political from which one may understand the unfolding of the social. Second, this process generates a "constitution." Rosanvallon is of course not referring to a constitution as a formal legal structure, but rather to the idea that the society is "constituted" – elsewhere he uses the term "instituted." With this idea, he means that within the democratic political, society "works on itself" giving meaning to its activities, institutions, and infrastructures. Finally, Rosanvallon suggests that this constitution is accepted through norms of *participation and deliberation*. In other words, this constitution is a collective production. To be clear, this does not mean that everyone agrees, that there is an originary point of unanimity or that there is ever a moment of complete agreement. To the contrary, the contention and oppositions continue and indeed structure the political as a historical process.

"One can even argue that the approach takes as its object the most intimate and decisive matters of social experience. Indeed, in modern society the forms of collective life exist in a permanent and constitutive tension with representations, since the structure of society is no longer a product of either nature or history, but needs to be continuously constructed and criticized." (Ibid: 73)

However, while there is a constant tension underlying all social experience, the political becomes a meaningful site of social transformation in democracy through social inclusion in the form of participation and deliberation.

Within this conceptualization, Rosanvallon further defines the political by making a series of distinctions, one of the most important of which is the separation between "the political" [*le politique*] and "politics" [*la politique*]. "In speaking of 'the political,'" Rosanvallon argues, "I thus mean [...] a form of collective action that is implicitly distinct from the functioning of politics" (ibid: 36). He elaborates this idea elsewhere arguing:

"The definition of a new philosophical history of the political rests on a definition of the political domain different from the one generally assumed by political science. For this inherited field, politics constitutes a subset of the social system as a whole." (Ibid: 60)

This distinction has been constitutive of his methodological vision since his early attempts to elaborate the field of inquiry proper to the democratic political. In an interview on his methodology published in the journal *L'Esprit* in 1995, Rosanvallon explained that his approach was distinct from political science to the extent that "I try to think about the political as a block, as the site of action of society on itself," whereas political scientists, he argued, "aim to elaborate separately their understanding of each element of the major structural components of political life: elections, parties, media, intellectuals, language, etc." (Rosanvallon 1995: 27). Rosanvallon's political historical conception may therefore explore such questions as elections or political parties, as he did in his trilogy on French democracy in the nineteenth century. However, instead of focusing on who won a given district or the percentage of voter turnout or modes of electoral behavior, he seeks, for example, to understand how social division in all of its forms (political parties, factions, associations, trade unions) shifted from being seen as a threat to a shared conception of political life to becoming "organizing thirds" in the last decades of the nineteenth century (Rosanvallon 1992; 1998; 2000).

"Politics" was therefore consistently given only a marginal place in Rosanvallon's work of the 1970s through the early 2000s.

"The history of the political as practiced in this spirit is distinct in the first place, and by its very object of study, from the history of politics. The latter, beyond the recovery of the chronological unfolding of events, analyzes the functioning of institutions, unravels the mechanisms of public decisionmaking, illuminates the reasoning of actors and the way they interacted, and describes the rites and symbols that punctuate life." (Ibid: 39)

One may therefore characterize the more marginal realm of politics in Rosanvallon's work as a space of sequential time ("chronology"), a source of functional resources and infrastructures ("institutions"), and a mode of collective and individual action ("decision making"). While he accords that these elements play an important role in social organization, they are a subset of the full range of social activities that constituted the political. That is, they do not constitute the realm in which the social confronts and transforms itself and gives meaning to the diversity of its actions. Politics are, so to speak, surface or epiphenomena that may be studied, but do not allow one to understand how collective life is organized or the structural aporias that shape it.

Here, we also come upon an important parallel between Rosanvallon's method and his self-presentation and practice as a public intellectual. Rosanvallon has expressed clearly in a number of interviews, and more recently in his lectures of 2016-2018 at the Collège de France[3] that he explicitly refused the political career that was opened to him on a number of occasions between 1977 and 1981, preferring instead to focus on his intellectual endeavors. The distinction between the relatively base activity of politics and the more noble realm of the political therefore goes far beyond a mere mode of analysis. Indeed, it would seem constitutive of the very way Rosanvallon conceived of the relationship between his own life decisions and his historical and theoretical investigations. He formalized this point when he stated:

"The strength of this history of the political is that it conceives academic life in such a way that it becomes an integral part of the civic experience. It suggests, in effect, a new form of civil engagement [...]. It is the very nature of intellectual labor that amounts to political engagement [...]. Knowledge becomes a form of action [...]. Intellectual labor is a form of political practice." (Rosanvallon 2006a: 70)

Rather than engage in the life of a politician, Rosanvallon therefore self-consciously chose to elaborate the shared collective experience of the political.

THE POLITICAL, THE EXCEPTIONAL AND THE RELIGIOUS

There is then, it would appear, on the one hand a sphere, the political, in which collective life is constructed and debated, and a more quotidian sphere, politics, which is a subset of it. On other occasions, Rosanvallon provides further insight

---

3   These lectures appear in his book (cp. 2018b) Notre histoire intellectuelle et politique – 1968-2018.

into this distinction by paying an intellectual debt to Claude Lefort[4] who, he suggests, played an essential role in pushing *le politique* toward the center of an innovative history of democracy:

"The philosophical history of the political implies (as Claude Lefort has put it) 'the notion that relations between human beings and the world are generated by a principle or body of principles.' Seen from this angle, it is not simply a matter of drawing a line between the political and the social, taking the symbolic dimension characteristic of society as the point of reference. If setting the political within this symbolic framework is hardly contestable (it leads, one can note in passing, to viewing the relationship between the political and the religious as fundamental), more precision is nonetheless required." (Ibid: 60)

There are two important elements to this assessment. First, Rosanvallon insists that in order to understand how the relations between individuals may be constituted through the political – instead of politics, or forms of social domination (such as capital, for example) – it is insufficient to simply assert the autonomy of the political from the social, economic or cultural. Rather, it is a question of grounding the political in the "symbolic dimension of society." Moreover, it is precisely because it operates in a symbolic register that the political and the religious play similar roles.

As Rosanvallon suggests, Lefort provided an important theorization of the proximity of the political and the religious. In his important article "Permanence du théologico-politique?", Lefort states this idea in words that would later inspire Rosanvallon's concept of the political:

"At the beginning of the nineteenth century, a debate of an entirely new scope took shape as a result of the French Revolution. It is out of the memory of this event that a rupture in time occurred, that established a new relationship with time as such, and out of which emerged a mystery of History. This rupture was not contained within the field of political, economic, or social institutions, but in relation to institution as such, out of which a mystery of society emerged. The religious meaning of this rupture then haunted the mind." (Lefort 1986: 275-76)

There are at least three key elements here that informed Rosanvallon's work. First, the idea that the Revolution marked an exceptional break in the ways that French

---

4 Claude Lefort placed the relationship between le politique and le religieux at the center of his philosophical investigation of political modernity (cp. Lefort 1986).

society apprehended itself. Second, this rupture was not merely within some particular field such as economic, political or social institutions, but rather within the very process of the institution of the social. Finally, out of this extraordinary transformation a mystery appeared which was of a profoundly religious, though secularized, type.

This emphasis on the political as a secularized religious realm can be found in a number of places in Rosanvallon's oeuvre. In some cases, it takes the language of a sacralization. He argues, for example, that by "sacralizing the will against the order of nature or that of history, modern politics entrusts power to the people at the very moment that the project of emancipation that it furthers leads in parallel to making the social more and more abstract" (Rosanvallon 2006a: 42). He further speaks of sacralization in the context of his history of universal suffrage in nineteenth-century France:

"History in such a case is thus not only marked by a conflict between high and low in society, but is also structured by an implicit tension about the very notion of political suffrage: a tension, namely, between suffrage as a symbol of social inclusion, the sacralization of equal citizenship (which therefore gives rise to the imperative of its universalization), and suffrage as an expression of social power, a form of social governance." (Ibid: 41)

In both of these cases, Rosanvallon uses the idea of the emergence of a "sacred" conceptualization of suffrage in the nineteenth century as the symbolic framework through which the political is structured.

It is out of this conception of a secularized sacralization that Rosanvallon constructed the first book in his trilogy on nineteenth-century French democracy on the history of universal suffrage, *Le sacre du citoyen* [*The sacralization/sacrement of the citizen*]. In this work, he argues that it was the sacralization of the idea of universal suffrage that made it an absolute ideal for French democratic and republican movements leading up to the Revolution of 1848. By becoming sacred, the vote became the symbolic context for all forms of political and social change among republicans and democratic socialists. Thus far from emphasizing specific electoral successes, for example, Rosanvallon demonstrates the incapacities of those aspiring for democratic change to imagine that universal suffrage would not magically overcome all social and political division.

Rosanvallon's conceptual history of nineteenth-century French democracy argues then that these secularized religious concepts which guided collective action emerged out of extraordinary or exceptional moments, such as revolution. He makes this claim directly when he writes: "The relationship between social history and conceptual history is parallel to that between ordinary and revolutionary periods." (ibid: 73) Social history, he suggests, invests society as the site from which one is able to make sense of quotidian power relations, modes of domination, and modes of action. He therefore clearly presents social history as pertaining to a subset of the conceptual history of the political, which is primarily concerned with the exceptional or "revolutionary" moments when society confronts itself and "institutes" a meaningful – in the deepest sense of the word – "set of procedures that institute the social." Or stated differently: "understood in this way," Rosanvallon argues, "the political stems from the need to establish a rule outside the ordinary" (ibid: 61).

One cannot, then, or so it would seem, understand the process of social institution of the political by merely exploring the ordinary moments of everyday life. "This ordinary pattern," Rosanvallon suggests, "acquires a meaning only when relocated within the process of transformation of institutions and ways of thinking" (ibid: 74). It is only through an exploration of the exceptional moments of social institution that the political can be studied. In the trilogy, it is the Revolution that provides the exceptional moment which structures the political across the nineteenth century until the second decade of the Third French Republic in the 1880s.

Rosanvallon states this point explicitly in the second volume of his trilogy, *Le peuple introuvable*, where he discusses the aporias of representative government in democracy that emerge from the revolutionary moment. Here Rosanvallon refers directly to Schmitt's argument that popular representation took two forms: "symbolic figuration" and "mandate." According to Schmitt, while the symbolic representation of the people required a symbolic figure that transcended the individual features of its popular source in order to incarnate the sovereign people as a whole, the mandate required an attentiveness and similitude to specific groups and individuals that challenged this transcendence. Schmitt argued then that these two forms were only reconcilable in a great leader. Rosanvallon elaborated this same aporia in his own terms, suggesting that the notion of the people captured a larger tension at the heart of all democratic organization, rooted in what he refers to as the "unfigurable people":

"By sacralizing the will against the natural order or history, political modernity entrusted the people with the power at the same time that the emancipatory project that resided within the people generated a social abstraction. There is therefore a contradiction between the political principle of democracy and its sociological principle. The political principle gives power to the collective subject at the same time that the sociological principle dissolves its coherence and reduces its visibility." (Rosanvallon 1998: 12)

After highlighting this tension between the abstract and concrete dimensions of representative power, he then writes:

"There is no reason to further insist here on the important theological-political dimension of this conception of representation-personification. There is no better authority on this question, since we cannot develop it in this context, than the work of Carl Schmitt and notably his analysis of the Church as a 'power of representation' in its capacity to superimpose aesthetic, juridical and political forms." (Ibid: 16)

With this conception of the political, Rosanvallon thus seems to be treading dangerously close to some of Carl Schmitt's key conceptual ideas. In particular, one may find a close relationship between Rosanvallon and Lefort's conception and Schmitt's *Political Theology* where Schmitt famously asserted that it was precisely the secularized theological foundations of rule that pushed the exception to the center of the modern political:

"All significant concepts of the modern theory of the state are secularized theological concepts not only because of their historical development – in which they were transferred from theology to the theory of the state, whereby, for example, the omnipotent god became the omnipotent lawgiver – but also because of their systematic structure, the recognition of which is necessary for a sociological consideration of these concepts." (Schmitt 1985[1922]: 36)

In one sense, the proximity between Rosanvallon (as well as Lefort) and some of Schmitt's conceptualizations of the political and the theological is not surprising. Indeed, as the quotation above suggests, some of the key concepts in his history of democracy come directly from his reading of Schmitt. Moreover, in itself, building from the powerful conception of Schmitt to explore the foundations of the democratic is not necessarily problematic. Rosanvallon is certainly not the only historian or theorist of democracy to find resources in Schmitt's work. Interestingly, however, his use of Schmittian categories would seem to have become more burdensome as he moved away from a focus on the Revolutionary period and the nineteenth century and toward an interest in the problems of contemporary democracy that occupied his tetralogy. Within this transition there seems to have been a reconsideration of the utility of understanding the political as the exceptional product of processes of secularized religious social institution.

THE PRAGMATIC RECONSTRUCTION
OF THE POLITICAL

A careful look at Rosanvallon and Lefort's work reveals signs that the sharp distinction between the political and politics, or between the exceptional and the ordinary, or between the secularized religious concepts and profane modes of action were not as clear-cut as they at times argued. There is an interesting passage in Rosanvallon's inaugural lecture on this point:

"It is not through taking refuge in the supposedly tranquil sky of concepts that one could really claim to understand the sources and difficulties of instituting the polity. Those cannot be grasped except through study of ordinary contingencies, always coated as they are by the veneer of events. This has to be acknowledged. But it is necessary to emphasize forcefully, all the same, that one cannot remain at that level to reach the enigma of the political." (Ibid: 40)

Indeed, Rosanvallon seems to walk right up to the very point where politics and the political merge only to turn back and insist on the fundamental distinction between the two both as subjects of inquiry and modes of understanding. Lefort goes even further in an interview in 1996 when in response to a question by Pierre Manent on his work on Machiavelli, he reconsiders his earlier arguments stating: "from that perspective there is not this distinction between the noble object of reflection, the political and that which is trivial, that is politics." [5]

This is not to suggest that there is no distinction between the two, nor that it has not been useful for their (and our) understanding democratic modernity. But these apparent hesitations do raise our awareness on the ways that the political and everyday, ordinary practices may have intermingled in their work. In particular, as Rosanvallon moved away from a focus on the nineteenth-century problems of democracy in the trilogy and began moving toward contemporary problems of democracy, he developed a new interest in accounting for everyday ordinary forms of political action, which he had previously marginalized within the lesser sphere of politics. Setting his cites more directly on the present-day crisis of democracy,

---

5   "Il n'y a pas cette distinction entre ce qui serait le noble objet de réflexion, le politique, et ce qui serait triviale, c'est à dire la politique". Pour la citation et l'idée du rapport entre l'institution et l'action en politique chez Machiavel voir Pensée politique et histoire: entretien avec Claude Lefort, "Actualité de Machiavel": https://www.canal-u.tv/video/ehess/pensee_politique_et_histoire_entretien_avec_claude_lefort.14106, 1h10-1h25mn.

a shift is therefore perceptible from an investment in the extraordinary and secularized religious function of the political to a more quotidian pragmatic conception.

In his essay, "The Transformation of Democracy and the Future of Europe," originally written in 2002, he framed the problem of contemporary democracy in historical terms. "Political theory," Rosanvallon noted,

"has recently begun to emphasize the distinction between ordinary and extraordinary politics, making clear that if the first sometimes seemed to be relegated to everyday housekeeping, the theatrical dimension of the will could sometimes return in the heat of exceptional circumstances [...] The felt decline of politics, from this perspective, has to be placed in the perspective of such 'cycles.' But it also corresponds, more profoundly to a 'disenchantment' of the will." (Rosanvallon 2006a: 226)

In this passage, Rosanvallon brings together a number of themes that have been essential to his conceptual history of the political: the distinction between extraordinary or exceptional circumstances and the ordinary or everyday and the consequent bifurcation between politics on the one hand and the political on the other. Furthermore, he stakes his claim that the increasing attention being paid to the politics of the everyday has been consonant with the decline of the "theatrical dimension of the will." Finally, it is the loss of will, or its "disenchantment" as he calls it, that is responsible for the declining fortunes of the political and therefore meaningful public engagement and a growing distrust of the very possibility of the institution of the social. He makes a similar argument elsewhere, suggesting that it is because of the loss of a sacred or spiritual value of the political that democracy has fallen on such difficult times: "Such is the lesson of the social sciences, one spread to such an extent that it has forced the retreat of 'magical' visions of the political." (ibid: 226)

This does not mean, however, that Rosanvallon jettisoned the importance of the political. "Against the overly cautious vision of a definitively disenchanted democracy, it is indeed necessary to find a new emphasis on and centrality for the political." (ibid: 197) This reinvestment in the political led him then to a fundamental question in his later work: "If the future of democracy proceeds down this route, it is the problem of resymbolization that becomes the decisive challenge." (ibid: 204) This observation calls for analytical pause. For, needless to say, one might not blame the attentive reader for gasping at the idea that it is necessary to overcome a disenchanted democracy by reasserting and especially *resymbolizing* the political – one cannot help noting, once again, the proximity to a Schmittian diagnosis, especially considering the concoction of the sacred, the religious and even the magical in his previous notion of the exceptional construction of the political.

Of course, Rosanvallon recognized this danger. And it is precisely in his attempt to avoid this pitfall while at the same time providing a more robust conception of the political that an important, if subtle, shift seems to have emerged within his history of the political. Rosanvallon clearly states that any attempt to resymbolize the democratic is a potentially dangerous operation. He insists therefore that he is "far from calling for a hypothetical 'return of the will' of a powerful state that would tower over men and transcend their differences" (Rosanvallon 2006a: 213). The question then arises: How does one achieve a resymbolization without falling into the Schmittian trap of a return of the singular secularized-theological will?

Rosanvallon's editorial projects and the original perspective on the transformations of contemporary democracy in the realms of citizenship, legitimacy, equality and government have all participated in a broader attempt to provide a capacious, historically-grounded response to this problem of resymbolization. He first stated the ambition of this project clearly in the conclusion of the last book of the trilogy, *La démocratie inachevée*:

"The symbolization of politics will not be a florid transfiguration and enchantment of reality, but the enterprise of perpetually recalling a task to be carried out: the constitution of an unlocalizable people in a living political community." (Ibid: 204)

He makes a similar claim when he suggests, for example, that creating a social imaginary will be possible "on condition, to be sure, that it is rethought and reformulated from the ground up" (ibid: 197). So what exactly does this reconstruction entail and did it mark a practical displacement away from some of his earlier conceptions in both his trilogy and his major methodological statements?

Rosanvallon explains what he means by this process of resymbolization when he writes:

"There is a whole range of practical works of resymbolization, of the production of generality, of translation, and of the interpretation of reality that has to be undertaken. Against exceptionalist conceptions of the political, the return of the political would have to be understood as proceeding from an ensemble of actions and discourses for producing commonality and making the system of social interactions both more legible and more visible." (Ibid: 250)

He continues arguing that such a process requires "giving meaning back to politics." It is, he argues, "above all a matter of publicly reconstituting and exposing, in order to pave the way for their evaluation and modification, the effective modes by which the social system is produced" (ibid: 250).

There are a number of important dimensions to this assessment that require careful consideration for understanding the process of resymbolization in which Rosanvallon was engaged during his tenure at the Collège de France. First, within this process, he argues, the very act and process of writing and researching on the democratic play a fundamental role:

"There is a work to be shouldered of writing and publication that in this regard amounts to the very foundation of the political. It would aim to give a vocabulary to social experience and to outline for it the framework in which it takes on meaning – and thus allow for it to reform itself." (Ibid: 250)

Here Rosanvallon reconnects with a consistent theme throughout his career. In 1995, he already affirmed:

"This way of understanding the historian's profession leads to a reconsideration of the relationship between academic work and civic participation. The force of this history of the political is that it conceives of university work as participating directly in civic engagement." (Rosanvallon 1995: 36)

However, in the later formulation he closes the gap even further between the *vita activa* and the *vita scientia* by highlighting the role that his works play in the re-enchantment of the political itself. From this perspective, the tetralogy was not a mere process of further historical, political and social investigation. It also attempted to provide a vocabulary for engaging our democratic present. In this sense, it is hardly through some extraordinary act or decision, but rather through the everyday, and even serial activities of research, writing and editing that Rosanvallon – and others thinking about the democratic – contribute to the production of a more vibrant concept of the political.

Second, Rosanvallon argues that this process of re-enchantment "calls for an authentic rediscovery of ordinary politics, conceived in terms that are at once simple, radical and profound" (Rosanvallon 2006a: 250). It is here that Rosanvallon seems to have stepped furthest from his conception of the political in the nineteenth century. Rosanvallon explicitly shifted toward a revalorization of "ordinary politics" which he claims need to be "rediscovered." For in this new context, it is no longer the extraordinary that may provide the foundation for access to the political, but rather a reinvestment in the normal pursuit of everyday politics. As he wrote in the second volume of the tetralogy for example: "Today it is necessary to invent an equivalent [of old political parties] in order to better organize the everyday and more disseminated relationship between power and society." (Rosanvallon 2008b)[6] While they remain "simple," these engagements in everyday politics may nonetheless have "radical and profound" consequences. In a context of wide-ranging democratic disenchantment, the normal pursuits of political engagement take on a new, deeper meaning. Politics become pragmatic in this instance to the extent that they serve an end that has little to do with politics in itself. It is rather the way they may help reconstruct the political if understood in a certain light as a mode of collective engagement.

Third, and finally, this new process of resymbolization involves "practical engagements in a democracy conceived as a social activity" (ibid: 250). Thus Rosanvallon elaborates a more thorough investment in practical matters. The attempt to participate in certain everyday activities take on a new meaning if they are perceived as having a "social" relevance. Once again, it is the decidedly pragmatic focus of this later conception that is striking. The symbolic order no longer seems to emerge out of exceptional or secularized religious moments born of revolution. Instead, the symbolic emerges directly out of everyday ordinary practices and engagements that may now gain meaning as a means of instituting the social.

This shift helps understand the ambitions of one of Rosanvallon's later editorial projects, *Raconter la vie*, a relatively short-lived, but ambitious and timely book series launched in 2014 under the direction of Pauline Peretz. The project, as he presented it in his book *Le parlement des invisibles* was inspired by the nineteenth-century endeavors of social observation, in particular the series "the French painted by themselves." According to Rosanvallon,

"confronted with the 'mal-representation' by political parties that leads to the ideological and caricatured presentations of reality, it is necessary to build a *narrative-representation* so that the democratic ideals take on new life and form. The time has come to propose a series of responses to the expectations of recognition that are manifest, in order to constitute them into an explicit movement, and give them a positive meaning and coherence." (Rosanvallon 2014)

---

6   "Il faut aujourd'hui inventer l'équivalent pour mieux organiser le rapport plus quotidien et plus disséminé entre pouvoir et société." The published translation doesn't translate the term "quotidien", so I have translated this passage myself.

Pierre Rosanvallon's Pragmatic Turn | 243

It is hard to imagine a stronger statement of the process of resymbolization at the heart of Rosanvallon's later works and civic engagements.

However, what is equally striking is the form this new series of representations took. Indeed, the subject of the series seems almost diametrically opposed to the kinds of questions Rosanvallon explored in his trilogy in which the French Revolution gave birth to a lasting set of secularized religious categories that shaped the history of democracy. A list of subjects from the *Raconter la vie* series suffice to demonstrate the new investment in the everyday in the twenty-first century: *Chercheur au quotidien* (*The Everyday Researcher*); *Moi, Anthony, ouvrier d'aujourd'hui* (*I, Anthony, Today's Worker*); *La femme aux chats* (*The Woman with Cats*); *Le corps des autres* (*The Body of Others*); *La Barbe* (*The Beard*); *Dans l'oeil du gardien* (*Through the Eyes of the Watchman*); *Un homme à la crèche* (*A Man at Daycare*), etc. Through each one of these books, from exploring the life of a father dropping off his child at daycare to portraying the life of a worker in a beauty salon, wearing a beard or presenting the everyday life of a researcher, *Raconter la vie* was motivated by an ambition to increase social legibility in an age of profound transformation, but also to contribute to the formation of a new social imaginary and thus participate in the everyday resymbolization (or what he calls in this case a *narrative*-representation) necessary for a contemporary reinvention of the political.

Through this project, and others, Rosanvallon was obviously building on the ideas presented in his conceptual history of the political. However, it would seem that there was a shift in how the political becomes the meaningful category for understanding human existence. By reinvesting everyday actions and practices, and framing them as modes of social engagement, the political no longer emerged as secularized sacred forms born of exceptional circumstances.[7] In short, Rosanvallon increasingly embraced a more pragmatic conception of the political. By pragmatic conception of the political, I mean that Rosanvallon accorded a new value to ordinary, everyday activities. The political no longer exists as distinct

---

7   Rosanvallon would seem to share at least some common ground with certain perspectives on radical democracy that have attempted to integrated a pragmatic perspective along side a more highly symbolized, or "visionary" conception of the political. One may for example, establish a proximity with Roman Coles's recent work on *Visionary Pragmatism* in which he argues: "Visionary pragmatism is oriented by a profound sense that the alternative resonances, flows, and system dynamics associated with the political work and action of a radical democratic habitus can be indispensable for opening out senses and enhancing our capacities for theorizing and scholarship." (*Visionary Pragmatism*)

from everyday practices but rather emerges out of the ways that ordinary modes of action institute it; there is no political outside of its everyday usages.

Within this shift toward a pragmatic conception of the everyday, one may venture a further more speculative question: What everyday activities may be considered appropriate for this process of resymbolization? And perhaps more mischievously, but importantly, we might follow this question back to the very distinction between the political and politics in Rosanvallon's earlier formulations. Rosanvallon clearly calls for an "authentic rediscovery of ordinary politics." In this case, one might reasonably ask if the daily life of a politician, community activist or party militant might not also be considered to participate in a process of resymbolization? Or stated in slightly different terms: Could there have been a book in the *Raconter la vie* series entitled *A Day at the National Assembly* or *The Everyday life of a Political Militant*? If indeed the political itself emerges out of our everyday political activities and practices, then how might politics participate in the construction of a new institution of the social? A turn toward the pragmatic conception of the political may therefore, and perhaps paradoxically, lead us back to a reevaluation of the intrigues, the rivalries, the instrumentalizations that make up the stuff of everyday politics that we know so well, that fascinate us too easily, and that sometimes infuriate us.

The more pragmatic conception that has animated Rosanvallon's later projects may then, in the end, force us to reconsider the value of banal politics and the importance of the political game in the construction of our collective lives. While Rosanvallon largely dismissed such practices in his earlier work, it would seem that as our democracies increasingly flirt with new forms of authoritarianism – in spite of and sometimes thanks to the elections or parties that have constituted the realm of politics – the political and politics are increasingly intertwined. More and more, we seem to be confronted with the permanent entanglements of the realms of social life that have constituted the political – in public law, the state, and the nation – and the unpredictable and permanent maneuverings of those who seek political power. From this perspective, Rosanvallon's pragmatic turn would seem to offer a promising point of departure for future studies of political practice.

BIBLIOGRAPHY

Godmer, Laurent/Smadja, David (2011): "Entretien avec Pierre Rosanvallon." In: Raisons politiques 44, pp. 173-199.
Lefort, Claude (1986): "Permanence du théologico-politique?" In: Claude Lefort, Essais sur le politique, XIXe-XXe siècles, Paris: Seuil, pp. 275-329.

Rosanvallon, Pierre (1986): "Pour une histoire conceptuelle du politique (note de travail)." In: Revue de synthèse 107/1-2, pp. 93-105.
Rosanvallon, Pierre (1990): L'Etat en France de 1789 à nos jours, Paris: Seuil.
Rosanvallon, Pierre (1992): Le sacre du citoyen. Histoire du suffrage universel en France, Paris: Gallimard.
Rosanvallon, Pierre (1994): La Monarchie impossible. Histoire des Chartes de 1814 et 1830, Paris: Fayard.
Rosanvallon, Pierre (1995), "Faire l'Histoire du politique." In: Esprit, février, pp. 25-42.
Rosanvallon, Pierre (1998): Le peuple introuvable. Histoire de la représentation démocratique en France, Paris: Gallimard.
Rosanvallon, Pierre (2000): La démocratie inachevée. Histoire de la souveraineté du peuple en France, Paris: Gallimard.
Rosanvallon, Pierre (2001): "Entretien. Sur quelques chemins de traverse de la pensée du politique en France." In: Raisons politiques 1. pp. 49-62.
Rosanvallon, Pierre (2003): Pour une histoire conceptuelle du politique. Leçon inaugurale faite au Collège de France le jeudi 28 mars 2002, Paris: Seuil.
Rosanvallon, Pierre (2004): Le modèle politique français. La société civile contre le jacobinisme de 1789 à nos jours, Paris: Seuil.
Rosanvallon, Pierre (2006a): Democracy Past and Future, Samuel Moyn (ed.), New York: Columbia University Press.
Rosanvallon, Pierre (2006b): La contre-démocratie. La politique à l'âge de la défiance, Paris: Seuil.
Rosanvallon, Pierre (2007): The Demands of Liberty. Civil Society in France since the Revolution, Cambridge: Harvard University Press.
Rosanvallon, Pierre (2008a): Counter-Democracy: Politics in an Age of Distrust, Cambridge: Cambridge University Press.
Rosanvallon, Pierre (2008b): La légitimité démocratique. Impartialité, réflexivité, proximité, Paris: Seuil.
Rosanvallon, Pierre (2011a): Democratic Legitimacy: Impartiality, Reflexivity, Proximity, Cambridge: Harvard University Press.
Rosanvallon, Pierre (2011b): La société des égaux, Paris: Seuil.
Rosanvallon, Pierre (2011c): "Ecrire une histoire générale de la démocratie (entretien)." In: Participations 1, pp. 335-347.
Rosanvallon, Pierre (2013): The Society of Equals, Cambridge: Harvard University Press.
Rosanvallon, Pierre (2014a): Le Parlement des invisibles, Paris: Seuil, Raconter la vie.
Rosanvallon, Pierre (2015): Le bon gouvernement, Paris: Seuil.

Rosanvallon, Pierre (2018a): Good Government: Democracy beyond Elections, Cambridge: Harvard University Press.

Rosanvallon, Pierre (2018b): Notre histoire intellectuelle et politique – 968-2018, Paris: Seuil.

Schmitt, Carl (1985[1922]): Political Theology: Four Chapters on the Concept of Sovereignty, George Schwab (trans.), Cambridge: MIT Press.

Weymans, Wim (2016): "Radical Democracy's Past and Future: Histories of the Symbolic." In: Modern Intellectual History 13/3, pp. 841-851.

The Authors

Alain Chatriot is Professor of History at Sciences Po Paris (Centre d'histoire de Sciences Po).

Greg Conti is Assistant Professor of Politics at Princeton University.

Paula Diehl (PhD Humboldt University) is responsible for the area "Theory, History, Culture of the Political" at the History Department of the University of Bielefeld.

Michel Dormal is a Postdoctoral Researcher in Political Science at RWTH Aachen University.

Oliver Flügel-Martinsen is Professor of Political Theory and History of Political Thought at Bielefeld University.

Felix Heidenreich is a Scientific Coordinator at the University of Stuttgart and teaches Political Science.

Anna Hollendung is Research Associate at Christian-Albrechts-University Kiel.

Franziska Martinsen is Deputy Professor of Political Science at Christian-Albrechts-University Kiel.

Samuel Moyn is Professor of Law and Professor of History at Yale University.

Pierre Rosanvallon is Directeur d'études at the École des Hautes Études en Sciences Sociales and holds the Chair of Early Modern and Modern History of the Political at the Collège de France.

Stephen W. Sawyer is Professor of History at the American University of Paris.

Daniel Schulz is Visiting Professor for Political Theory and the History of Ideas at the Technical University Dresden.

Wim Weymans holds the Velge Chair in European Values at UCLouvain (Louvain-la-Neuve, Belgium).

GPSR Authorized Representative: Easy Access System Europe, Mustamäe tee 50, 10621 Tallinn, Estonia, gpsr.requests@easproject.com